Becoming a Professional Counselor

Becoming a Professional Counselor

Preparing for Certification and Comprehensive Exams

Sheri A. Wallace Michael D. Lewis

SAGE Publications
International Educational and Professional Publisher
Newbury Park   London   New Delhi

For information address:

SAGE Publications, Inc.
2455 Teller Road
Newbury Park, California 91320
E-mail: order@sagepub.com

SAGE Publications Ltd.
6 Bonhill Street
London EC2A 4PU
United Kingdom

SAGE Publications India Pvt. Ltd.
M-32 Market
Greater Kailash I
New Delhi 110 048 India

Printed in the United States of America

Library of Congress Cataloging-in-Publication Data

Wallace, Sheri A.
    Becoming a professional counselor : preparing for certification
and comprehensive exams / by Sheri A. Wallace and Michael D. Lewis.
        p.   cm.
    Includes bibliographical references.
    ISBN 0-8039-3565-X.
    1. Counseling.   2. Counseling—Examinations—Study guides.
3. Counselors—Certification—United States.   I. Lewis, Michael D.,
1937-   . II. Title.
BF637.C6W28   1990
361.3'23—dc20

90-32750
CIP

96 97 98 99 00 01 13 12 11 10 9 8 7

Sage Production Editor: Diane S. Foster

Contents

Preface 7

1. Human Growth and Development 9
2. Social and Cultural Foundations 32
3. The Helping Relationship 55
4. Group Dynamics, Process, and Counseling 78
5. Life-Style and Career Development 99
6. Appraisal of the Individual 121
7. Research and Evaluation 144
8. Professional Orientation 166

Study Tips 188

Glossary 193

Appendix A. NBCC Code of Ethics 197

Appendix B. Ethical Guidelines for Group Counselors 205

Appendix C. Responsibilities of Users of Standardized Tests 213

Appendix D. Counseling Services: Consumer Rights
and Responsibilities 225

References 227

About the Authors 234

Preface

This book provides a comprehensive review of the counseling profession. You may be using this book as a review in preparation for becoming a national certified counselor or to prepare for comprehensive exams in a doctoral, specialist, or master's degree program in counseling or counselor education. In either case, you will find that the eight content areas represented by the chapters in this volume conform with those prescribed by the Council for the Accreditation of Counseling and Related Education Programs (CACREP) and the National Board for Certified Counselors (NBCC) and represent material covered by a dozen or more graduate courses.

All of the eight chapters follow the same format. Each begins with a table of contents that is essentially an outline of the content area to be discussed, according to the AACD *Standards of Preparation* for counselor training programs. This serves as an advanced organizer and provides an overview of the chapter. Next, a summary of the content area is provided, followed by a list of learning objectives and a time line. A list of important terms and names is also provided; many of the terms listed are further defined in the volume Glossary. Several practice tests are included in each chapter: fill in the blanks and matching tests, a case study analysis, and a multiple-choice test (the NBCC exam is a multiple-choice test). An answer key is provided at the end of each chapter.

Due to the tremendous volume of information covered, you may find new material in any section of a chapter. Do not expect to find every practice test answer in the chapter summary. If you identify weak areas, you may want to review your course notes or textbooks in order to strengthen your knowledge base. For further reading, you might refer to the comprehensive reference section provided in this volume.

Your familiarity with the material and your use of smart study strategies, as suggested in the Study Tips, increase the likelihood that you will successfully complete your upcoming exam. The pages of this book have been perforated so that you may remove and reorganize them according to your individual preferences. This format lends itself to class or study group work as well. We wish you success and welcome you to the world of professional counseling.

Your choice to be a counselor tells the world a lot about you. It expresses the value that you think people are important and have a right to make educated and informed choices in their lives. You have chosen to become a professional counselor by demonstrating to your peers that you have learned the basic tenets of this profession and that you are committed to continued educational and professional growth. With this thought in mind, one of the authors of this book has set up a scholarship at Governors State University to advocate for the prevention of mental illness and thus for the promotion of mental health. His royalties from the sale of this book will go into that scholarship. He hopes that each and every one of you who becomes a national certified counselor will spend some of your valuable professional time in the area of prevention.

We would like to express our thanks to the many individuals who contributed to the preparation of this volume. Thanks to the professionals who took time to read various chapters and offer helpful comments: Larry Gerstein,

Richard Hayes, Larry Litwack, and Steve Weinrach. The students of Governors State University's Division of Psychology and Counseling gave some of the tests a trial run and provided useful feedback. We especially appreciate our reviewer, Dr. George Leddick, who supplied us with a valuable chapter-by-chapter critique. We would also like to thank our family members, especially Brian, Jim, Sheila, and Mindy, who had to share Mom's attention with the computer for many months. Finally, Terry Hendrix, Christine Smedley, and the staff at Sage Publications offered us support and encouragement throughout the project.

—Sheri A. Wallace
—Michael D. Lewis

CHAPTER 1

Human Growth and Development

SUMMARY   11
  Human Development   **11**
    Worldviews   11
    Developmental Theories   11
  Abnormal Behavior   **13**
    Biological Viewpoint   14
    Psychosocial and Sociocultural Viewpoint   14
    Causes   14
    Patterns   15
  Personality Theory   **15**
    Psychoanalytic Theories   15
    Trait Theories   16
    Humanistic Theories   16
    Cognitive Theories   17
  Learning Theory   **17**
    Classical Conditioning   17
    Operant Conditioning   17
    Vicarious Conditioning   18
LEARNING OBJECTIVES   19
TIME LINE   20
TERMS AND NAMES TO REMEMBER   21
  Terms   **21**
  Names   **21**
FILL IN THE BLANKS   22
MATCHING TEST   24

CASE STUDY   25
   Analysis   25
MULTIPLE-CHOICE TEST   28
ANSWER KEY   31
   Fill in the Blanks   31
   Matching   31
   Multiple-Choice   31

SUMMARY

Human growth and development includes studies that provide a broad understanding of the nature and needs of individuals at all developmental levels. Emphasis is placed on psychological, sociological, and physiological approaches. Also included are areas such as human behavior (normal and abnormal), personality theory, and learning theory. (Loesch & Vacc, 1986, p. 13)

Human Development

The phrase *human growth and development* refers to change and maturation not only of the biological and physical systems of people, but also of their social, emotional, and personality systems. The traditional approach to human development includes significant change from birth to adolescence, stability during adulthood, and decline in old age. However, as the life span of human beings increased and theorists began to realize that much significant growth and change can take place throughout adult life, the life-cycle approach to human development began to emerge. This view addresses eight periods of life-span development: (a) prenatal, (b) infancy, (c) early childhood, (d) middle and late childhood, (e) adolescence, (f) early adulthood, (g) middle adulthood, and (h) late adulthood (Santrock, 1986).

Worldviews

An understanding of human development may be gained by studying the differing worldviews that have been advanced to explain human growth and development throughout the life span.

Behavioral worldview. The behavioral (Hayes, 1986) or mechanistic (Santrock, 1986) worldview sees individuals as passive reactors to the environment who have little control over their own destinies. This view emphasizes social and environmental experiences and minimizes biological, mental, and cognitive activity.

Organismic worldview. The organismic worldview explained by Santrock (1986) sees individuals as active, mindful producers of their own destiny. Individuals have a strong biological foundation of development, and the social environment provides the setting, rather than the cause, for development. Hayes (1986) further divides the organismic view into *maturational* and *structural* paradigms. The maturational view attributes change to growth and differentiation, limited, not directed, by environmental influences. The structural view sees individuals producing their own development through active interaction with the environment, while keeping the maturational, social, and physical factors in balance.

Interactional worldview. Santrock (1986) applies the term *contextual* to the interactional worldview. The individual is neither purely active nor purely passive, but in an interactive relationship with the environment. This dialectical approach sees the individual as continually responding to and acting upon various contexts (environmental, sociohistorical, biological, and so on) that are also in a continuous state of change. Riegel (1975) stresses change and disequilibrium as the hallmarks of development. Because humans are changing beings in a changing world, they are constantly in a state of flux. Once a goal seems to be reached, rather than achieving balance, the individual faces new challenges.

Developmental Theories

In order to explain human growth and development, various theories have been advanced. These theories have traditionally been grouped according to their common underlying principles. For the purpose of this chapter, four types of theories will be highlighted: (a) biological and physical, (b) psychodynamic, (c) cognitive, and (d) behavioral.

Biological/physical theories. Biological theories emphasize the importance of genetics to explain individual growth and development. The 46 sets of chromosomes individuals inherit from their parents contain thousands of genes that determine the individuals' patterns of development and personal characteristics. Gessell (1925) uses the theory of maturation to explain common developmental patterns that are internally controlled rather than influenced by the external environment. Although the genetic code is a powerful determinant of behavior, individual maturation patterns require a supportive environment and may be somewhat influenced by experience.

Thomas and Chess (1977) cite activity rate, rhythmicity, adaptability to new experiences, general mood, and intensity of response as facets of inherited temperament; Buss and Plomin (1975) view temperament as a set of dichotomies—active versus passive, emotional versus impassive, gregarious versus detached, and impulsive versus deliberate. Whatever the view, the individual's temperament influences not only the way the individual approaches the world, but also the way the world responds to the individual (Santrock, 1986).

Psychodynamic theories. Psychodynamic theories include the psychoanalytic theory of Sigmund Freud and the neopsychoanalytic theories of Freud's followers—Jung, Adler, and Erikson, among others. Freud's (1925/1961) work has had a greater impact on the study of human development than that of any other theorist. Central to Freud's theory is the concept of libido, the sexual energy that influences human behavior and development.

Freud's personality structures include the id, ego, and superego. The id represents an instinctual need for immediate gratification and tension reduction, and it operates under the pleasure principle. The ego represents a system of thought that regulates the demands of the id, and it operates under the reality principle. The third structure, the superego, consists of conscience and ego ideal, a set of standards toward which the individual strives.

Freud's is a stage theory that hypothesizes that human personality is formed within the first five years of life, with each stage representing certain developmental issues. The five stages are as follows: (a) oral, up to age 2; (b) anal, ages 2 to 3; (c) phallic, ages 3 to 6; (d) latency, age 6 to puberty; and (e) genital, from puberty through old age.

Neopsychoanalytic theories have been developed by a number of Freud's followers. Among these, the works of Jung, Adler, and Erikson are having a profound effect upon the practice of counseling today (Hayes, 1986). Jung's (1928) theory, analytic psychology, disagrees with Freud's emphasis on the nature of libido, viewing it as general psychic energy instead of sexual energy. Jung believed that humans also possess an instinct toward individuation that pushes them to achieve wholeness. Just as one's inner forces guide physiological development, the individuation instinct guides psychological development, constantly seeking to fulfill the truest self and to find one's meaning in life. Personal growth takes place as the individual gains more awareness and becomes more conscious by uncovering more of the unconscious. Jung's method of exploring the unconscious is through dream analysis. Unconscious products (dreams, fantasies, artistic productions) are interpreted not only in terms of antecedent causes, but primarily as directing the way to further development (Kaufmann, 1979).

Adler's (1963) *individual psychology* takes a holistic view of development. According to Adler, more than environment and heredity, one's striving toward individual goals determines one's behavior and life-style. Thus rather than "being," the individual is constantly "becoming," striving to achieve the self-ideal. When there is a discrepancy between the self and the self-ideal, feelings of inferiority result. Although these feelings are universal and normal, when taken to the extreme, the pathological inferiority complex results (Mosak, 1979). The social context in which the individual operates, primarily the family constellation, motivates the child to master the environment while searching for significance. The child forms conclusions about him- or herself and others and acts upon them as if they were true. When these perceptions are faulty, the person can learn, through the encouragement of therapy, to have faith in him- or herself, to trust, and to love.

Erikson (1963) proposed a stage theory of development including eight psychosocial stages that extend over the life span. Development consists of the individual's search for a mature sense of identity. At each stage, the individual must master a particular task or dilemma. As each stage task is resolved, the individual moves on to the next stage. The eight stages and tasks are discussed more fully in the section in Chapter 2 on age roles.

Cognitive theories. Among cognitive theorists, Piaget has had the greatest impact upon developmental psychology. Working with children, Piaget (1936/1952) concludes that development is a process of adaptation and active seeking to understand the environment. Adaptation includes assimilation (noticing and understanding), accommodation (changing concepts based upon new information), and equilibration (forming new theories in order to achieve balance). Piaget identifies four stages of cognitive development: (a) sensorimotor, ages 0-2; (b) preoperational, ages 2-6; (c) concrete operations, ages 6-12; and (d) formal operations, age 12 and up. Progression through the stages requires experience as well as interaction with the environment.

Piaget's cognitive development is a prerequisite of moral, ethical, and ego development. Kohlberg (1984) expands upon Piaget's notions and seeks to determine the individual's stage of justice reasoning. His model consists of three levels: (a) the preconventional level, where individuals act out of self-centered, rather than social, motives; (b) the conventional level, where individuals do as they are supposed to, according to the rules of society; and (c) the postconventional level, where individuals act upon principles (moral, legal, ethical) rather than rules.

Loevinger's (1976) theory of ego development contains seven stages and two transitions, each characterized by particular types of character development, interpersonal style, conscious preoccupations, and cognitive style. The progression is as follows: (a) presocial, symbiotic; (b) impulsive; (c) self-protective; (d) conformist; (e) conscientious-conformist; (f) conscientious; (g) individualistic; (h) autonomous; and (i) integrated.

Perry (1970) provides a cognitive-developmental sequence of stages to identify intellectual and ethical development in college students. He categorizes the stages as dualism, relativism, and commitment. Dualism takes a dichotomous view of the world: All things are either right or wrong. Relativism involves abstract thinking and the realization that there is no absolute right or wrong. Commitment involves responsibility for resolving the right-wrong dilemma within oneself.

Kegan (1982) takes a life-span developmental approach in which the individual constantly engages in the cognitive process of meaning making, attempting to make sense of events in order to grow. Kegan's stages consist of the following: (a) incorporative, (b) impulsive, (c) imperial, (d) institutional, and (e) interindividual.

For a summary of the human development stages discussed by the theorists mentioned above, see Table 1.1.

Behavioral theories. Behavioral theories stress the importance of environmental, rather than biological or cognitive, factors as determinants of development. In order to promote development and to predict or control human behavior, it is necessary to become aware of the environmental conditions of the individual. Because all behavior is presumed to result from learning, the general therapeutic goal is to create new conditions for learning (Hayes, 1986). The three basic models of learning—classical conditioning, operant conditioning, and vicarious conditioning—will be discussed later in this chapter in the section on learning theory.

Abnormal Behavior

Theoretically based on the developmental model, professional counseling focuses on group interventions, "giving skills away" (assertiveness, parenting, communication, and so on), training and educational interventions, work on family and societal problems, and preventive community interventions (Aubrey, 1986) with "normal" individuals and groups experiencing developmental or environmental difficulties. However, many counseling settings adhere to the medical model, which requires counselors to make accurate assessments of their clientele based on the American Psychiatric Association's (1987) *Diagnostic and Statistical Manual of Mental Orders* (third edition, revised) (DSM-III-R). Thus counselors need to be aware of *abnormal* as well as normal behavior in human development.

TABLE 1.1: Summary of Human Development Stages

Theorist	Stage 1	Stage 2	Stage 3	Stage 4	Stage 5	Stage 6
Freud	oral	anal	phallic	latency	genital	—
Piaget	sensorimotor	preoperational	concrete operational	early formal operations	full formal operations	postformal operations
Erikson	autonomy versus shame/doubt	initiative versus guilt	industry versus inferiority	identity versus role confusion	intimacy versus isolation	integrity versus despair
Maslow	survival	security	safety	love, belongingness	self-esteem	self-actualization
Perry	—	—	dualism	relativism	commitment	—
Loevinger	presocial	impulsive	opportunistic	conformist	conscientious	autonomous
Kegan	incorporative	impulsive	imperial	interpersonal	institutional	interindividual
Kohlberg	egocentric	concrete individual	interpersonal	social conscience	moral/legal conflict	ethical principles

Abnormal behavior may be defined either as "a deviation from the social norms," or as "maladaptive behavior which interferes with optimal functioning and growth of the individual and, ultimately, the society." Maladaptive behavior may include not only traditional disorders such as alcoholism, neuroses, and psychoses, but also prejudice and discrimination, pollution, violence, corruption, and other behaviors that eventually lead to personal distress and group conflict (Coleman, Butcher, & Carson, 1980).

Biological Viewpoint

In early times maladaptive behavior was attributed to demonology, mass madness, and witchcraft, and was punished accordingly. Scientific advances during the eighteenth century led to the development of the biological viewpoint—that is, the idea of mental disorder as an illness based on pathology of an organ, namely, the brain. Through the work of William Griesinger (1817-1868) and Emil Kraeplin (1859-1926), the biological viewpoint was widely accepted in the medical community, a system of classification was begun, and research was initiated to determine the role of

organic processes in mental disorders (Coleman et al., 1980).

Psychosocial and Sociocultural Viewpoint

Although the field of psychology was in its infancy in the early 1900s, there was a growing interest in determining the role of psychological factors in maladaptive behavior. Coleman et al. (1980) have examined five explanations of human nature and behavior that lead to the development of the psychosocial viewpoint of abnormal behavior: (a) psychoanalytic, (b) behavioristic, (c) humanistic, (d) existential, and (e) interpersonal.

Causes

Discovering the etiology of abnormal behavior is a complicated, if not impossible, task. A wide variety of biological as well as environmental factors come into play, and there is no universal reaction to any of these factors. Depending upon the viewpoint of the researcher or clinician, various aspects of causation may be emphasized.

Proponents of the biological viewpoint stress the importance of genetic makeup, biochemical functions, and brain pathology. Constitutional liabilities such as physical handicaps and physical deprivation may also contribute to the development of abnormal behavior. From the psychosocial perspective, a number of interacting factors may influence an individual to behave abnormally. Some of these factors are childhood trauma, parental deprivation, dysfunctional parent-child relationships, dysfunctional family systems, and stress. In addition to these, various sociocultural factors may come into play. These include war and violence, deviant social roles, prejudice and discrimination, and economic and employment difficulties, as well as rapid changes in technology and societal norms and values (Coleman et al., 1980).

Patterns

Patterns of abnormal behavior are classified according to the DSM-III-R (American Psychiatric Association, 1987), which uses a multiaxial evaluation system. Each client is evaluated on five axes: Axis I—Clinical Syndromes and V Codes (for conditions not attributable to a mental disorder that are a focus of attention or treatment); Axis II—Developmental Disorders and Personality Disorders; Axis III—Physical Disorders and Conditions (including substance use disorders); Axis IV—Severity of Psychosocial Stressors; and Axis V—Global Assessment of Functioning. Although the official diagnostic assessment is determined by the first three axes, the last two provide environmental and functional information that may be useful for treatment planning that addresses the whole person rather than a single presenting problem.

Personality Theory

Theories of personality have been developed in an attempt to describe and explain the behavior of individuals. Unlike other scientific theories, which are based upon prediction and control, personality theories are based upon uncontrolled observations, which gives them a philosophical, rather than scientific, tone. Personality theories discussed in this section will

be classified as (a) psychoanalytic, (b) trait, (c) humanistic, and (d) cognitive. Learning theories are taken up in the following section.

Psychoanalytic Theories

The early personality theories of Freud, Jung, and Sullivan developed out of the psychoanalytic school of thought.

Freud. As discussed above, Freud based his theory on the three systems of personality he called id, ego, and superego. He believed that the crucial time for personality development occurs during the first five years of life. According to Freud, problems in the early stages of development can cause an individual to become fixated at that stage and to retain the personality type associated with that particular stage—that is, oral, anal, or phallic.

Jung. Through his analytic theory, discussed above, Jung made two major contributions to the field of personality theory: the word-association technique and the concept of introversion-extroversion. He developed a projective personality assessment using free association with a list of 100 words, and he proposed four dimensions to explain personality structure: introversion-extroversion, sensing-intuition, thinking-feeling, and judgment-perception. Individuals' personality types are indicated by their positions along these dimensions. This work influenced the development of a major personality inventory, the Myers-Briggs Type Indicator (Myers, 1962), which is widely used in counseling, education, and research (Drummond, 1988).

Sullivan. Sullivan's (1953) interpersonal theory of personality development stresses observable interactions among people. Sullivan views individuals as progressing through seven stages of personality development extending throughout the lifetime as they strive for psychological health. Sullivan focused on the dynamism of self, which is greatly influenced by expectations of the outside world. The individual's perceptions of self (me) and others (not me) are called *personifications.* Depending upon the individual's experiences, opposing personifications may develop simultaneously, and the individual must struggle to find a balance between good-me and bad-me (Byrne & Kelley, 1981).

Trait Theories

The following categories of personality theories were developed from a psychological, rather than psychoanalytic, perspective. The first category, trait theories, attempts to classify individuals according to a series of personality constructs, or traits, that can be used to predict behavior under given circumstances. Murray and Allport, two of the trait theorists working at Harvard University in the 1930s, created and defined the academic field of personality psychology.

Murray. Murray's (1938) theory attempted to explain human motivation in terms of two types of needs: (a) basic, or primary, needs; and (b) learned, or secondary, needs. As individuals strive to get these needs met, external events, called *press,* may either hinder or help in the achievement of the need. The combination of need and press is called *thema.* Based upon Murray's theory, two personality assessments have been developed: the Thematic Apperception Test (TAT) and the Edwards Personal Preference Schedule (EPPS).

Allport. Allport's theory of personality is based on the concept of traits (see Allport & Odbert, 1936). According to Allport, personality is an internal, dynamic process that changes throughout life, rather than a reaction to external events. Personality traits fall along a continuum from specific, a particular behavior, to general, a habit of being a certain way. Allport designates three types of traits: (a) common traits, used to compare people in a given culture; (b) personal traits, usually five to ten characteristics used to define individual personality; and (c) cardinal traits, used to describe one dominant characteristic in an individual's personality. Allport believed that one could determine an individual's philosophy of life by looking at a set of underlying values. Allport, Vernon, and Lindzey's (1960) *Study of Values* was designed to measure an individual's value orientation according to six basic evaluative attitudes: theoretical, economic, aesthetic, social, political, and religious.

Cattell. Cattell (1946) attempted to define personality by compiling a list of 171 personality traits on which an individual could be rated. He used factor analysis and intercorrelation of these ratings to reduce the list to 16 dimensions along which individuals differ. These underlying *source traits* are expressed by an individual's observable behaviors, or *surface traits.* Source traits can be measured by the Sixteen Personality Factor Questionnaire (Cattell, Eber, & Tatsuoka, 1970), which Cattell claims identifies the basic elements of personality. Although Cattell's theory has been widely researched, his use of factor analysis to identify basic personality dimensions has not been universally accepted. More empirical validation is needed (Anastasi, 1988).

Humanistic Theories

In opposition to the psychoanalysts, test builders, and behaviorists, Maslow and Rogers took a humanistic approach to personality theory. They believed in the basic goodness of human nature and the inherent desire of individuals to achieve higher levels of functioning.

Maslow. Maslow interviewed high-functioning individuals in order to determine characteristics of self-actualized people. His theory was based upon a hierarchy of needs, consisting of lower-order needs (physiological necessities and safety) and higher-order needs (belongingness and love, self-esteem and, finally, *self-actualization*) (Maslow, 1962). Given a supportive environment, Maslow believed that all humans would naturally move toward self-actualization, which is characterized by creativity, happiness, autonomy, and a democratic attitude.

Rogers. Through his work in client-centered therapy, Rogers (1951) developed a self-theory of personality. According to Rogers (1961), difficulties arise when there is a discrepancy between one's real self (self-concept) and one's ideal self. The actualizing tendency moves individuals to eliminate the discrepancies and reach their highest potential. Rogers recognized a need for *unconditional positive regard* from important others as well as positive self-regard. Contrary to the behaviorist point of view, Rogers stressed internally, rather than externally, directed behavior.

Cognitive Theories

Cognitive approaches to personality theory stress the importance of rational thought processes and the phenomenological approach. People react individually to situations based upon their perceptions rather than objective reality. Lewin (1951), an early proponent of this approach, viewed human behavior as a function of individuals and their psychological environment, or life space. Another cognitive approach, Festinger's (1957) theory of cognitive dissonance, proposed that individuals strive for consistency in cognitive structure, and that the unpleasantness of inconsistency, or dissonance, motivates them to avoid or reduce it.

Kelly's (1955) psychology of personal constructs takes a cognitive approach to personality. Kelly believes that individuals create their own concepts or constructs in an attempt to make sense of their environment. The ability to choose options—onstructive alternativism— influences the individual's decisions and behavior. The Role Construct Repertory Test (Rep Test) developed by Kelly (1955) yields information about how individuals organize their interpersonal worlds, their degree of cognitive complexity, and certain personality and cognitive variables. In order to make progress in counseling, it may be necessary for an individual to build new constructs and to discard some old constructs (Anastasi, 1988).

Learning Theory

Another set of personality theories, learning theories, focus on perception, learning, and cognition as a way of explaining human development.

Classical Conditioning

Pavlov (1927), a Russian psychologist, first introduced the concept of classical conditioning. In his laboratory work with dogs, Pavlov discovered the important role of antecedents in determining behavior. In some cases, certain antecedents (i.e., unconditioned stimuli) produced unconditioned, or natural, responses.

For example, when presented with meat powder, Pavlov's dogs automatically salivated. Classical conditioning occurs when a neutral stimulus, such as the ringing of a bell, is paired with an unconditioned stimulus, such as meat powder, to provoke the unconditioned response, in this case, salivation. Repetition of this process eventually results in the neutral stimulus becoming a conditioned stimulus provoking a conditioned response. Thus in Pavlov's experiments the dogs salivated upon hearing the bell.

Important concepts. Some other concepts important to understanding classical conditioning include stimulus generalization, extinction, and counterconditioning. *Stimulus generalization* occurs when a conditioned stimulus is repeatedly paired with another similar stimulus until the subject responds to the other stimulus presented alone. *Extinction* occurs as the conditioned response weakens over time because the conditioned stimulus is repeatedly presented without the unconditioned stimulus. In *counterconditioning*, the conditioned stimulus is paired with a stimulus that elicits a response that is incompatible with the unwanted conditioned response. Research on classical conditioning, which has revealed that many emotional responses are the result of classical conditioning, has helped explain such problems as prejudice and irrational fears, and has altered some ideas about human nature (Chance, 1979).

Early applications. Early behaviorists in the United States include Watson and Wolpe. Watson (1919), the first American behaviorist, used classical conditioning methods to treat phobias. He believed that individuals' behavior could be shaped through conditioning. Wolpe (1966) used classical conditioning theory in psychotherapy. He introduced the concepts of reciprocal inhibition and systematic desensitization, which he applied in order to reduce anxiety. In treatment he paired relaxation with an anxiety-provoking stimulus until the stimulus no longer produced anxiety.

Operant Conditioning

Rather than focusing on antecedents, as in classical conditioning, operant conditioning focuses on the consequences of behavior. This idea was first advanced by Thorndike (1913), with his "law of effect." He believed the strength of the stimulus-response connection was either increased when followed by a "satisfying state of affairs" (reward) or decreased when followed by an "annoying state of affairs" (punishment).

Reinforcement principle. Skinner (1953) renamed Thorndike's law "the principle of reinforcement" and called this type of learning "operant conditioning." Learning takes place as individuals experience the consequences of their behaviors—either reinforcement or punishment. Reinforcement increases the likelihood of the behavior reoccurring, while punishment decreases the likelihood. A consequence that is added is positive; one that is withdrawn is negative.

Reinforcement schedules. The term *schedule of reinforcement* refers to the pattern of response consequences and has a powerful effect upon the learning of new behaviors. When a response is reinforced every time it occurs, it is called *continuous reinforcement.* When the behavior is reinforced sometimes, but not always, it is called either *partial reinforcement* or an *intermittent schedule of reinforcement.*

There are four kinds of intermittent schedules: (a) fixed interval, in which reinforcement occurs only after a given amount of time, such as at 10-second intervals; (b) variable interval, in which reinforcement occurs after varying amounts of time, such as after 2 seconds, then 8 seconds, then 5 seconds, and so on; (c) fixed ratio, in which reinforcement occurs at regular response intervals, such as after every fifth response; and (d) variable ratio, in which reinforcement occurs at a particular rate, such as 5:1 on average, but the actual number of responses for any one reinforcement may be more or less than 5 (i.e., [7 + 3 + 2 + 8]/4 = 5).

Important terms. Some other concepts in operant conditioning include token economy, shaping, extinction, and differential reinforcement. *Token economy* involves reinforcing desirable behavior with objects (such as stars, money, or poker chips) that can be exchanged

for some other reinforcer, such as an outing, a movie, or other treat. Rather than waiting for the desired response to occur spontaneously, behavior can be *shaped* by rewarding closer and closer approximations to the desired behavior.

To eliminate undesirable behavior, extinction or differential reinforcement may be used. *Extinction* usually involves withholding reinforcement for the response, and, to be effective, all the reinforcers following an undesirable response must be removed all the time. *Differential reinforcement* consists of putting the unwanted response on extinction while reinforcing desirable behavior (Chance, 1979).

Vicarious Conditioning

Although Thorndike and Watson ruled out the idea of vicarious conditioning (observational learning) through their laboratory experiments, interest was renewed when Bandura (1977) proposed his social learning theory. His work with children led him to believe that children can learn simply by observing the behavior of others, who serve as models. In primary vicarious conditioning the observer learns new behavior by watching a model undergo classical or instrumental conditioning. Vicarious reinforcement occurs when the observer sees the model's behavior being reinforced and then performs the reinforced behavior; vicarious punishment occurs when the observer sees the model's behavior being punished and then refrains from the behavior.

When the stimuli and responses are not actually demonstrated, but are represented in some symbolic fashion, secondary vicarious conditioning may take place. Thus an individual may learn to do something by reading about it, by seeing some graphic demonstration, such as a map, of it (imagistic symbols), or by receiving verbal instructions from another (linguistic symbols). In secondary vicarious reinforcement and punishment, the consequences are also represented symbolically. Behavior acquired through observation can be modified through the direct conditioning procedures used in classical and operant conditioning (Chance, 1979).

LEARNING OBJECTIVES

After studying the material in this chapter, you should be able to do the following:

(1) Understand three worldviews relevant to human development.
(2) Explain the four major categories of developmental theory: biological, psychodynamic, cognitive, behavioral.
(3) Define *abnormal behavior*.
(4) Discuss the biological, psychosocial, and sociocultural viewpoints on maladaptive behavior.
(5) List three biological causes of abnormal behavior.
(6) Name some sociocultural causes of abnormal behavior.
(7) List some psychosocial causes of abnormal behavior.
(8) Discuss some common patterns of abnormal behavior.
(9) Link specific theories of personality with their major proponents.
(10) Compare and contrast classical, operant, and vicarious conditioning.
(11) Explain the various types of reinforcement.
(12) Discuss some application of learning theory that could be used in counseling.

TIME LINE

You should be aware of important developments in the area of human growth and development.

1913	Thorndike, law of effect	1955	Kelly, psychology of personal constructs
1919	Watson coins the term *behaviorism*		
1925	Freud, psychoanalytic theory	1962	Maslow, hierarchy of needs
1927	Pavlov, classical conditioning	1963	Adler, individual psychology
1928	Jung, analytic psychology	1968	Erikson, psychosocial development
1936	Allport, trait theory	1970	Perry, ethical development
1938	Murray, needs theory	1971	Bandura, social learning theory
1946	Cattell, 171 personality traits	1976	Loevinger, ego development
1951	Rogers, client-centered therapy	1982	Kegan, life-span developmental approach
1952	Piaget, developmental psychology		
1953	Skinner, operant conditioning	1984	Kohlberg, moral development

TERMS AND NAMES
TO REMEMBER

Terms

You should have an understanding of the following terms and be able to define them in your own words.

abnormal behavior
antecedent
anxiety
behavioral worldview
biological viewpoint
classical conditioning
cognitive dissonance
consequences
constructive alternativism
counterconditioning
defense mechanism
ego
etiology
extinction
extroversion
generalization
id
inferiority complex
interactional worldview
introversion

learning theory
libido
maturation
modeling
neurosis
operant conditioning
phenomenological
pleasure principle
psychosis
psychosocial viewpoint
punishment
reality principle
reinforcement
self-actualization
shaping
superego
trait theory
token economy
unconditional positive regard
vicarious conditioning

Names

You should be familiar with these people and be aware of their contributions to the counseling profession with regard to human growth and development.

Adler
Allport
Bandura
Cattell
Erikson
Festinger
Freud
Jung
Kegan
Kelly
Kohlberg
Lewin

Loevinger
Maslow
Murray
Pavlov
Perry
Piaget
Rogers
Skinner
Sullivan
Thorndike
Watson
Wolpe

FILL IN THE BLANKS

The following section reviews some of the major points in this content area. Check your knowledge of the area by filling in the appropriate name, term, or concept in each blank provided. Answer choices are found above, in the section containing terms and names to remember. You will find the correct answers at the end of the chapter.

(1) The ego's need for immediate gratification is known as the _Pleasure Principle_.

(2) _Shaping_ of behavior is accomplished by rewarding successive approximations of the desired behavior.

(3) The causation, or _etiology_, of abnormal behavior is difficult to determine in most cases.

(4) An individual who has achieved _Self-actualization_ is happy, autonomous, and creative.

(5) According to Rogers, _Unconditional positive regard_ from parents is necessary for children to develop healthy self-concepts.

(6) A method of learning that involves the conditioning of new stimuli to existing responses is _Classical Conditioning_.

(7) In behavior modification, use continuous _reinforcement_ to establish a new behavior.

(8) The designations *common, personal,* and *cardinal* refer to _trait theory_.

(9) In the _Contextual worldview_ individuals are in an interactional relationship with their environment.

(10) Freud believed that human behavior is primarily motivated by the psychosexual energy he called _libido_.

(11) Relearning by using a particular stimulus to establish a new, more adaptive response is _Counterconditioning_.

(12) Kelly's concept of _Constructive alternativism_ alludes to the idea that there are many different ways of interpreting events, each interpretation leading to different behaviors.

(13) _Psychosis_ is a severe psychological disorder involving loss of contact with reality.

(14) The process of development and body change resulting from heredity rather than learning is _Maturation_.

(15) Vicarious conditioning occurs through observed _Modeling_
_____ of the desired behavior.

(16) The unpleasantness of _Cognitive dissonance_ motivates
individuals to avoid or reduce inconsistencies in cognitive structure.

(17) Individuals use _defense Mechanisms_ in order to
maintain their feelings of adequacy and self-worth rather than cope
directly with a stressful situation.

(18) A counselor might use systematic desensitization to help reduce the
Anxiety experienced by an agoraphobic
client.

(19) Skinner believes that the social environment provides a wide variety of
Consequences that help shape human behavior.

(20) Patterns of _abnormal behavior_ may be organic,
psychological, or sociocultural in origin.

(21) In Jung's theory, _Introversion_ is the tendency
toward subjective functioning, with the self being of greatest importance.

(22) Behavior modification programs in schools or group homes often use
token economy to motivate participants.

(23) The _phenomenological_ approach to human
functioning stresses the importance of each individual's perception of
reality.

(24) The _Biological Viewpoint_ emphasizes the importance
of genetic and physical contributors to maladaptive behavior.

(25) Through _extinction_, undesirable behavior
may be eliminated.

MATCHING TEST

Match the names in the left-hand column with the appropriate concepts in the right-hand column.

___	(1) Adler	(a)	id, ego, superego
___	(2) Allport	(b)	introversion-extroversion
___	(3) Bandura	(c)	use of family constellation
___	(4) Cattell	(d)	stage theory of development
___	(5) Erikson	(e)	original child psychologist
___	(6) Festinger	(f)	justice reasoning
___	(7) Freud	(g)	seven-stage ego development
___	(8) Jung	(h)	dualism, relativism, commitment
___	(9) Kegan	(i)	cognitive meaning making
___	(10) Kelly	(j)	Thematic Apperception Test
___	(11) Kohlberg	(k)	traits and values
___	(12) Lewin	(l)	Sixteen Personality Factor Questionnaire
___	(13) Loevinger	(m)	life space
___	(14) Maslow	(n)	cognitive dissonance
___	(15) Murray	(o)	Role Construct Repertory Test
___	(16) Pavlov	(p)	systematic desensitization
___	(17) Perry	(q)	principle of reinforcement
___	(18) Piaget	(r)	Russian psychologist
___	(19) Rogers	(s)	vicarious conditioning
___	(20) Skinner	(t)	interpersonal personality theory
___	(21) Sullivan	(u)	self-actualization
___	(22) Thorndike	(v)	actualizing tendency
___	(23) Watson	(w)	father of American behaviorism
___	(24) Wolpe	(x)	stimulus-response-consequence

CASE STUDY

Bill is a 40-year-old divorced man who was just released from a week-long stay at the crisis stabilization unit (CSU) following a suicide attempt. Bill discussed his situation during a few sessions with a psychotherapist at the CSU. He was able to overcome some of the guilt he felt for the suicide attempt, but he realized he would need more help to work on the depression and low self-esteem that had led him to the attempt in the first place. Bill arranged for outpatient therapy before being released from the hospital.

Bill revealed that he was very dissatisfied with life in general. He had married at a young age, hoping to escape his father's criticism and become a "real man." He tried to satisfy his wife's desire to have a child, but after three years without success, she left him for another man. For several years Bill made feeble attempts at dating, but never established a close relationship with a woman. He reports his current social life is almost nonexistent. He has not been out with a woman in over four years. Occasionally, he goes out to dinner, a movie, or a card game with a few men from work. He often spends weekend afternoons watching sports on TV with his brother, the one family member with whom he keeps in contact.

Bill's intelligence is average, and he is very skilled in his trade as a carpenter. He reports a series of jobs that have been secure, but unchallenging. He thinks he has the skills and expertise to be foreman. He often sees better and more proficient ways of getting the job done, but his fear of failure and lack of assertiveness keep him from approaching his boss with suggestions. Asking for a promotion is entirely out of the question. Due to his lack of social support, frustration on the job, and general dissatisfaction with life, Bill had become so depressed that he attempted to commit suicide. Further analysis revealed that Bill's attempt was more a cry for help and attention than a serious desire to do away with himself.

Analysis

(1) Given the information above, write three treatment goals for Bill.

_____

_____

_____

_____

_____

_____

(2) In terms of the cognitive theories of development, which stage or level do you think Bill has achieved, and how would you help him move to the next level proposed by Loevinger?

_____

_____

Kegan?

_____

Kohlberg?

_____

(3) How would you analyze Bill's situation from the biological viewpoint?

_____

_____

psychosocial viewpoint?

_____

_____

sociocultural viewpoint?

_____

_____

(4) Describe how you would use systematic desensitization to help Bill overcome the anxiety related to speaking up to his boss.

_____

_____

_____

_____

(5) Discuss some behavioral techniques you could use to help Bill improve his social life. Use the concepts of reinforcement, vicarious conditioning, and modeling.

_____

_____

Notes

MULTIPLE-CHOICE TEST

Check your understanding of this content area by responding to the following questions. You will find the answer key at the end of the chapter.

1. Social learning theory uses the concept of modeling to explain some aspects of human behavior. The concept that best explains how modeling works within this theory is

   a. primary reinforcement
   b. secondary reinforcement
   c. vicarious reinforcement
   d. intermittent reinforcement

2. Counselors who follow Maslow's theory believe people's behaviors are directed by

   a. oral gratification
   b. pleasure principle
   c. pleasing others
   d. need gratification

3. Motivation and reinforcement may come from within a person or from sources external to the person. According to Rotter, people's behavior is determined by their belief that reinforcements are either internally or externally controlled. This concept is called

   a. locus of control
   b. reinforcement contingency
   c. goal orientation
   d. expectancy level

4. A client who reverts to old behavior patterns is said to be

   a. projecting
   b. compensating
   c. actualizing
   d. regressing

5. As a counselor in a community mental health center, you receive a paycheck every other Friday. This is an example of which reinforcement schedule?

   a. variable interval
   b. fixed interval
   c. variable ratio
   d. fixed ratio

6. Jung's work forms the basis for many personality concepts of interest today. Among these are

   a. introversion-extroversion
   b. collective unconscious
   c. individuation
   d. all of the above

7. In adult development, mid-life is characterized by

   a. androgyny
   b. decline in intellectual functioning
   c. a sense of time running out
   d. peer pressure

8. Piaget identifies four major stages of child development. Which of the following refers to the period during which the child develops the abilities to classify and seriate objects and to maintain relationships between objects despite their physical manipulation?

   a. formal operations
   b. concrete operations
   c. preoperational
   d. sensorimotor

9. Which of the following describes Rogers's view of humanity?

   a. People are rational.
   b. People are irresponsible.
   c. People are inherently good.
   d. People are externally controlled.

10. According to Kohlberg's theory of moral development,

    a. most fail to go beyond the conventional level
    b. moral development precedes logical development
    c. structure and content are synonymous
    d. society's rules are superior to personal ethics

11. Festinger is known for the concept of cognitive dissonance. He believes individuals

    a. cannot accept differences of opinion
    b. tend to change their attitudes irrationally
    c. seek consistency in cognitive structure
    d. reject discrepancies between the real and ideal

12. The first theorist to acknowledge continued development during adulthood was

    a. Jung
    b. Adler
    c. Piaget
    d. Loevinger

13. A childhood disturbance characterized by withdrawal, a blurred sense of self, and obsessive self-stimulation (head banging, rocking, and so on) is known as

    a. infantile dementia
    b. hyperkinesis
    c. retardation
    d. autism

14. According to Adler's theory of individual psychology, when an individual's real self and self-ideal do not match,

    a. the reality principle becomes evident
    b. the individual will seek ego gratification
    c. the preconventional level has been reached
    d. feelings of inferiority arise

15. Behavioral theory is to humanistic theory as

    a. preoperational thinking is to formal operational thinking
    b. unconscious motivation is to conscious motivation
    c. external locus of control is to internal locus of control
    d. extinction is to generalization

16. In order to describe and explain human behavior,

    a. reinforcement contingencies have been established
    b. personality theories have been developed
    c. needs gratification is essential
    d. projective personality tests must be given

17. As a new counselor in a community mental health center, you have been assigned to a client whose diagnosis is "anorexia nervosa." You would expect the client to be

    a. male rather than female
    b. middle-aged rather then adolescent
    c. extroverted rather than introverted
    d. none of the above

18. Two theorists who believe human beings are motivated by needs are

    a. Adler and Allport
    b. Maslow and Rogers
    c. Murray and Maslow
    d. Moreno and Murray

19. When working with clients, counselors need to be aware of defense mechanisms. Clients who refuse to take responsibility for their own actions or situations often attribute their unacceptable desires or impulses to others. This is an example of

    a. regression
    b. projection
    c. repression
    d. protection

20. The term cardinal trait, used by Allport in his personality theory, means

    a. a dominant characteristic of the individual
    b. a "red flag" for counselors
    c. a highly developed value system
    d. one of five or ten characteristics that best describe an individual

21. A counselor whose methods are based on learning theory approaches treatment

    a. with an emphasis on rational thinking
    b. by focusing on emotional content
    c. from a behavioral standpoint
    d. in a holistic manner

22. Lewin theorizes that an individual's behavior is a function of the person and his or her psychological environment, or life space. This approach to human development may be called

    a. psychosociological
    b. phenomenological
    c. rational-emotive
    d. cognitive-behavioral

23. Harry Stack Sullivan's psychiatry of interpersonal relations focuses on

    a. family constellations
    b. communication between persons
    c. stages of ethical development
    d. psychosexual functioning

24. Which of these is not a particular theorist's expression of high-level functioning?

    a. Rogers, self-ideal
    b. Maslow, self-actualization
    c. Loevinger, integrated
    d. Kohlberg, postconventional

25. A major category of maladaptive behavior is known as addictive disorders. Some examples of these include

    a. alcoholism, enuresis, drug abuse
    b. gambling, obesity, homosexuality
    c. neurosis, marijuana abuse, dependence
    d. alcoholism, obesity, drug abuse

ANSWER KEY

Fill in the Blanks

(1) pleasure principle
(2) shaping
(3) etiology
(4) self-actualization
(5) unconditional positive regard
(6) classical conditioning
(7) reinforcement
(8) trait theory
(9) contextual worldview
(10) libido
(11) counterconditioning
(12) constructive alternativism
(13) psychosis
(14) maturation
(15) modeling
(16) cognitive dissonance
(17) defense mechanisms
(18) anxiety
(19) consequences
(20) abnormal behavior
(21) introversion
(22) token economy
(23) phenomenological
(24) biological viewpoint
(25) extinction

Matching

(1) c
(2) k
(3) s
(4) l
(5) d
(6) n
(7) a
(8) b
(9) i
(10) o
(11) f
(12) m
(13) g
(14) u
(15) j
(16) r
(17) h
(18) e
(19) v
(20) q
(21) t
(22) x
(23) w
(24) p

Multiple-Choice

1. c
2. d
3. a
4. d
5. b
6. d
7. c
8. b
9. c
10. a
11. c
12. a
13. d
14. d
15. c
16. b
17. d
18. c
19. b
20. a
21. c
22. b
23. b
24. a
25. d

CHAPTER 2

Social and Cultural Foundations

SUMMARY   34
   Human Roles   **34**
      Age Roles   34
      Sex Roles   34
      Family Roles   35
      Work Roles   36
      Role Integration   36
   Ethnic and Cultural Issues   **36**
      Cross-Cultural Perspective   36
      Profiles of Ethnic Minorities   37
      Discrimination and Stereotyping   38
      Diagnosis and Intervention   38
   Social Issues and Mores   **39**
      Aging   39
      Loss and Grief   39
      Inequality   39
      Disabilities   39
      Abuse   40
      Substance Abuse   40
   Life-Styles and Patterns   **40**
      Family Life   40
      Nonfamily Households   41
      Gay Life-Style   41
   Conclusion   **41**
LEARNING OBJECTIVES   42
TIME LINE   43

TERMS AND NAMES TO REMEMBER   44
   Terms   **44**
   Names   **44**
FILL IN THE BLANKS   45
MATCHING TEST   47
CASE STUDY   48
   Analysis   **48**
MULTIPLE-CHOICE TEST   51
ANSWER KEY   54
   Fill in the Blanks   **54**
   Matching   **54**
   Multiple-Choice   **54**

SUMMARY

Social and cultural foundations include studies of change, ethnic groups, subcultures, changing roles of women, sexism, urban and rural societies, population patterns, cultural mores, use of leisure time, and differing life patterns. Disciplines such as the behavioral sciences, economics, and political science are involved. (Loesch & Vacc, 1986, p. 13)

Human Roles

Because social systems are made up of a series of interlocking positions, or roles, role theory is a useful way of looking at human development. Bee and Mitchell (1984) offer a useful definition: "A role is the content of a position or the behavioral implications of occupying that position" (pp. 22-23). They discuss three important properties of roles: (a) Roles are culturally defined and may change within a culture; (b) roles occur in complementary pairs, such as teacher-student, parent-child; and (c) individuals occupy more than one role at a time, sometimes creating role conflict. Human roles, including age roles, sex roles, work roles, and family roles, change as individuals develop over the life span.

Age Roles

Two developmental theorists, Erikson (1963) and Levinson (1978) view human development as a progression through stages and eras, respectively. Erikson identifies eight developmental stages, while Levinson divides the life span into five eras.

Erikson. To understand age roles better, consider Erikson's (1963) developmental stages, each having an approximate age limit and a central theme. As individuals master Erikson's five childhood and three adult stages, depicted in Table 2.1, role changes can be expected.

Transitions. Each stage is associated with particular role expectations determined by the culture. Children are expected to behave one way, young adults another, and the elderly still another. *Transition* refers to the changing of roles over the ages. Some role strain and accompanying disorganization and anxiety are normal as individuals shift from one role, or one set of roles, to another (Hultsch & Deutsch, 1981).

Levinson. Levinson (1978) has paid particular attention to the adult life cycle and has identified five eras of the life span. The first is that of childhood; the other four focus on adult developmental periods and transitions. The five eras include (a) preadulthood, ages 0-22; (b) early adulthood, ages 17-45; (c) middle adulthood, ages 40-65; (d) late adulthood, ages 60-85; and (e) late late adulthood, age 85 and older. Each era is marked by a stable period followed by a transition. During stable periods roles are set and individuals build their life structures. During transition periods, roles are less stable, as individuals explore possibilities for change and make choices that provide the basis for a new life structure (Hultsch & Deutsch, 1981).

Sex Roles

In the past, sex roles were more clearly defined and stable over the life span than they are today. Within the first few years of life a child could determine whether he or she was male or female and could learn the basic cultural expectations associated with her or his gender role, expecting little change. However, recent research has shown that there have been some shifts in the "job descriptions" for men and women. While male and female sex roles are relatively distinct in childhood and early adulthood, they appear to be more alike among older adults (Bee & Mitchell, 1984).

Myths. A number of myths surround the notion of sex differences. Maccoby and Jacklin (1974) have found few facts to support the myths. The fact is that females have greater verbal ability, while males excel in visual-spatial ability and mathematics and are more aggressive. The myths say that females are more sociable and suggestible, have lower self-

TABLE 2.1: Erikson's Life Stages

Age (years)	Stage	Central Theme
Birth–1	early infancy	trust versus mistrust
1–2	later infancy	autonomy versus shame and doubt
3–5	early childhood	initiative versus guilt
6–11	middle childhood	industry versus inferiority
12–20	adolescence	identity versus role confusion
20–35	early adulthood	intimacy versus isolation
35–65	middle adulthood	generativity versus stagnation
65+	late adulthood	integrity versus despair

esteem, are better at rote learning and simple repetitive tasks, are more affected by heredity, lack achievement motivation, and are more auditory than males. Myths about males include that they are more analytic, can better inhibit previously learned responses, are better at higher-level cognitive processes, are more affected by the environment, and are more visual. Only when these myths are dispelled and individuals are no longer judged by their biological characteristics, but valued for their unique contributions, can equality of the sexes be achieved (Van Hoose & Worth, 1982).

Challenges. Although traditional sex roles had some practical value when men's primary responsibility was working in the fields or in business and women's responsibilities centered on home and children, Van Hoose and Worth (1982) point out that the traditional division of sex roles (a) limits human potential by confining individuals to sex-appropriate behaviors and (b) gives more status, power, and desirability to the male role. This division is reinforced by mass media, which continue to imply male superiority and female passivity. Today, however, this notion is being challenged by those who believe that the range of behaviors for both sexes should be expanded.

Stereotyping versus androgyny. Bem (1975) argues that sex role stereotyping is unhealthy. Based upon research using the Bem Sex Role Inventory, she concludes that in adults both high femininity and high masculinity correlate with high anxiety and low self-acceptance; in children, highly feminine girls and highly masculine boys are lower in intelligence, spatial ability, and creativity. Bem asserts that men and women can function better in complex societies when they are free from rigid sex roles and are

allowed to be androgynous (from *andro*, male, and *gyne*, female). Androgyny is the incorporation of both feminine and masculine attributes in one personality, allowing the person to express feelings and behaviors of either sex, as the situation warrants, without feeling threatened. Van Hoose and Worth (1982), who expect that androgyny will increase as societal values evolve, espouse a wider range of behavior for both sexes.

Family Roles

As the divorce rate increases, the number of single-parent families and stepfamilies in this society continues to grow. However, according to Bee and Mitchell (1984), changes in family roles provide the most visible changes for the majority of people, who, at least for part of their adult lives, experience traditional family life.

Family stages. Adults who marry and have children move through a distinct set of roles in a specific order known as "family life-cycle stages." These eight stages can be characterized as follows:

(1) *Newly married with no children:* The major new role is that of spouse.

(2) *New parents:* The first child is still an infant, and the new role of parent has been added. The infant takes on the child role.

(3) *Families with preschool children:* The oldest child is not yet in school. The parental role is changing as the child gets older. The child takes on the sibling role.

(4) *Oldest child in school:* Again the role shifts as parents deal with the child's

new characteristics and with the school system. The child assumes the role of student.

(5) *Oldest child takes on teenager role:* As the teenager goes through puberty and begins to push for independence, the parents' role shifts again.

(6) *Oldest child has left home:* Some authors describe the family during this period as a "launching center." Children take on the role of single adult or go to stage 1 above.

(7) *All children gone from home:* This involves the loss of a good portion of the role of parent, although other elements remain. This is often described as the postparental period.

(8) *Aging families:* This may include the roles of retired person and, as children take on the parent role, grandparent.

Work Roles

Work roles occupy most of an individual's life, usually beginning in the teenage years and continuing into retirement. The importance of work in human experience prompted Frank Parsons to initiate the counseling profession (see Chapter 5). Because the majority of people in most societies define themselves by the nature of their work, the worker role fills social and psychological needs in addition to subsistence needs (Vacc & Loesch, 1987). Work roles can progress from novice to mid-level worker to skilled worker. Experienced workers may assume the roles of manager, mentor, and/or trainer, while younger workers assume a student-type role (Bee & Mitchell, 1984).

Role Integration

Role integration is necessary for good mental health. Though some roles may be dominant at particular times in life, healthy adults work toward a balance of attention to their various roles. Super's (1980) life-career rainbow depicts how various roles emerge and interact across the life span. Role conflict results when the demands of an individual's many different roles do not fit together. Individuals who attempt to emphasize too many roles at one time (such as those caught up in the "super-

woman syndrome" of wife, mother, career woman, and community volunteer roles) may suffer from role strain. Counselors can assist clients in alleviating role strain and resolving role conflict by helping them make decisions about which roles to take on at any one time.

Ethnic and Cultural Issues

Counselors have traditionally taken into account the cultural and social backgrounds of their clients, but only recently has cross-cultural, intercultural, or multicultural counseling been recognized as a subspecialty of the counseling profession.

Cross-Cultural Perspective

In cross-cultural counseling there are distinct differences between counselor and client regarding cultural, racial, ethnic, and/or socioeconomic environments (Vontress, 1986). A cross-cultural perspective is necessary in counseling if counselors are to become sensitized to the unique needs and experiences of minority individuals. To achieve this end, counselors must learn to overcome the three barriers to all cross-cultural counseling situations discussed by Atkinson, Morten, and Sue (1983): (a) language differences, (b) class-bound values, and (c) culture-bound values.

Language differences. An understanding of language differences, both verbal and nonverbal, requires counselors to rely less on verbal skills for rapport building and to recognize that minority clients may benefit more from proactive counseling than from talk therapy. When serving clients of other cultures, it is most effective to use clear, direct language and avoid the use of professional jargon.

Class-bound values. Because traditional counseling techniques are oriented toward the upper and middle classes, class-bound values may interfere with the counseling process in such areas as making and keeping appointments. Lower-class clients expect advice and suggestions for immediate solutions (Sue & Sue, 1977) and shun the White middle-class values of promptness, planning, and protocol (Vontress, 1973). The attempt to impose middle-class religious and sexual mores on upper- and lower-class clients will also interfere with the counseling process (Atkinson et al., 1983).

Culture-bound values. Counselors who impose their own culture-bound values involving customs, attitudes, beliefs, and institutions lack sensitivity to their clients' values. Attitudes toward sexual orientation, self-disclosure, and structure in the counseling sessions may impede rapport building in the counseling relationship (Atkinson et al., 1983).

Profiles of Ethnic Minorities

The main ethnic minority groups in the United States include Asian Americans, Black Americans, Hispanic Americans, and Native Americans. For counselors to be effective helpers of these diverse populations they must gain an understanding of the attitudes, values, traditions, and norms that each group brings to the counseling relationship. The following brief profiles of these groups will highlight issues about which counselors must be aware in helping ethnic minority clients.

Asian culture. In working with Asian Americans, counselors must be aware of the effects of racism on the clients' psychological development. Attention must be paid to the highly interdependent nature of the Asian American family, the restraint of emotional expression, obligation to family, high value of achievement, and the use of shame and guilt to control behavior. As Asian Americans become acculturated and assimilated into mainstream American culture, they find themselves spanning two cultures and may find it difficult to reconcile the effects on their personalities. It is advocated that counselors help these clients resolve the ensuing culture conflict by attempting to integrate aspects of both cultures that the clients believe are functional to their own self-esteem and identity (Sue, 1973/1983b).

Black culture. Knowledge of the cultural diversity among members of the Black American population may serve to facilitate communication between counselors and Black clients. Although Blacks run the whole socioeconomic gamut in U.S. society, they generally share a past of ethnocentric oppression, prejudice, and discrimination. They are often degraded for their family structure, educational level, and "nonstandard" speech (Dillard, 1983). In order to work effectively with Black clients, counselors must pay attention to the identified strengths of Black families—(a) strong kinship bonds, (b) adaptability of family roles, (c) high achievement orientation, (d) strong work orientation, and (e) religious orientation (Hill, 1972)—as well as their problems—(a) low pay, (b) ethnocentric bias in hiring practices, (c) monocultural education modes, (d) poor housing facilities, and (e) inadequate state and federal social services (Dillard, 1983).

Hispanic culture. The majority of Hispanic Americans are Cuban, Mexican, and Puerto Rican immigrants or the U.S.-born children of those immigrants. Though some important differences must be noted among these groups, they share cultural and socioeconomic similarities. Due to the lack of bilingual as well as bicultural training of helpers, Hispanic Americans may perceive helping institutions as alien and hostile. Because they are only partially acculturated and marginally integrated economically, those in this group are subject to high-stress factors indicating the need for treatment. However, unless counselors are able to communicate effectively and help to resolve problems of a social nature actively rather than using passive intrapsychic techniques, Hispanic Americans will continue to underutilize mental health services (Padilla, Ruiz, & Alvarez, 1983).

Native American culture. Native Americans have been underserved by the social service system in this country due to lack of understanding of Native American culture, retention of stereotyped images of Native Americans, and use of standard techniques and approaches. If professional counselors wish to overcome these barriers, they must acquire knowledge about Native American culture. Contrary to mainstream American values, the values of Native Americans include some elements about which counselors need to be aware to avoid misinterpretation. These include (a) the concept of sharing rather than accumulating, (b) the priority that interpersonal relations have over punctuality, (c) resilience in the face of suffering, (d) "optimistic toughness" and humor rather than pessimism, (e) inner serenity rather than stoicism, and

(f) patience rather than laziness. Besides taking these traits into consideration, counselors must communicate mutual consideration, respect, and noncoercion to be helpful to Native Americans (Lewis & Ho, 1975).

Discrimination and Stereotyping

A common thread running through the literature on minority groups is the problems they encounter due to discrimination, stereotyping, and prejudice. Indeed, Atkinson et al. (1983) reject the view that minorities are such because they are identifiable groups represented numerically, and suggest instead that the key factor in identifying minorities is oppression.

Prejudice. Axelson (1985) defines prejudice as "an irrational attitude or behavior directed against an individual or a group, or their supposed characteristics" (p. 120). He calls prejudice the most serious psychological and social problem in U.S. society. Before counselors can be helpful to minority groups, they must become aware of their hidden prejudices and begin to develop rational open-mindedness toward minority clients.

Minority identity development. Counselors can use the minority identity development (MID) model (Atkinson et al., 1983) to understand the stages oppressed people experience as they struggle to understand themselves. The stages are briefly defined below.

(1) *conformity:* appreciation toward the dominant culture; depreciation toward own group; discrimination toward other minorities

(2) *dissonance:* conflict between depreciation and appreciation for self, own group, and dominant group; conflict between dominant-held view toward other minorities and feelings of shared experience

(3) *resistance and immersion:* appreciation toward self and own group; conflict between empathy and ethnocentrism toward other minorities; depreciation toward dominant group

(4) *introspection:* concern with basis of self- and own-group appreciation; concern with ethnocentric judging of others;

concern with basis of dominant group depreciation

(5) *synergetic articulation and awareness:* appreciation toward self, own group, and other minorities; selective appreciation toward dominant group

Counselors can utilize this model to understand minority client behavior in order to make accurate diagnoses and to choose interventions applicable to the various stages. Diagnosis calls for counselors to make judgments about their clients regarding past and present behavior, thought processes, and emotional states. In order to diagnose clients from other cultures accurately, counselors need to know the distinctive qualities of those ethnic or socioeconomic cultures (i.e., what is normal or abnormal) and to understand and empathize with the social history of their clients (Vontress, 1986).

Diagnosis and Intervention

Intervention, or the very act of making a difference in the life of the client, cannot be achieved without a positive relationship between the client and the counselor and a tenable diagnosis (Vontress, 1985). Many traditional counseling intervention techniques (eye contact, revelation of feelings, talk rather than action, and so on) are either ineffective with or threatening to minority clients. Diagnoses made without respect to the cultural norms and values of each individual client may well be inaccurate or inadequate. Thus a faulty, and therefore ineffective, course of treatment may be undertaken.

Intervention models. Padilla et al. (1983) suggest three effective models for intervening with Hispanic Americans that may have value for other minorities as well. These models include such elements as bilingual and bicultural staff; easy accessibility; consultation with community organizations for prevention; short-term, crisis-oriented treatment; informal atmosphere; and liaison services with other agencies, including medical, legal, financial, and vocational.

Cross-cultural views. The emergence of two differing views of cross-cultural counseling have significant effects upon the counseling relationship, diagnosis, and methodology. One focuses on the emic-etic distinction and the other on the autoplastic-alloplastic dilemma (Draguns, 1981). The emic view emphasizes individual differences, taking a culture-specific approach; the etic view focuses on the sameness of all humanity, applying the same theories and methodology to all clients. Counselors who take the autoplastic view encourage clients to change themselves to accommodate the external circumstances; the alloplastic view suggests imposing changes on the outside world. Usually a combination of approaches is necessary as the client adapts to the dominant culture by some degree of change, and counselor and client work together to improve negative conditions.

Social Issues and Mores

Though the counseling profession has its heritage in school counseling, today it is difficult to identify settings where counselors do not work (Vacc & Loesch, 1987). As counselors expand their influence in all levels of educational institutions, community agencies, business and industry, religious organizations, legal systems, and private practice, they are confronted with the full range of social and personal issues faced by people in this society.

Taking the multicultural approach, counselors are mandated to consider the individual personality in interaction with the environment as they help clients adjust to a wide range of social and personal issues (Axelson, 1985). Some of the issues that are relevant today include aging, loss and grief, equality, disabilities, violence, and substance abuse.

Aging

Riker (1981) calls attention to the counseling needs of the aging population, citing high rates of alcoholism and suicide, besides difficulties with health, finances, and living conditions, as major problems to be addressed by gerontological counselors. In addition to experiencing a wide range of life problems, the elderly must be helped to cope with the sense of time running out, the fact that ageism is still prevalent in this

society, and the decrease in their cohort group. Butler (1974) describes the life review process as a way of helping the elderly reintegrate life experience and prepare for death.

Loss and Grief

Loss refers to many kinds of deprivation, while *grief* is the normal psychological reaction to any distressing situation, including loss (Van Hoose & Worth, 1982). Many who seek counseling may be suffering from unresolved grief due to loss of a loved one through death or the loss of a relationship, job, money, skill, or any important element of their lives. Counselors can help clients adjust to their losses by understanding the grieving process. Kübler-Ross (1969) identifies five common stages in the grieving process: (a) denial, (b) anger, (c) bargaining, (d) depression, and (e) acceptance. Though the client may not progress through these stages in this order, the goal of counseling is to reach acceptance.

Inequality

Inequality is an issue for a wide variety of clients. As discussed earlier in this chapter, ethnic minorities (through racism) as well as the elderly (through ageism) may be victims of inequality in such areas as employment, housing, medical treatment, and educational opportunities. Despite the reemergence of the women's movement over the last two decades, changing sex roles, and the theoretical achievement of equal rights, women, too, are still subject to discriminatory practices (sexism) in several life areas. Counselors must be aware of the specific needs and concerns of each of these groups to help them achieve their potentials and adjust to their changing roles, while advocating for societal change to make equality a reality for all.

Disabilities

The needs of another minority group, disabled persons, gained attention with the passage of the Education for All Handicapped Children Act (Public Law 94-142; 1980), which mandates educational and counseling services for handicapped children. This act expanded the role of the school counselor and increased the awareness of other counseling profession-als regarding disabled persons. Counselors can assist those with disabilities in solving social and emotional problems and in developing independent living skills. They can also advo-cate for changes in social and physical environ-ments, accessible buildings and transportation, fair housing, and the right to independent, unencumbered living (Lewis & Lewis, 1983).

Abuse

As the incidence of interpersonal violence and abuse of all types increases, counselors are being called upon to alleviate the resulting psy-chological trauma. This type of care is remedial in nature, urgent in terms of immediacy, and collaborative with medical, law enforcement, and/or legal professionals. Abused clients may be victims of physical, verbal, and/or sexual abuse and may be young or old, male or female, and of any racial, ethnic, or social group (Vacc & Loesch, 1987). The need for comprehensive services for these clients is being met in part by family violence shelters (for spouse abuse vic-tims), foster care and parent aid programs (for child abuse victims and parents at risk of becoming abusers), and rape victim advocate programs (for victims of sexual abuse). The ultimate goal in working with abused clients, according to Axelson (1985), is to rebuild their self-confidence and self-belief.

Substance Abuse

Substance abuse, another problem that affects nearly every member of our society either directly or indirectly, is one with which counselors in all settings will be confronted. Therefore, all counselors need to be able to recognize substance abuse and to use counsel-ing or referral skills in helping clients (Lewis, Dana, & Blevins, 1988). Depending upon the severity of the problem, substance abuse may be treated on an outpatient or inpatient basis, in agencies, schools, and business and industry settings, as well as through self-help groups, including Alcoholics/Narcotics Anonymous, Al-Anon, Narc-Anon, Ala-Teen, and Adult Children of Alcoholics. Counselors working with substance abuse problems should advo-cate for the least restrictive environment and a systems approach.

Life-Styles and Patterns

Because most adults marry and most become parents, the family life cycle provides a useful framework for examining life-styles and patterns. However, societal changes over the past 20 to 30 years have increased the vari-ability in family forms as well as the chronolog-ical ages associated with stages in the family life cycle (Goldhaber, 1986). Today's counselors may be called upon to help clients resolve issues related to traditional as well as nontradi-tional family life, single living, or gay/lesbian life-style.

Axelson (1985) defines *family* as a group of two or more people related by birth, marriage, or adoption and residing together. According to the 1980 census, nearly three-fourths of all U.S. households fit this category.

Family Life

Many family types exist, each with special issues:

(1) *Traditional nuclear family:* Includes only wife, husband, and their own or adopted children. Issues in counseling may include problems of a working mother, marital conflict, wife's per-sonal needs for expression, conflict with extended family, empty-nest syn-drome.

(2) *Single-parent family:* Includes either father or mother (single, widowed, or divorced) and his or her own children. Issues in counseling may include postdivorce problems, depression, economic and/or sociosexual prob-lems of the parent, school achievement and behavioral difficulties for chil-dren.

(3) *Blended family:* Results from marriage of a divorced man and/or divorced woman and includes his and/or her children. Issues include readjustment to parent/child roles, role-appropriate relations between new parents and half-children and among stepsiblings.

(4) *Extended family:* Includes other rela-tives or in-laws who share the house-

hold with the nuclear family (a family form especially fostered by ethnic groups). Issues may include power, authority, discipline of children, and independence, but a general aura of sustenance and support prevails.

(5) *Augmented family:* Includes nonrelatives, such as boarders, friends, or other long-term guests, who share the household with the family and have some influence on family life. Issues include power, trust, economics, and relationship problems.

(6) *Shared household:* Includes two or more relatives or nonrelated persons of the same or opposite sex living together. Examples include brother and sister, unmarried couples, or two adults and one or more children. Relationship and economic issues are important.

Nonfamily Households

According to the 1980 census, nonfamily households represent about one-fourth of all U.S. households. These households include persons living alone (86%) or with nonrelatives. A large increase in persons living alone is attributed to several factors: More elderly persons are continuing to maintain their own homes after the deaths of their spouses; divorce and marital separation rates have increased; and the trend has been toward later marriage among young adults. Counseling issues for singles may include loneliness, depression, and sociosexual relations.

Gay Life-Style

The homosexual population is one minority group that is growing in size as well as visibility. Conservatively speaking, gay men and lesbian women constitute a significant minority, more than 10% of the U.S. population (Bell & Weinberg, 1978). Historically, the gay population has been oppressed by many societal groups, including the helping professions (Woodman & Lenna, 1980). The prevalence of homophobia (Weinberg, 1972), a wide range of negative feelings, attitudes, and behaviors directed toward homosexuals, affects the identity development of gay men and lesbians.

Only in 1973 did the American Psychiatric Association remove homosexuality from the *Diagnostic and Statistical Manual of Mental Disorders* (second edition). This was a major step in removing the stigma of pathology attached to homosexuality. It opened the door for reexamining views of psychotherapy and counseling with gay clients and societal acceptance of homosexuality as a viable life-style (Krajewski, 1986).

In counseling, the presenting problems of gay men and lesbian women may include coming out to self and others. Beyond this issue, Woodman and Lenna (1980) list a wide range of problems concerning homosexual clients' relationships that are not unlike nongay concerns. Some of the issues in counseling may include problems in maintaining committed relationships, problems with family relationships, problems due to separation, and problems of later life.

To be effective helpers for gay clients, counselors need to help them identify and use support systems such as intimate others, family members, nongay friends, and legal and medical resources. Counselors must also confront their own prejudices, oppose homophobic individuals and institutions, and use creativity in developing supports where they are lacking (Woodman & Lenna, 1980).

Conclusion

The area of social and cultural foundations of the counseling profession challenges counselors to help clients recognize and reconcile the various roles they play in life. It calls for sensitivity to the ethnic and cultural concerns of a multicultural society and familiarity with a wide range of social issues in the ever-changing environment. Finally, counselors must be cognizant of the many life-style alternatives in today's world if they are to help in resolving the counseling issues related to those life-styles.

LEARNING OBJECTIVES

After studying the material in this chapter, you should be able to do the following:

(1) Discuss human roles in terms of age, sex, family, and work roles.
(2) Understand the concept of role integration.
(3) Explain the cross-cultural perspective in counseling.
(4) Name the four major ethnic minority groups in the United States.
(5) List characteristics of the main minority groups.
(6) Understand discrimination and stereotyping from a personal as well as a societal standpoint.
(7) Discuss diagnosis and intervention regarding minority clients.
(8) List relevant issues regarding aging, loss and grief, equality, disabilities, interpersonal violence, and substance abuse.
(9) Describe various types of family and nonfamily households.
(10) Discuss issues relevant to household types.
(11) Discuss the gay population as a minority group.
(12) List several counseling issues of gay clients.

TIME LINE

You should be aware of important developments in the area of social and cultural foundations.

1963	Erikson, developmental stages	1978	10% of U.S. population homosexual
1968	U.S. National Advisory Commission on Civil Disorders	1980	U.S. census, 75% of households are families
1969	Kübler-Ross, grieving process	1981	Draguns, emic-etic, alloplastic-autoplastic view
1972	Association for Non-White Concerns in Personnel and Guidance	1982	Vontress, class-based language usage
1973	homosexuality removed from DSM-II	1983	minority identity development model
1975	Bem, sex role stereotyping	1985	Vontress, intervention barriers
1978	Levinson, life-span eras		

TERMS AND NAMES
TO REMEMBER

Terms

You should have an understanding of the following terms and be able to define them in your own words.

abuse
ageism
alloplastic
androgyny
augmented family
autoplastic
bicultural
bilingual
blended family
class-bound values
cohort group
coming out
cross-cultural
culture-bound values
disabled
discrimination
emic
ethnic
etic
extended family
family roles

handicap
homophobia
homosexual
intervention
least restrictive environment
nonverbal
nuclear family
oppression
prejudice
racism
role conflict
role integration
role strain
sex roles
sexism
single-parent family
stereotyping
systems approach
transitions
verbal
work roles

Names

You should be familiar with these people and be aware of their contributions to the counseling profession with regard to social and cultural foundations.

Asian Americans
Atkinson, Morten, and Sue
Bem
Black Americans
Butler
Draguns

Erikson
Hispanic Americans
Kübler-Ross
Levinson
Native Americans
Super

FILL IN THE BLANKS

The following section reviews some of the major points in this content area. Check your knowledge of the area by filling in the appropriate name, term, or concept in each blank provided. Answer choices are found above, in the section containing terms and names to remember. You will find the correct answers at the end of the chapter.

(1) _____ is the main factor in defining a minority.

(2) In order to serve Hispanic American clients better, more counselors need to be _____ and _____ _____.

(3) Counselors who do not resolve their own _____ _____ will undermine their own work with minority clients.

(4) The "superwoman syndrome" is an example of _____ _____.

(5) When too many demands come from various areas of an individual's life, _____ results.

(6) Sex role _____ is unhealthy, whereas _____ promotes better functioning.

(7) Times of change from one role or stage to the next are referred to as _____.

(8) Discrimination against the elderly, _____ _____, makes employment, housing, medical, and other services difficult to obtain.

(9) _____ is detrimental to a counselor's work with gay men and lesbian women.

(10) In determining treatment situations for clients, counselors should look for the _____.

(11) Public Law 94-192 improved services for children with _____ _____.

(12) Gender roles, or _____, are more distinct in early life and more alike in the elderly.

(13) In building rapport with minority clients, counselors need to be especially aware of _____ communication.

(14)   The major _____ are child, parent, and
       grandparent.

(15)   Females actually have greater _____
       ability than males.

(16)   A balance among work life, family life, and leisure is known as

       _____.

(17)   _____ dictate the customs, attitudes,
       and beliefs of a particular racial or ethnic group.

(18)   Culture conflict is a major issue for many _____

       _____.

(19)   Stereotypes of _____ include
       pessimism, stoicism, and laziness.

(20)   Before effective _____ can take place,
       the counselor must accurately diagnose the problem, taking cultural mores
       into consideration.

(21)   Counselors who take the _____ view
       believe clients should change to fit the environment, while the _____
       _____ view suggests changing the
       outside world.

(22)   In dealing with _____, counselors are
       often called upon to collaborate with medical and legal personnel.

(23)   The traditional _____ is declining as
       nontraditional families increase.

(24)   As one's age increases, one's _____
       decreases.

(25)   In the process of _____, homosexuals
       reveal their sexual orientation to themselves and/or to others.

MATCHING TEST

Match the names in the left-hand column with the appropriate concepts in the right-hand column.

___	(1) Asian Americans	(a)	grieving process
___	(2) Atkinson, Morten, and Sue	(b)	emic-etic dilemma
___	(3) Bem	(c)	life-career rainbow
___	(4) Black Americans	(d)	primarily from China, Japan, and the Philippines
___	(5) Butler	(e)	life review therapy
___	(6) Draguns	(f)	American Indian
___	(7) Erikson	(g)	primarily African
___	(8) Hispanic Americans	(h)	development stages
___	(9) Kübler-Ross	(i)	MID model
___	(10) Levinson	(j)	Sex Role Inventory
___	(11) Native Americans	(k)	primarily Cuban, Mexican, and Puerto Rican
___	(12) Super	(l)	five life-span eras

CASE STUDY

Fong identifies himself as a Chinese American. His ancestors have resided in California for several generations, originally in San Francisco's Chinatown, but more recently in a suburban area with a high concentration of Asians. Fong's family speaks Chinese in the home, but he is quite articulate in English as well. He is the youngest child in the family, and has two older sisters. The oldest sister is married and lives in another state and his closest sibling is in her last year of nursing school. Fong's paternal grandparents also live with his family. Fong's father, grandfather, and mother work in the family business.

Fong's childhood development was normal. He had no major illnesses or injuries, seemed well adjusted in school, and had a circle of close friends, both Chinese and white. Fong had attended a local community college, where he received his A.S. degree. He transferred to a state university, where he is seeking a degree in computer science. He came to the University Counseling Center shortly after midterms during the first semester of his junior year on the recommendation of his academic adviser.

Although Fong gravitated toward the other Chinese students in his classes, he sometimes found it difficult to relate to them. As he got to know some of the white students, he felt alienated from some of his Chinese counterparts, who did not approve of his behavior. He felt guilty when he spent time with white classmates, yet he was not satisfied with his Chinese friends.

In his first counseling interview Fong related his conflict with friends. He also alluded to difficulties adjusting to life away from his family. He had never experienced such responsibility and independence before. He was used to being under the direction of his father and was ashamed to admit to his family that he was unsure of his ability to complete his college education. Fong had previously been an A student, but this semester he barely made Cs in a couple of his classes. Consequently, he had begun to spend most of his time alone in his room trying to study. However, he related that he found it difficult to concentrate and sometimes wasted hours just staring at a book or out the window.

Analysis

(1)   What kind of intrapsychic difficulties might Fong be experiencing, considering that he is a college junior away from home for the first time?

_____

_____

(2)   What recommendations would you make for resolving these difficulties?

_____

_____

_____

_____

_____

(3)   In view of your knowledge about Chinese Americans, discuss Fong's identity issues:
      cultural identity/degree of acculturation:

_____

_____

_____

      personal identity:

_____

_____

_____

(4)   Keeping Asian cultural values in mind, what approach would you take in helping Fong resolve his conflicting cultural identity?

_____

_____

_____

_____

_____

(5)   Discuss your counseling approach and the rationale for the approach to resolving Fong's personal identity crisis.

_____

_____

Notes

MULTIPLE-CHOICE TEST

Check your understanding of this content area by responding to the following questions. You will find the answer key at the end of the chapter.

1. In working with clients, counselors need to be aware of both verbal and nonverbal communications because

    a. verbal communication is always superior
    b. discrepancies between verbals and nonverbals indicate distress
    c. nonverbals can usually be disregarded
    d. verbals and nonverbals give identical messages

2. The term *mainstreaming* in educational systems refers to

    a. tracking students by ability
    b. using the "Pygmalion principle" for slower children
    c. placing mentally handicapped children in regular classrooms for as much as they can benefit from the experience
    d. using the major amount of the educational budget for average children because they are the majority

3. *Culturally different* means

    a. counselor and client both belong to a minority culture
    b. the counselor is helping the client adopt the majority culture
    c. the counselor is helping the client reject the majority culture
    d. counselor and client belong to two different cultural groups

4. The legal definition of a handicapped person as "categorical with functional limitations" demonstrates that

    a. categorically disabled persons have the same functional limitations
    b. the specific category determines the service provided
    c. both of the above
    d. neither of the above

5. Research findings concerning sex role stereotyping indicate that both male and female respondents believe males are

    a. unpredictable in their emotional sensitivity
    b. equally as emotionally sensitive as females
    c. less emotionally sensitive than females
    d. more emotionally sensitive than females

6. Which of the following are not influenced by cultural and social factors?

    a. client-counselor fit
    b. intervention strategies
    c. notions about appropriate help-givers
    d. all of the above are influenced by social and cultural factors

7. Ideally, an interpreter on a counseling staff should be

    a. bilingual and bicultural
    b. Hispanic
    c. part of mainstream America
    d. a transference figure

8. According to Havighurst, there are specific developmental tasks of older adulthood. One of these is

    a. separation from parents
    b. adjustment to decreased physical strength
    c. crystallization of intelligence
    d. establishment of career goals

9. The concept of *propinquity* explains

   a. the decline in racial prejudice when Whites live next door to minority persons
   b. social norms of particular neighborhoods
   c. prejudicial behavior of minorities toward other minorities
   d. the negative attitude of minority clients toward counselors

10. Widespread prejudice and ethnic bigotry in society can be explained by

    a. the crime rate of minority students
    b. the effects of the race riots of the 1960s
    c. ignorance of the histories, cultures, and life-styles of other groups
    d. personal experience with violent members of other groups

11. The differential treatment of males and females at all levels of maturation in American society explains

    a. androgynous roles in adulthood
    b. sex role identification and sexism
    c. the incidence of homosexuality
    d. sex role identification and sexual abuse

12. In order to label a multicultural client's behavior *normal* or *abnormal*, a counselor must first

    a. compare the client's behavior to the dominant culture
    b. check the DSM-III-R
    c. judge the client's behavior against the norms of the client's cultural group
    d. consult with the staff psychologist about the personality development of the client

13. Which of the following is an example of role conflict?

    a. a negative parent-child interaction
    b. a dispute between a supervisor and a counselor

c. prejudicial behavior of one culture or race toward another
d. a single parent who is a full-time student and also has a career

14. An understanding of the concept of "least restrictive environment" would prompt a counselor to

    a. recommend outpatient therapy over inpatient therapy
    b. move to a more spacious office
    c. collaborate with social service agencies for client housing
    d. advocate for wheelchair-accessible facilities

15. According to Bem's research using her Sex Role Inventory, the most well-adjusted adults are

    a. androgynous
    b. highly masculine males
    c. highly feminine females
    d. males or females with low masculine and low feminine scores

16. In their work with minority clients, Atkinson, Morten, and Sue identified three major barriers to cross-cultural counseling. These include

    a. verbal, nonverbal, and nonstandard language
    b. class-bound values, nonverbal language, and ethnicity
    c. nonstandard language, nonstandard values, and nonstandard mores
    d. culture-bound values, class-bound values, and language differences

17. Minority clients seem to respond best to

    a. action-oriented therapy
    b. psychodynamic methods
    c. same-sex counselors of the dominant group
    d. opposite-sex counselors of any minority group

18. Which of the following has not contrib-
    uted to the failure of social service
    systems to serve minority clients
    adequately?
    a. lack of bilingual, bicultural
       counselors
    b. lack of needs by minority populations
    c. oppression
    d. prejudice

19. According to Kübler-Ross, the grieving
    process consists of five stages. Which of
    these are not part of the process?
    a. denial and acceptance
    b. resolution and relief
    c. anger and bargaining
    d. acceptance and depression

20. Generally speaking, victims of abuse lack
    a. emotional response capacity
    b. knowledge of the abuser
    c. self-recrimination and self-denial
    d. self-confidence and self-belief

21. Alcoholics Anonymous is an example of
    a. an outpatient program
    b. a culture-free organization
    c. a closed group
    d. a self-help organization

22. Homosexuality is
    a. a diagnosable pathology
    b. the norm for single adults
    c. an alternative life-style
    d. curable through counseling

23. According to Erikson,
    a. human development continues
       through the life span
    b. by middle adulthood, all
       developmental issues are resolved
    c. transitions allow one to skip over a
       stage
    d. the task of one adult stage is
       interchangeable with the task of any
       other adult stage

24. A theorist whose major focus is adult
    development is
    a. Satir
    b. Levinson
    c. Super
    d. Erikson

25. Conformity is the first stage in
    a. the life review process
    b. sex role identification
    c. minority identity development
    d. the grieving process

ANSWER KEY

Fill in the Blanks

(1) oppression
(2) bilingual, bicultural
(3) prejudices
(4) role strain
(5) role conflict
(6) stereotyping, androgyny
(7) transitions
(8) ageism
(9) homophobia
(10) least restrictive environment
(11) handicaps
(12) sex roles
(13) nonverbal
(14) family roles
(15) verbal
(16) role integration
(17) culture-bound values
(18) Asian Americans
(19) Native Americans
(20) intervention
(21) autoplastic, alloplastic
(22) abuse
(23) nuclear family
(24) cohort
(25) coming out

Matching

(1) d
(2) i
(3) j
(4) g
(5) e
(6) b
(7) h
(8) k
(9) a
(10) l
(11) f
(12) c

Multiple-Choice

1.	b	10.	c	18.	b
2.	c	11.	b	19.	b
3.	d	12.	c	20.	d
4.	b	13.	d	21.	d
5.	c	14.	a	22.	c
6.	d	15.	a	23.	a
7.	a	16.	d	24.	b
8.	b	17.	a	25.	c
9.	a				

CHAPTER 3

The Helping Relationship

SUMMARY	57
Philosophic Bases of the Helping Relationship	**57**
Four General Tenets	57
Four Core Elements	57
Three Underlying Premises	59
Three Basic Propositions	59
Counseling Theory and Practice	**59**
Psychodynamic Approaches	60
Humanistic Approaches	60
Cognitive Approaches	61
Behavioral Approaches	63
Systems Approaches	63
Consultation Theory and Practice	**63**
Triadic Consultation	64
Mental Health Consultation	64
Behavioral Consultation	64
Process Consultation	64
Supervision	65
LEARNING OBJECTIVES	66
TERMS AND NAMES TO REMEMBER	67
Terms	**67**
Names	**67**
FILL IN THE BLANKS	68
MATCHING TEST	70
CASE STUDY	71
Analysis	**72**

MULTIPLE-CHOICE TEST   74
ANSWER KEY   77
    Fill in the Blanks   77
    Matching   77
    Multiple-Choice   77

SUMMARY

The helping relationship includes philosophic bases of the helping relationship, counseling theory and application, consultation theory and application, and an emphasis on development of counselor and client (or consultee) self-awareness and self-understanding. (Loesch & Vacc, 1986, p. 13)

Philosophic Bases of the Helping Relationship

Although "natural helpers" have been an integral part of human existence throughout time, counseling by professional helpers is unique to the twentieth century. The counseling profession has roots in the school and community guidance programs pioneered by Jesse B. Davis (1914) and Frank Parsons (1909), known as the "father of guidance." It also draws from such diverse fields as social work, clinical psychology, psychiatry, learning theory, psychoanalysis, and pastoral counseling. While this varied background offers counselors an array of tools and techniques, it does little to consolidate the professional identity of counselors (Aubrey, 1986).

Given this diverse background, a few writers have attempted to identify the philosophical bases upon which the helping relationship rests, but there has been little agreement. The task of defining the helping relationship and drawing boundaries between helping professions is a difficult one that is further complicated by overlap, conflict, and competition between psychology and counseling.

Four General Tenets

Hershenson and Power (1987) offer four general tenets that form the philosophic bases of mental health counseling. The first states that behavior is an interaction between clients and their environments at a particular point in time. Thus client behaviors must be considered in the context in which they occur. Second, human development naturally tends toward healthy growth. This developmental approach seeks to help normal people with problems of living, rather than to diagnose them as mentally ill. Third, the helping relationship consists of a partnership of counselor and client working together to solve client problems by activating client assets, developing client skills, and utilizing environmental resources in order to decrease client problems and increase client coping skills. Fourth, counselors seek to help clients by using skills, techniques, and methods that research has shown to be effective.

Four Core Elements

To effect positive client change, a quality counselor-client relationship based upon caring and reciprocity must be established. The counselor's characteristic ways of thinking, feeling, and behaving form the basis for an interdependent helping relationship that is both positive and beneficial to the client. Kurpius (1986) defines four core elements upon which this relationship is built: (a) human relations, (b) social influence, (c) skills, and (d) theory.

Human relations. The human relations core must be based upon empathy, respect, and genuineness. Empathy involves active listening, focusing on both expressed and unexpressed feelings and meanings experienced by the client. Since empathy is considered to be the key element in the helping relationship (Carkhuff, 1969; Rogers, 1961), guidelines for formulating empathic responses and a scale for measuring levels of empathy have been developed (Carkhuff, 1969). Empathic responses reflect the content, emotional tone, and language style of the client. They focus on nonverbal expressions in order to expand and clarify the verbal and behavioral messages of the client. Ivey (1988) delineates three types of empathy: (a) subtractive, in which the counselor response subtracts from the helping process and takes something away from the client; (b) basic, in which the counselor response parallels the client statement; and (c) additive, in which the counselor response expands upon the ideas and feelings of the client.

Respect assumes the counselor maintains a nonjudgmental attitude toward the client. The important elements of respect include holding the client in high regard, accepting the client unconditionally, and valuing the client as a person of dignity and worth (Rogers, 1961). The counselor's communication of respect may be ranked from least to most facilitative on a 5-point scale (Carkhuff, 1969), with a rank of 3 as a minimum of acceptability.

Genuineness implies being true to self in the client-counselor relationship. The genuine counselor's ideas, feelings, and behaviors remain consistent with his or her value system, theoretical orientation, and philosophical position. This counselor maintains confidence and remains comfortable with self-disclosure. Genuineness, too, can be rated on a 5-point scale (Carkhuff, 1969) from least to most facilitative, with 3 the minimum acceptable level.

Social influence. The social influence core represents another arena of importance in the helping relationship. This core includes helper self-image—competence, power, and intimacy—and helpee receptiveness to helper—trustworthiness, attractiveness, and expertness. These six qualities are influential in the change process.

Competence in this context is the counselor's ability to accept his or her own limitations, to behave positively toward clients, and to set realistic expectations for them. Power has to do with the counselor's ability to influence the client without controlling him or her. Intimacy is the counselor's ability to enter into the relationship sincerely and openly, without fear of rejection. When the counselor exhibits expertness, the client believes the helper has the proper training, reputation, and behaviors to be helpful. Counselor attractiveness is based on the client's positive thinking and feeling about the counselor. Over time, the counselor's trustworthiness is established as the client perceives congruence in the helper's verbal and nonverbal behavior (Kurpius, 1986).

Skills. The skills core consists of basic interviewing abilities necessary for the counselor to interact with the client. Egan (1988) emphasizes

the need for competency-based counselor training programs that focus on skill acquisition. He lists eight groups of skills that effective helpers need to develop: (a) establishing working relationships, (b) basic and advanced communication skills, (c) helping clients challenge themselves, (d) problem clarification, (e) goal setting, (f) program development, (g) program implementation, and (h) ongoing evaluation. Skilled helpers also need to help clients develop the skills of problem solving and self-responsibility.

Ivey (1988) presents a microskills hierarchy for intentional interviewing. From attending behaviors, counselors progress to the basic listening sequence, which, when mastered, enables them to conduct well-formed interviews. The more advanced skills in the hierarchy include confrontation, focusing, and reflection of meaning, as well as a set of influencing skills. Once counselors have progressed to this point, they are capable of skill integration that allows them to use various combinations and patterns of the basic skills to fit the particular setting, situation, client, and theoretical orientation.

Gazda's (1973) process of helping is based on Carkhuff's (1969) model and includes three phases of helping: facilitation, transition, and action. The facilitation phase promotes understanding and self-exploration and includes three core skills: empathy, respect, and warmth. The transition phase utilizes the next three skills—concreteness, genuineness, and self-disclosure—to bring about self-understanding and a commitment to change. The action phase emphasizes two skills, confrontation and immediacy, to encourage more appropriate action or direction.

Gazda's model includes the Global Scale for Rating Helper Responses as well as a scale for each of the eight basic skills. Counselor responses are rated as follows: 1.0, harmful; 2.0, ineffective; 3.0, facilitative; or 4.0, additive. Acceptable responses are rated 3.0 or higher. Facilitative responses establish a trusting relationship and help clients get an accurate picture of themselves. Additive responses promote problem solving by the client and allow the counselor to help.

Theory. Finally, knowledge of the theory core enables the counselor to be more helpful to a greater number of clients in a wider variety of situations. Different theories provide the counselor with a wide range of perspectives from which to view the client and a large repertoire of interventions from which to choose. Though well over a hundred different theories of helping exist, they can be organized into categories according to their general approaches. The section below on theories and practice presents four different approaches—psychodynamic, humanistic, cognitive, and behavioral—and discusses some representative theories in each of the four categories.

Three Underlying Premises

Belkin (1988) asserts that "the counseling way" rejects the medical model as it works with the whole person, including environmental as well as intrapsychic components of the client's experience. Assuming an anti-illness stance, counselors seek to develop a helping relationship free of bias and preconceptions, a relationship based upon understanding clients within their own realities. Assuming this stance, the helping relationship relies on three underlying philosophic premises: ontology, epistemology, and axiology.

The first, the ontological basis of counseling, is concerned with problems of existence. It compares the client's reality with the objective reality of the world and tries to determine inner qualities and higher purposes in life. The epistemological core of counseling examines truth and knowledge. It questions the client's learning behaviors and compares client knowledge with generally accepted truths. The axiological premise is concerned with values, ethics, and conscience. Questions that arise in these three areas of philosophy challenge counselors to evaluate their relationships with their clients, themselves, and the institutions in which they are employed (Belkin, 1988).

Three Basic Propositions

According to Blocher (1987), counseling exists as a separate, distinct enterprise and is defined by several major sets of philosophical concerns and commitments that distinguish the process of counseling from psychotherapy, teaching, social work, and other related services. The philosophy of the counseling profession can be expressed in three basic propositions:

(1) The primary commitment of counselors is to facilitate human development.

(2) Counseling must take into account the social, psychological, and physical environments of the client.

(3) The goal of counseling is to facilitate a dynamic fit between person and environment.

In order to facilitate human development, counselors work to help clients develop awareness of their psychosocial selves and attain higher levels of functioning. As clients learn problem-solving and decision-making skills, they become empowered to manage the inevitable changes of life with maximum long-term control. It is these very interactions between clients and their environments that necessitate the contextual approach characteristic of the counselor-client helping relationship. Attending to the psychosocial, rather than the intrapsychic, aspects of growth and development, counselors can utilize the concepts of social roles and behaviors, coping behaviors, and developmental tasks in helping clients master their environments. Finally, when they see that client problems arise from the community, counselors may intervene in the larger environment for remediation as well as prevention, thus improving the person-environment fit (Blocher, 1987).

Counseling Theory and Practice

No discussion of counseling theory would be complete without acknowledging the tremendous contribution to the fields of psychiatry, psychology, and counseling made by Sigmund Freud, who pioneered the field of psychoanalysis beginning in the 1880s. Early in his work with hysterical patients, Freud discovered the efficacy of the "talking cure" that forms the basis of most modern psychotherapy and counseling practice.

Psychodynamic Approaches

Many doctors and scholars studied the psychoanalytic approach developed by Freud. Among Freud's many followers and students, most notable were Alfred Adler, Carl Jung, and Karen Horney, all of whom eventually broke away from Freud in order to develop their own psychodynamic theories.

Freud. Freud's (1925/1961) theory of psychoanalysis focuses on the client's past. According to Freud, a child's personality is determined by the time he or she is 5 years old, and subsequent problems can be traced back to one of five stages of development occurring in childhood—oral, anal, phallic, latency, or puberty. Difficulties can be traced to psychic conflict within the structures of the mind that Freud calls id, ego, and superego. Id represents unconscious sexual and aggressive impulses; ego mediates between id and the outside world as it struggles to keep id under control; and superego acts as a conscience.

Using such techniques as dream analysis and free association, psychodynamic counselors seek to help clients overcome the neurotic use of defense mechanisms (repression, projection, reaction formation, intellectualization, denial, isolation, rationalization, displacement, regression, introjection, and identification) and to resolve interpersonal problems through the analysis of transference.

Adler. Alfred Adler's (1930/1963) individual psychology is an example of a more recent psychodynamic theory. Adler views humans as social beings, "striving for superiority," always in the process of "becoming." Some concepts that Adler has contributed to the counseling profession include style of life, inferiority complex, compensation, birth order, and private logic. Many of Adler's concepts were far ahead of his time. His recurring emphasis on social factors was an important precursor to other dynamic personality theories, and has added immeasurably to the growing acceptance of psychoanalysis in the counseling profession (Belkin, 1988).

Jung. Another psychodynamic approach, Jung's (1964) analytical psychotherapy is an attempt to create, by means of a symbolic approach, a relationship between the conscious and the unconscious. The psyche is viewed as a self-regulating system naturally moving toward a life of fuller awareness (Kaufmann, 1979). Some concepts credited to Jung include those of a collective unconscious, animus and anima, persona, archetypes, and the shadow. Unlike psychoanalysis, which was originated to treat neurotic symptoms and character disorders, analytical psychotherapy fits the counseling mandate of facilitating human development as it applies primarily to "adjusted" clients attempting to find meaning in life, especially in middle age.

Although long-term Freudian psychoanalysis is not suitable in the counseling setting, it has influenced many counselors in their development and/or practice. Many of the concepts of psychoanalysis, as well as the psychodynamic orientation, can be applied by counselors in vocational, family, and group settings (Belkin, 1988).

Humanistic Approaches

The humanistic approaches, such as existential, gestalt, and client-centered counseling, developed as a reaction to psychoanalysis and behavioral psychology. The major proponents of humanistic psychology in the United States have included Carl Rogers, Eugene Gendlin, Rollo May, Eric Fromm, Victor Frankl, Frederick Perls, Abraham Maslow, and Gordon Allport. Maslow (1954) typifies the humanistic approach as he argues that psychology should start by examining the normal, healthy personality rather than the abnormal.

Existential counseling. Existential counseling evolved from Kierkegaard's philosophy, which became known as existentialism. The basic theory purports the belief that humans are inherently good and that they are responsible for their own destinies. Belkin (1988) points out three main tasks of the existential counselor: to help clients (a) discover valid meanings in their existence, (b) develop the freedom to shape their own destinies, and (c) handle interpersonal encounters more effectively.

In practice, existential counselors may use a wide variety of techniques to fit particular situations. Traditional approaches such as free association, dream analysis, verbal interchange, and development of a relationship are common. Two specific existential techniques that have been developed are Frankl's (1967) paradoxical intention and Gendlin's (1981) focusing.

Gestalt counseling. Gestalt counseling, based upon the academic discipline of Gestalt psychology, came into popular use through the efforts of Fritz Perls. Clients are encouraged to focus on the here-and-now process, rather than to search for meanings or causes from the past. An individual's personality is said to be like an onion—each time a layer is peeled away, there is still another layer, until one finally comes to the core (Simkin, 1979).

Although the gestalt approach is used with individuals, its widest application is in groups. Kempler (1974) describes gestalt counseling with families, and Rhyne (1973) advocates integrating art with gestalt work. Some other applications include crisis intervention, mental health, education, the dying, and organizational development (Simkin, 1979). Some of the concepts and terminology highlighted by gestalt counseling include figure-ground, the I-thou relationship, hot seat, empty chair, and contact and support.

Person-centered counseling. Another humanistic approach, person- or client-centered counseling, is based on the theory of Carl Rogers. "In the history of counseling there was a time when professionals were polarized by orientation. Psychiatrists were psychoanalytic, psychologists were behavioral, and counselors were client-centered. Thus Rogers's impact on counseling has been extensive, perhaps immeasurable" (G. Leddick, personal communication, 1989).

Rejecting the psychoanalytic view, which focuses on the past and sees humans as irrational, the Rogerian approach attends to the present experience of the client and views humans as basically good, growth-seeking organisms with a natural tendency toward self-actualization. Counselor traits of unconditional positive regard, genuineness, and empathy are central

to the counselor-client relationship. When these attitudes are present, positive personality change will occur in the client (Rogers, 1957).

Believing in the self-directing capacity of their clients, in practice person-centered counselors are nondirective. They allow the inner experiencing of the client to set the pace and direction of the counseling relationship. These counselors focus on the feelings of the clients and experience their own feelings in the relationship. Because the main purpose of the helper is to facilitate positive change in the helpee, this approach cuts through complex diagnostic definitions, webs of theory, and protocols of techniques, making it attractive to professionals in a wide variety of fields. The person who can be real, caring, and understanding can count on being an effective facilitator of growth in a helping relationship (Meador & Rogers, 1984).

Cognitive Approaches

Cognitive approaches, such as rational-emotive therapy (RET), cognitive therapy, reality therapy, and transactional analysis (TA), have had a powerful impact on the counseling profession in America. These approaches stress the use of the client's thought process in overcoming emotional difficulties. They integrate a variety of dynamic and behavioral constructs by helping clients to rethink assumptions and restructure cognitions (Belkin, 1988).

Rational-emotive therapy. RET, developed by Albert Ellis in the 1950s, purports that when a highly charged emotional consequence (C) follows a significant activating event (A), A may seem to, but actually does not, cause C. Instead, emotional consequences are largely created by B, that is, the individual's belief system. Because the undesirable emotions can be traced to irrational beliefs, these beliefs can be attacked rationally, thus eliminating the disturbed emotions (Ellis, 1979).

The goal of RET is to show unconditional acceptance of clients while trying to correct their illogical beliefs and irrational feelings. The RET counselor takes an authoritative stance, acts in a very directive manner, and tries to teach clients effective self-analysis. RET combines cognitive therapy to change beliefs, emotive-evocative therapy to change core values, and behavior therapy to help clients change their dysfunctional symptoms. It employs such techniques as role play, modeling, exhortation, and even humor. RET is used for individual, group, marathon encounter, marriage and family, and brief therapy (Ellis, 1979).

Cognitive therapy. The cognitive therapy developed and tested by Aaron Beck has gained wide acceptance over the past 15 years, especially for the treatment of phobias and depression. Beck's premise is that the client's problem stems from a distorted construction of reality. These distortions occur at three levels: (a) view of self, (b) view of experiences, and (c) view of the future. Beck (1985) asserts that changes in thinking produce biochemical changes in the brain, which in turn make the client feel less depressed.

In practice, the cognitive counselor uses a variety of techniques, such as Meichenbaum's (1977) "self-talk," to help clients examine automatic, illogical thoughts, reevaluate those thoughts, and modify the assumptions underlying them. Clients are trained to keep a daily record of their dysfunctional thoughts. This forces them to identify the situation, specify the emotion aroused, articulate the automatic thought, identify a rational response, and evaluate the outcome. Thus the client can identify illogical thoughts and work with the counselor to generate alternative thoughts and behaviors that are more adaptive and satisfying than the previous ones (Belkin, 1988).

Reality therapy. Reality therapy, the approach developed by William Glasser in the 1950s, is founded upon the premise that individuals are responsible for what they do. Glasser's (1981) control theory espouses that individuals' brains act as control systems, attempting to control the outside world in such a way as to satisfy individuals' needs. This theory rejects the conventional concept of mental illness. Instead, Glasser believes people experience psychological disorders because they are unable to control the world in such a way as to satisfy their basic human needs for survival, belonging, power, fun, and freedom.

Reality therapists help clients to see themselves accurately, find appropriate ways to meet their needs, and take personal responsibility for their own behavior. This is done in a straightforward, sensible manner that pushes aside rationalizations, excuses, explanations, and distortions by artfully applying logic and environmental realities. Reality therapy has proven effective for groups as well as for individuals, in educational settings, with institutionalized patients, and for marriage and family counseling.

Glasser (1984) presents the eight steps of reality therapy:

(1) Make friends and ask clients what they want.
(2) Ask, What are you doing now?
(3) Is what clients choose to do getting them what they want?
(4) Make a plan to do better.
(5) Get a commitment to follow the plan.
(6) No excuses.
(7) No punishment.
(8) Never give up.

Transactional analysis. The last cognitive approach to be discussed is transactional analysis (TA), a system developed by Eric Berne and popularized through two best-selling books: Berne's (1964) *Games People Play* and Thomas A. Harris's (1969) *I'm OK—You're OK.* TA analyzes human transaction in terms of three ego states: (a) the Parent, the authoritative state characterized by values, injunctions, and shoulds, critical versus nurturant; (b) the Adult, the rational, objective state that processes and files information; and (c) the Child, the uninhibited state that is free to respond naturally without making judgments; free child versus adapted child.

TA presents four life positions: (a) I'm not OK—You're OK; (b) I'm not OK—You're not OK; (c) I'm OK—You're not OK; and (d) I'm OK—You're OK. The goal of counseling is for the client to reach the fourth life position. This is done by analyzing structural interactions, interpreting them in terms of the client's life script, and altering the script to enable the client to function on a mature adult level. TA is clearly a cognitive-dynamic counseling approach that asserts that a certain level of rational functioning (expressed by the interaction Adult-Adult) is the epitome of psychological health and the goal of the counseling (Belkin, 1988).

Behavioral Approaches

Behavioral approaches to counseling evolved from the behavioral psychology principles developed by John B. Watson and Edward L. Thorndike. Behavioral therapy, based on the work of Joseph Wolpe, follows the classical conditioning model, while B. F. Skinner's behavior modification derives from operant conditioning. Albert Bandura added the idea of vicarious conditioning through observational learning. All these behavioral techniques seek to teach clients more desirable behaviors to replace affective, cognitive, or motoric behaviors that are problematic (Chambless & Goldstein, 1979). The goal of behavioral counseling, then, is to remove the presenting problem, allowing more healthy patterns of behavior to emerge (Bandura, 1969).

Behavioral counselors view clients as products of their conditioning. The counselor's task is to design a program to modify conditioned behaviors that are problematic. The client's task is to learn new responses to old situations. In order to facilitate this, specific goals must be stated and a contract must be set up. A number of techniques may be used to bring about the desired change. Some of these are systematic desensitization, extinction, positive and negative reinforcement, punishment, shaping, modeling, and time-out. These techniques have proven effective for juvenile delinquency, alcoholism, anxiety, and other symptoms in a wide variety of settings, including hospitals, schools, rehabilitation centers, and prisons (Belkin, 1988).

Systems Approaches

Systems theory presents a general framework for therapy that involves shifting the focus from the individual "identified patient" (IP) to the dysfunctional system. This approach is widely used in family therapy, where the IP is viewed as a symptom of the dysfunctional family. Thus the family system itself is seen as the client and interventions are designed to change the system of relationships in order to bring about desired change in individuals.

Satir (1983) classifies systems as "open" or "closed." In closed systems the members are all expected to have the same thoughts, feelings, and opinions, whether they actually do or not. Individuality is stifled, along with personal growth and health, which results in emotional or behavioral disturbance. Open systems, on the other hand, allow honest self-expression and promote personal growth, and are characterized by a willingness to compromise and take turns. Utilizing a systems approach, the goal of family therapy would be to move from a pathological system of interaction to a growth-producing one.

Consultation Theory and Practice

A unique type of helping relationship is that which develops between consultants and their consultees. Just as effective counseling relies upon the strength of the helping relationship, the success of consultation is built on a good, solid working relationship. While counseling usually takes place within some type of human service setting, most consultation occurs in the workplace. Consultants aim to assist consultees with immediate problems while helping them to improve long-term problem-solving abilities. Consultation may focus either on organizational issues or on service delivery. In either case the relationship is voluntary, professional, and essentially egalitarian (Lewis & Lewis, 1987).

Though consultation has long been a part of mental health professional activity, no unified theory of the consultation process has been developed. Gallesich (1985) cites several impediments to the development of a cogent theory: (a) the assumption that unique principles and conceptions are not needed to consult, (b) the rapidly changing nature of consulting practice, (c) difficulty in selecting variables and relationships to investigate, (d) lack of meaningful process measures, and (e) the triadic structure of the consulting relationship, which makes outcome research difficult. She suggests the need for a metatheory that would better conceptualize the consultation process. This would give counseling professionals a chance to use their expertise in relationship building and maintenance and in theory and research related to helping roles, relationships, and processes to move consultation out of its developmental impasse.

Despite the lack of theory, a number of consultation models have been developed to guide practitioners in the consultation process. Some widely used consultation models include triadic consultation, mental health consultation, behavioral consultation, and process consultation.

Triadic Consultation

Triadic consultation (Tharp & Wetzel, 1969) involves three distinct roles: the consultant, the mediator, and the client. The consultant works with the mediator in solving professional, rather than personal, problems. The mediator in turn delivers the service to the ultimate client. In some cases the consultant never even sees the client. In others, the consultant provides direct service to clients identified by the mediator. Kurpius (1978) identifies four modalities of this type: (a) provision mode, (b) prescriptive mode, (c) collaboration mode, and (d) mediation mode.

Mental Health Consultation

Mental health consultation focuses on such work problems as the management or treatment of clients or the planning or implementation of a program to cater to such clients. In most mental health consultation responsibility for the client lies with the consultee. The consultant aims to solve current problems while enhancing skills to enable consultees to handle this type of problem in the future. A unique type of mental health consultation, supervision, places more direct, ethical, and legally binding responsibility for the client on the consultant (supervisor) than on the consultee (counselor).

Caplan (1963) identifies four types of mental health consultation: (a) client-centered case consultation, (b) program-centered administrative consultation, (c) consultee-centered case consultation, and (d) consultee-centered

administrative consultation. Caplan also cites four categories of consultee problems that might require consultation: (a) lack of understanding of the psychological factors in the case, (b) lack of skill or resources to deal with the problems involved, (c) lack of professional objectivity in handling the case, and (d) lack of confidence and self-esteem due to fatigue, illness, inexperience, youth, or old age.

Behavioral Consultation

Behavioral consultation is based on social learning theory. As more and more helping professionals employ behavioral techniques in schools, hospitals, prisons, group homes, and other settings, there is a growing need for help in designing and implementing behavior change programs. The behavioral consultant works with the consultee (teacher, doctor, parent, counselor) who has direct contact with the client (student, patient, child). The consultee then implements a program to alter the client's behavior. The goal of behavioral consultation is to reduce or eliminate the client's presenting problematic behavior and to initiate and maintain the consultee behaviors necessary to implement the client's behavior change program (Russell, 1978).

Process Consultation

In Schein's (1969) view, process consultation, or organizational consultation, is a way of delivering services to an organization that is intended to increase the effectiveness of a work group in attaining its goals. Schein defines process consultation as a set of consultant activities that help the client to perceive, understand, and act upon process events that occur in the client's environment.

Process consultation differs from other types because the consultant and consultee come to a joint diagnosis about which processes need improvement. In contrast, the purchase model involves hiring a consultant to solve a particular problem or perform a specific task already identified by the organization as the target problem; the doctor-patient model involves asking the consultant to find out what is wrong with what part of the organization. These two methods are doomed to failure because they put the consultee in a passive role and the consultant in a position of high authority, rather than one of process facilitator (Schein, 1969). No matter what type of counseling or consultation, the helper must always be aware that it is a sound working relationship that forms the basis for effective helping to occur.

Supervision

Experienced counselors are often in a position to serve as consultants to novice or less experienced counselors. This supervisory role involves not only consultation, but also teaching and counseling with the supervisee. According to Borders and Leddick (1987), several tasks need to be accomplished early in the supervisory relationship:

(1) Establish a working relationship.

(2) Assess the supervisee's counseling skills.

(3) Agree to a contract for the conduct of supervisory sessions.

(4) Establish learning goals for the supervisee.

Once these tasks are accomplished, interventions can be chosen based on the needs and experience of the counselor. Ongoing feedback and final evaluation, including self-evaluation, are integral parts of the supervisory process. "Competent supervision is more likely to result in competent counseling and, in turn, more fully-functioning clients" (Borders & Leddick, 1987).

LEARNING OBJECTIVES

After studying the material in this chapter, you should be able to do the following:

(1) Understand the philosophical bases of the helping relationship in terms of basic propositions, underlying premises, general tenets, and core elements.

(2) Name counselor characteristics that contribute to the helping relationship.

(3) Define the psychodynamic approach to helping and give examples of how it is used in practice.

(4) Define the humanistic approach to helping and give examples of how it is used in practice.

(5) Define the cognitive approach to helping and give examples of how it is used in practice.

(6) Define the behavioral approach to helping and give examples of how it is used in practice.

(7) Identify significant contributors to counseling practice according to their particular contributions.

(8) Identify and explain four models for consultation.

(9) Compare and contrast counseling and consultation.

TERMS AND NAMES
TO REMEMBER

Terms

You should have an understanding of the following terms and be able to define them in your own words.

attending
attractiveness
authenticity
aversion
behavior modification
behavioral view
catharsis
client-centered view
cognitive mediators
cognitive restructuring
cognitive therapy
collaboration
consultation
dream analysis
eclectic
empathy
evaluation
existential-humanistic
expertness
free association

genuineness
inquiring
intervention
intimacy
listening skills
paradoxical intention
paraphrase
power
psychoanalytic view
psychodrama
reality therapy
reflection
regression
resistance
respect
self-actualization
termination
TA view
transference
unconditional positive regard

Names

You should be familiar with these people and be aware of their contributions to the counseling profession with regard to the helping relationship.

Adler
Bandura
Beck
Berne
Caplan
Carkhuff
Egan
Ellis
Frankl
Freud
Gendlin
Glasser

Horney
Ivey
Jung
Kurpius
Maslow
Moreno
Parsons
Perls
Rogers
Schein
Skinner
Wolpe

FILL IN THE BLANKS

The following section reviews some of the major points in this content area. Check your knowledge of the area by filling in the appropriate name, term, or concept in each blank provided. Answer choices are found above, in the section containing terms and names to remember. You will find the correct answers at the end of the chapter.

(1) _____ may be either basic, additive, or subtractive.

(2) Treatment using _____ focuses on the client's past.

(3) When counselors accept and value clients without reservation, they are demonstrating _____.

(4) _____ insists that clients take full responsibility for their actions.

(5) Humanistic counselors believe that clients are inherently moving toward _____.

(6) The _____ relationship is voluntary, professional, and egalitarian.

(7) Counselors who consistently behave in accordance with their own values and perceptions are exhibiting the trait called _____.

(8) The _____ counselor has a personal style that incorporates methods and techniques from a variety of theories and approaches.

(9) According to the _____, clients' current behaviors, feelings, and actions are based on their life scripts.

(10) _____ developed scales for measuring empathy, genuineness, and respect.

(11) Counselors who fear rejection or fear closeness and affection may have difficulty developing _____ in the helping relationship.

(12) When counselors use accurate _____ of content and feeling, client's feel that they have really been understood.

(13) The approach used by _____ is very effective for treating depression.

(14) Counselors who apply their complete thinking, feeling, and behavior toward the client are using the helping skill referred to as _____ _____.

(15) The _____ approach tries to explore what is affecting the client in the here and now.

(16) _____,
_____,
and _____ are examples of helping skills.

(17) _____ recognized the importance of a person's position in the family constellation.

(18) When a client directs toward the counselor feelings that were once attached to a significant other, _____ takes place.

(19) _____ introduced the concept of observational learning.

(20) _____ is a process of eliminating anxiety by pairing the anxiety-evoking situation with the relaxing response.

(21) A basic premise of _____ is that people are influenced by the consequences of their behavior.

(22) The _____ holds that individuals are essentially good in nature, with a tendency toward growth and productivity.

(23) Flooding the client with anxiety-producing stimuli within a safe setting is called _____.

(24) Counselors who keep confidentiality and who are reliable and dependable slowly develop _____.

(25) The concept of collective unconscious was introduced by _____.

MATCHING TEST

Match the names in the left-hand column with the appropriate concepts in the right-hand column.

___ (1) Adler	(a) paradoxical intention
___ (2) Bandura	(b) person-centered therapy
___ (3) Beck	(c) behavior therapy
___ (4) Berne	(d) individual psychology
___ (5) Caplan	(e) social learning theory
___ (6) Carkhuff	(f) gestalt
___ (7) Egan	(g) counselor response scales
___ (8) Ellis	(h) RET
___ (9) Frankl	(i) focusing
___ (10) Freud	(j) process consultation
___ (11) Gendlin	(k) psychodrama
___ (12) Glasser	(l) reality therapy
___ (13) Horney	(m) psychoanalysis
___ (14) Ivey	(n) mental health consultation
___ (15) Jung	(o) neo-Freudian
___ (16) Kurpius	(p) behavior modification
___ (17) Maslow	(q) analytical psychotherapy
___ (18) Moreno	(r) TA
___ (19) Parsons	(s) cognitive therapy
___ (20) Perls	(t) consultation modalities
___ (21) Rogers	(u) father of guidance
___ (22) Schein	(v) microskills
___ (23) Skinner	(w) hierarchy of needs
___ (24) Wolpe	(x) helping skills

CASE STUDY

Angela is a 34-year-old homemaker and mother of three school-aged children. She is a strict Catholic and comes into counseling at the recommendation of her parish priest. She states that she has had training as a nurse but has not worked since her first child was born ten years ago. She maintains full responsibility for the running of the household, including cleaning, cooking, shopping, paying bills, and doing yard work, not to mention most of the parenting. Her husband is a rather domineering man and she is somewhat afraid of him.

At this time Angela feels she is losing control of her life. She has difficulty keeping up with her housework, her children have become hard to handle, and all the intimacy has gone out of her marriage. She lacks energy when she gets up in the morning and lacks the motivation to repeat the mundane daily tasks of her life.

Angela would like to go back to work full-time now that her youngest child is in school all day, but she is afraid to ask her husband. He has been extremely critical of her efforts with the house and the children lately, and so she hesitates to say anything that might displease him. Upon questioning, she reveals her belief that her husband's attitude toward her and his lack of emotional support are all her fault. She would like to be able to "do better" with the help of counseling. Then she thinks she might be able to convince her husband that she is capable of handling a job.

Angela reports that she has few friends—just one or two neighbors with whom she can borrow back and forth and to whom she could turn in an emergency. Her husband does not really approve of these relationships; therefore Angela has not attempted to develop them further. She has become quite involved with her church and, even though her husband is not Catholic, their children attend the parish elementary school.

Concerning her family, Angela reports that her mother and sisters live a thousand miles away. Her father, who was quite special to her, died eight years ago while she was pregnant with her second child. She named this son after her father. Her mother does come to visit several times a year, but Angela reports a great deal of anxiety connected with those visits. She states that her mother indulges the children and lavishes Angela with gifts and lunches out, which makes Angela's husband quite irritable. Consequently, her mother's visits have become shorter and less frequent over the years.

Finally, Angela states that her goal in counseling is to become a better wife and a better mother so that she will be allowed to get a job using her nursing skills.

Analysis

(1)   After reading the story of Angela, name three techniques that you think might be helpful in
      her case. Choose one affective, one cognitive, and one behavioral technique and discuss how
      you would use each technique and what outcome you would expect.

      affective:

      _____

      use:

      _____

      _____

      outcome:

      _____

      _____

      cognitive:

      _____

      use:

      _____

      _____

      outcome:

      _____

      _____

      behavioral:

      _____

      use:

      _____

      _____

      outcome:

      _____

      _____

(2)   How would you define Angela's presenting problem?

      _____

      _____

      _____

(3) If you were a TA counselor, how would you describe the function of Angela's Parent, Adult, and Child?

_____

_____

_____

_____

_____

_____

(4) If you were a person-centered counselor, what would you say to express unconditional positive regard for Angela?

_____

_____

_____

_____

(5) If you were using behavior modification, which client behavior do you think would be easiest to change, and how would you help Angela achieve the change?

_____

_____

_____

_____

MULTIPLE-CHOICE TEST

Check your understanding of this content area by responding to the following questions. You will find the answer key at the end of the chapter.

1. Albert Ellis has developed a system of helping known as rational-emotive therapy. A basic premise of this theory is that
   a. irrational thought patterns are the result of depression
   b. the environment is the major determinant of behavior
   c. psychological problems arise from irrational thought patterns
   d. rational thinking leads to emotional deficits

2. Gestalt therapy (counseling) developed by Perls is based upon a number of principles. One of these is
   a. explore the clients problems in the here and now
   b. explore the client's past to uncover negative childhood experiences
   c. treat the client with unconditional positive regard
   d. provide reinforcement for behavior change

3. A major belief associated with psycho-analytic therapy holds that
   a. the counselor's ability to empathize with the client is most important
   b. the counselor and client work together as equals to solve client problems
   c. the counselor's task is to apply learning principles to change client behavior
   d. the client's task consists of discovering, reliving, and mastering conflicts from childhood

4. Glasser's Reality Therapy focuses on
   a. cognitions
   b. being
   c. actualization
   d. identity

5. Systematic desensitization is a technique whereby a client resolves irrational fears through gradual exposure to the fear-producing stimulus. It was first developed as a therapy technique by
   a. Rogers
   b. Wolpe
   c. Freud
   d. Bandura

6. Counselors need to pay attention not only to verbal but also to nonverbal behavior. They need to be aware that nonverbals
   a. represent the client's rational state
   b. accent and/or contradict verbals
   c. are identical across cultures
   d. are valid only when they support verbals

7. A counselor whose theoretical orientation comes from behavioral counseling believes
   a. most behavior is learned, and therefore subject to change through specifically designed techniques
   b. the counselor should help the client to achieve a sense of self-actualization
   c. the counselor-client relationship should mimic the parent-child relationship of the client's past
   d. the unconditional positive regard of the counselor toward the client will automatically produce positive behavior change

8. Carkhuff has developed scales for measuring the core conditions for effective counseling. Which of the following is not one of the core conditions?

   a. empathy
   b. respect
   c. insight
   d. genuineness

9. Particular counseling activities are usually associated with their primary proponents. For example, psychodrama is to Moreno as hot seat is to

   a. Freud
   b. Glasser
   c. Adler
   d. Perls

10. Some counseling techniques are appropriate for individual counseling, while others apply more to group counseling. Which of the following counselor skills applies to individual as well as group counseling?

    a. summarizing
    b. consensus taking
    c. moderating
    d. linking

11. Which of the following are neo-Freudians?

    a. Sullivan, Rogers, Ellis
    b. Adler, Sullivan, Horney
    c. Sullivan, Jung, Ellis
    d. Bandura, Jung, Horney

12. The counseling profession is based upon some general philosophical propositions. Which of these is not one of them?

    a. Counseling aims to promote human growth and development.
    b. Counseling considers physical as well as psychosocial environment.
    c. Counseling facilitates person-environment fit.
    d. Counseling is a clearly defined helping relationship.

13. Which counselor intervention most closely follows client verbalizations?

    a. reflection of feelings
    b. confrontation
    c. restatement of content
    d. positive regard

14. Which of these is not one of the core elements of the helping relationship?

    a. psychodynamics
    b. theory
    c. social influence
    d. human relations

15. According to Schein, the path to increasing organizational effectiveness is to focus on

    a. human processes
    b. time management
    c. productivity
    d. managerial diagnosis

16. Maslow believes that individuals are unable to reach self-actualization until they

    a. face reality
    b. identify irrational beliefs
    c. satisfy lower order needs
    d. resolve transference issues

17. Counselors who choose their approach and techniques according to the needs and capacity of each individual client are said to be

    a. humanistic
    b. affective
    c. cognitive
    d. eclectic

18. Carkhuff has defined the core dimensions of counseling. Some of these are

    a. concreteness, genuineness, self-disclosure, respect
    b. empathy, reflection, respect, immediacy
    c. genuineness, self-disclosure, empathy, assessment
    d. concreteness, responsiveness, respect, confrontation

19. The "mediator" is an important dimension of which type of consultation?

    a. mental health
    b. triadic
    c. process
    d. behavioral

20. When a counselor's response includes congruent ideas and feelings from another frame of reference to facilitate client exploration, Ivey would say the counselor is using

    a. basic empathy
    b. reflection of meaning
    c. additive empathy
    d. skill integration

21. Which of these does not apply to Beck's cognitive therapy?

    a. testing automatic thoughts
    b. attending to feelings
    c. identifying maladaptive assumptions
    d. generating alternative responses and behaviors

22. When clients ask decision-oriented questions, counselors serve them best by

    a. answering the question to the best of their ability
    b. offering the client two or three options to choose from
    c. reminding the client that this is inappropriate
    d. responding with questions back to the client

23. Consultation is an example of

    a. management training
    b. environmental intervention
    c. human development training
    d. indirect helping

24. Which statement applies to the social influence core of the helping relationship?

    a. Clients need to learn counseling principles to combat resistance.
    b. The counselor uses techniques from social learning theory.
    c. Two important elements are helper's self-image and client's perceptions of helper.
    d. The counselor utilizes basic interviewing skills to socialize the client.

25. Which of these is not compatible with the existential approach?

    a. personal responsibility
    b. predestination
    c. goodness of human nature
    d. meaning of life

ANSWER KEY

Fill in the Blanks

(1) empathy
(2) psychoanalysis
(3) unconditional positive regard
(4) reality therapy
(5) self-actualization
(6) consultation
(7) genuineness
(8) eclectic
(9) TA view
(10) Carkhuff
(11) intimacy
(12) reflection
(13) Beck

(14) attending
(15) gestalt
(16) listening, attending, inquiring
(17) Adler
(18) transference
(19) Bandura
(20) systematic desensitization
(21) behavior modification
(22) client-centered view
(23) implosive therapy
(24) trustworthiness
(25) Jung

Matching

(1) d	(9) a	(17) w
(2) e	(10) m	(18) k
(3) s	(11) i	(19) u
(4) r	(12) l	(20) f
(5) n	(13) o	(21) b
(6) g	(14) v	(22) j
(7) x	(15) q	(23) p
(8) h	(16) t	(24) c

Multiple-Choice

1. c	10. a	18. a
2. a	11. b	19. b
3. d	12. d	20. c
4. d	13. c	21. b
5. b	14. a	22. d
6. b	15. a	23. d
7. a	16. c	24. c
8. c	17. d	25. b
9. d		

CHAPTER 4

Group Dynamics, Process, and Counseling

SUMMARY   80
  Group Types, Dynamics, and Processes   **80**
   Types of Groups   80
   Group Dynamics   81
   Group Process   82
  Group Counseling Theory   **82**
   Theoretical Orientations   82
   Whole Group Versus Individual   83
   Outcome Versus Process   83
  Group Counseling Practice   **83**
   Ethics   83
   Training   84
   Current Issues   84
LEARNING OBJECTIVES   86
TIME LINE   87
TERMS AND NAMES TO REMEMBER   88
  Terms   **88**
  Names   **88**
FILL IN THE BLANKS   89
MATCHING TEST   91
CASE STUDY   92
  Analysis   **93**
MULTIPLE-CHOICE TEST   95

ANSWER KEY   98
  Fill in the Blanks   98
  Matching   98
  Multiple-Choice   98

SUMMARY

Groups includes theory and types of groups, as well as descriptions of group practices, methods, dynamics, and facilitative skills. (Loesch & Vacc, 1986, p. 13)

Group Types, Dynamics, and Processes

A group may be defined as an aggregate of people who are seen by themselves and others as psychologically interdependent and interactive in pursuit of a shared goal (Dagley, Gazda, & Pistole, 1986). The purpose of the group may be to prevent, to correct, or to enhance. It may offer guidance, counseling, or psychotherapy. As such, group work has been going on since the late 1800s, with ever-increasing importance in this century. Group counseling offers valuable opportunities for learning and growth that are not always available in the individual counseling mode.

Types of Groups

Group work is effective in a wide range of settings for a wide variety of purposes. Counselors need to have an understanding of various types of groups in order to become effective group leaders. Several writers have classified groups in terms of function, goal, technique, or membership.

Classification by task. Shaw (1981) distinguishes among three types of groups: (a) problem-solving groups, (b) educational groups, and (c) experiential groups. Problem-solving groups such as committees or task forces handle problems that could be attacked individually; however, group solutions offer greater diversity of resources, correct errors more frequently, and increase the motivation of group members. Educational groups are those formed to facilitate learning by group members. They are most effective, according to Shaw, when they are heterogeneous by ability and sociometric for mutual attraction, and employ team teaching methods. Experiential groups assume

that the individual will benefit from group membership itself. Examples of experiential groups include laboratory training groups (T-groups), sensitivity training groups, and therapy, encounter, and personal growth groups.

Therapeutic groups. Corey and Corey (1982) use the term "therapeutic group" to refer to group counseling, group therapy, T-groups, encounter groups, awareness groups, self-help and leaderless groups, consciousness-raising groups, sensitivity training groups, and personal growth groups, among others. Encounter, or personal growth, groups teach people about growth and development and, at the same time, help them achieve these goals. They are usually time limited and are characterized by risk-taking behavior. T-groups help people from organizational settings develop human relations skills by examining group process rather than personal growth. The focus is on experimentation, feedback, and problem-solving and decision-making skills that can be brought back to the organization.

Therapy versus counseling. Group therapy attends to people's unconscious needs and their past in an effort to bring about personality change. Traditionally, group therapy has been limited to people with specific emotional or behavioral problems, but recently, more emotionally healthy persons are turning to group therapy in an effort to get even healthier. Unlike leaders or facilitators of personal growth groups, whose training may be minimal, group therapists generally need a more advanced degree in counseling, psychology, social work, or psychiatry. Group counseling, on the other hand, focuses on conscious problems (not neurotic or psychotic disorders) that may be social, educational, vocational, or personal, and attempts to bring about resolution within a relatively short period of time.

Formed versus natural and treatment versus task. Toseland and Rivas (1984) classify groups according to two criteria: (a) formed or natural and (b) treatment or task. Natural groups, such as family, peer, gang, or friendship groups, come together spontaneously; formed groups come together for a particular purpose through some outside influence. Treatment groups differ from task groups with respect to roles. In treatment groups roles develop through the interaction of the members, whereas in task groups roles may be assigned. Communication patterns in treatment groups are more open and spontaneous; task group communication focuses mainly on the task at hand.

Level and purpose. Conyne (1985) classifies groups according to level and purpose. Intervention may occur at the individual, interpersonal, organizational, or community level. Interventions may be planned for correction or enhancement of either personal or task behavior. Personal correction includes psychotherapy, counseling, employee assistance, and mutual help groups. Personal enhancement includes groups for personal development, team development, life transition, and training (T-groups).

Gazda's typology. Gazda's (1984) group typology recognizes three distinct classifications of group work: (a) guidance, (b) counseling, and (c) psychotherapy. Group guidance and life skills training groups, which correspond with primary prevention, aim to prevent problems and promote health among high-risk populations. Various types of counseling groups (T-groups, encounter groups, sensitivity groups, organizational development groups) may be preventive or remedial. Because counseling utilizes early intervention to reduce the duration or depth of problems in identified populations, it corresponds with secondary prevention. Psychotherapy, which corresponds to tertiary prevention, seeks to rehabilitate, reeducate, or otherwise restore group members to health.

Group Dynamics

No matter what the type or purpose of the group, attention must be given to the interacting forces within the group—otherwise known as group dynamics. As the term *dynamic* implies, the forces that interact to influence individual behavior in groups are fluid and changing, not static (Dagley et al., 1986). Despite the changing nature of groups, counselors need to focus on four main areas of group dynamics in order to understand and work

effectively with groups. According to Toseland and Rivas (1984), these four areas include (a) the communication and interaction patterns occurring in groups, (b) the attraction of groups for their members, (c) the social controls that are exerted in groups, and (d) the culture that develops in groups.

Communication patterns. First, if counselors are aware of both verbal and nonverbal communication patterns among group members, they can intervene at appropriate times in order to facilitate the kind of helpful communication that moves the group toward the achievement of its goals.

Cohesiveness. Second, cohesiveness, or the group's attraction for its members, is a prime mode of help in the therapy experience. Highly cohesive groups have an overall higher outcome, higher levels of self-disclosure, and more group support and acceptance. These findings taken together strongly support the contention that group cohesiveness is an important determinant of positive therapeutic outcome (Yalom, 1975).

Social control. The third area of group dynamics, social control, concerns the methods by which the group gains sufficient compliance and conformity from its members to enable it to function in an orderly manner. Social control includes such dynamics as norms, roles, and status (Toseland & Rivas, 1984). A group's norms, or standard rules of conduct, may be spoken or silent, formal or informal, visible or invisible. The role of the counselor is to help the group avoid blind responses to the pressures to conformity. Norms that define how individuals operate within the group are known as role expectations. *Task* and *maintenance* roles help the group function effectively in the achievement of its goals, while *individual* roles are often selfish and therefore counterproductive to group goal achievement (Dagley et al., 1986). A person's status, or ranking, within the group is determined in part by the person's prestige or position outside of the group and in part by the person's behavior as a group member. Status affects the person's conformity (or lack of it) to the group norms.

Group culture. The fourth area, group culture, develops from the beliefs, customs, and values shared by the group members and also from the environment in which the group functions. Group culture influences the objectives of the group, the task the group decides to work on, the way members interact, and the methods the group uses to conduct its business (Toseland & Rivas, 1984). Because it is the group itself, as a therapeutic social system, that provides support, universality, advice, testing, learning, interpersonal feedback, opportunities for altruism, and hope, it is really the group that is the agent of change (Yalom, 1975).

Group Process

The functioning of the group, or group process, is a study of how groups work. Group process involves the functions of leadership, decision making, communication, and stages of group development. The study of group process involves observing, describing, and recording behavior as it occurs in the group and using the results of these observations to revise group process in order to make it more effective. To develop skill in the facilitation of group effectiveness, counselors must be aware of group process while participating in the group, and it is through observation practice that such skills are developed (Johnson & Johnson, 1987).

Stages of group development. An effective group leader can keep group process from getting bogged down. While maintaining sensitivity to the individual needs of group members, the counselor can use a variety of leadership techniques in order to facilitate the movement of the group through its developmental stages. Various writers have described the stages of group development. Although there are differences in the number and type of stages identified, it is agreed that groups definitely have a beginning, a middle, and an end. According to Corey and Corey (1982), group stages are as follows: (a) initial stage, (b) transition stage, (c) working stage, (d) final stage, and (e) postgroup stage. Tuckman (1963) calls the beginning "forming" and the middle "storming," "norming," and, finally, "performing." For Klein (1972), the beginning includes "orientation" and "resistance"; the middle includes "negotiation" and "intimacy"; and the end, "termination."

Group Counseling Theory

Because the field of group work is relatively young and quite diverse, and because it draws from a number of disciplines within the social sciences, it is influenced by a wide variety of theoretical approaches. Theoretical orientation seems to be situational rather than personal. Depending upon the type of group with which counselors are working or the type of research being done, they could be influenced by several different theoretical approaches. Cartwright and Zander (1968) suggest that although the different theories may sometimes appear to be in conflict with one another, a closer look reveals that they do not actually contradict, but rather augment and amplify one another. These authors suggest that a more unified theory of group dynamics will be forthcoming when more is known about the proper objects of study, observation techniques, and data collection, and their relationship to theory building.

Theoretical Orientations

Toseland and Rivas (1984) list five theories that influence group practice: (a) psychoanalytic theory (Freud, 1922), (b) learning theory (Bandura, 1977), (c) field theory (Lewin, 1951), (d) social exchange (or interaction) theory (Blau, 1964; Homans, 1961; Thibaut & Kelley, 1959), and (e) systems theory (Anderson, 1979; Olsen, 1968). Besides these, Cartwright and Zander (1968) include four others: (a) sociometric orientation (Jennings, 1943; Moreno, 1934), (b) general psychology orientation (applying individual theories to individuals within groups), (c) empiricist-statistical orientation (or group syntality theory; Cattell, 1948), and (d) formal models orientation (French & Snyder, 1959; Harary, Norman, & Cartwright, 1965; Simon, 1957).

Besides group syntality theory and social exchange theory, Shaw (1981) adds FIRO (a theory of interpersonal relations; Schutz, 1958) and group congruence theory (Benoit-Smullyan, 1944). He stresses the interrelationship of theory and research and suggests viewing each theory in terms of its contribution to the understanding of group behavior.

Eclectic approach. Recognizing the contributions various theorists have made to the field of group work, Corey and Corey (1982) subscribe to an eclectic approach to group counseling. They borrow various concepts and techniques from contemporary therapeutic models and adapt them to their own personal style. They recommend that counselors take into account the feeling, thinking, and behaving aspects of human beings, and develop their own individual philosophy of life, theory of group practice, and leadership style.

Whole Group Versus Individual

Irrespective of the theories upon which counselors base their work with groups, they need to decide upon a philosophical position concerning the issue of working with the group as a whole versus working with the individual within the group. For some group counselors it makes more sense to focus upon the group setting, group relationship building, group tasks, and group process. Yalom (1975) advocates the use of process comments in working with therapeutic groups. This technique serves two purposes: (a) to plunge the group into the here-and-now experience and (b) to draw attention to the implications of the nature of group members' relationships with one another. If successful, this method should serve to keep the group focused upon itself and moving toward group goals.

Other group counselors may attend to the individual client, paying little attention to other group members. In effect, they are doing individual counseling within the group setting. This approach may also be called *vertical* intervention, in contrast to *horizontal* intervention or attention to the group as a whole. Group counselors of either orientation may at times use either approach. They take their cues for intervention from the dynamic process, that is the interactions, of the group (Kissen, 1981).

Outcome Versus Process

Another issue in the study of group dynamics is that of outcome versus process. While outcome studies address the question, Do groups work? process studies try to answer the question, How do groups achieve their outcomes? Research conclusions in this area are quite tentative. Conclusions based upon a relatively small number of studies indicate that group counseling is more effective than no counseling at all, but there is little information to indicate the comparative effectiveness of groups as opposed to other forms of treatment. Though it seems apparent that groups do work, why or how they work is uncertain (Dagley et al., 1986).

Group Counseling Practice

Counselors who wish to pursue group work in the practice of their profession must pay special attention to the ethics of group work practice. They should be aware of their training and its possible limitations, and they need to stay apprised of the current issues in the profession.

Ethics

Group counselors need to be aware of the *Ethical Guidelines for Group Leaders* of the Association for Specialists in Group Work (ASGW) (American Association for Counseling and Development, 1980; see Appendix B). These guidelines expand upon the general ethical standards of AACD (1981) as they address three issues of importance to group leaders: (a) responsibility for providing information about group work and group services, (b) responsibility for providing group services to clients, and (c) responsibility for safeguarding ethical practice.

Information. The first responsibility has to do with information provided to clients by the group leader prior to clients' entering the group. Clients should be informed of the nature and goals of the group, the potential risks involved, and the types of group activities and experiences to be expected. Group members should be aware of the voluntary nature of group participation and should be coached on confidentiality.

Protection from harm. The second responsibility has to do with the protection of group members from harm by other members or by unethical leader behavior. It ensures clients' rights to an equal share of group resources while focusing on their own personal goals. It mandates between-session and termination follow-up consultation for group members who request or need it.

Enforcing the code of ethics. The third set of responsibilities requires group leaders to display the code of ethics. It further obligates group leaders to confront other group leaders who violate ethical procedure, to report those violations to ASGW, and to help the leaders correct their inappropriate behaviors.

Besides attention to the formal code of ethics for group workers, Corey and Corey (1982) warn counselors to base their practice on sound, informed, and responsible judgment. They suggest that counselors develop this judgment by getting experience in leading groups, by consulting with other professionals, and by continuing supervision and training during their early years of practice. Other ways of improving group leadership skills include keeping up with current literature, reading relevant journals, and attending training meetings, conventions, and workshops.

Group leaders must be responsible for representing themselves accurately to the populations they serve. They should take on only those groups for which their training and expertise are appropriate. Depending upon the type of group to be led, the setting in which the group meets, and characteristics of the group members, various types of training are required.

Training

In general, professional group leaders may have received their basic training in a number of fields, including, but not limited to, counseling, psychology, social work, addictions, and education. For counselors, the Council for the Accreditation of Counseling and Related Educational Programs (CACREP) follows a set of guidelines for reviewing the required competencies and training for group counselors. These standards include 9 knowledge competencies, 17 skill competencies, and 6 types of supervised experiences (AACD, 1986).

Knowledge core. Knowledge competencies include (a) theories, (b) group dynamics, (c) leadership qualities, (d) ethics, (e) research, (f) group modalities, (g) group process, (h) roles, and (i) appropriateness of group for specific circumstances.

Skills core. Skill competencies include (a) pre-group screening, (b) defining group counseling, (c) recognizing self-defeating behaviors, (d) selecting and conducting a clientele-appropriate model, (e) identifying nonverbal behavior, (f) exhibiting pacing skills, (g) effectively intervening in critical incidents, (h) working with disruptive members, (i) using strategies, techniques, and procedures of group counseling, (j) providing help for clients to transfer changes from group to natural environment, (k) using adjunct group structures (like homework), (l) using basic group leader interventions, (m) facilitating therapeutic conditions, (n) working cooperatively with coleader, (o) opening and closing sessions as well as terminating group, (p) providing follow-up, and (q) utilizing assessment procedures.

Supervised experience. The types of supervised experiences and hours required in each experience include (a) critiquing group tapes, 5 hours; (b) observing group counseling, 5 hours; (c) group membership, 15 hours; (d) coleading a group and receiving critical feedback, 15 hours; (e) group leadership practicum, 15 hours; and (f) fieldwork internship with on-site supervision, 25 hours.

Current Issues

Besides training standards, counselors need to be aware of a number of current issues in the profession. Dagley et al. (1986) address gender issues as well as life-span development and prevention. Much of the literature to date on gender issues focuses on women and the unique challenges and problems of women in the workplace, women's anger, sexuality, and so on. As yet, there is no unified theory, but rather a scattering of information from individual studies. In contrast, life skills training and prevention is a much more systematic fusion of research and practice. Such systems as Gazda's life skills training model use an educative mode to bring about remediation as well as prevention. This model is based on a developmental curriculum of life skills that can be implemented easily through schools and community mental health systems.

Other current issues in group membership include involuntary membership, informed consent, and confidentiality (Corey & Corey, 1982). Participation in groups in mental health, correctional, and educational settings is often mandatory rather than voluntary. In this case there may be a great deal of resistance. The group leader needs to let participants ventilate their feelings about this requirement and let them know that the extent of their participation is up to them. It is especially important in mandatory groups that group participants be clearly informed of the nature and goals of the group as well as their responsibilities and rights as group members.

Although confidentiality is a major issue in all aspects of the counseling profession, it takes on added importance in the context of group work. The group leader is responsible not only for keeping the confidences of the group members but also for getting the group members to keep one another's confidences. The confidentiality issue is particularly difficult in working with groups whose members are well known to each other, adolescent groups, and children's groups. Leaders must inform interested parties ahead of time about the limits to the information the leader may ethically disclose. Due to privileged communication, counselors are required by law to break confidence when child abuse is involved or when clients are likely to do serious harm to themselves or others. Before breaking confidentiality, consultation with other professionals is recommended (AACD, 1981).

LEARNING OBJECTIVES

After studying the material in this chapter, you should be able to do the following:

(1) Name several types of groups and tell their purposes.

(2) Understand the fundamental principles of group dynamics.

(3) Understand the fundamental principles of group process.

(4) Explain several models of group development (stages).

(5) Identify at least eight underlying theories upon which group work practice is built.

(6) Identify leadership techniques and strategies.

(7) Determine the advantages and disadvantages of vertical versus horizontal intervention.

(8) Explain the three main ethical responsibility areas for specialists in group work.

(9) Understand the skill, knowledge, and experiential competencies put forth by the Council for the Accreditation of Counseling and Related Educational Programs.

(10) Discuss group approaches to current counseling issues.

(11) Explain the concept of confidentiality as it relates to group counseling.

(12) Define at least 20 terms specific to group work.

TIME LINE

You should be aware of important developments in the evolution of group dynamics, process, and counseling.

1895   LeBon, group mind
1897   Triplett, schoolchildren working in groups
1920s   Adler, group guidance with families
1930s   Slavson, small therapy groups
1931   Moreno coins term *group therapy*
1936   Sherif, social norms study
1941   Moreno, American Society of Group Psychotherapy and Psychodrama
1942   Slavson, American Group Psychotherapy Association
1945   T-groups versus therapy groups
1951   Foulkes, group = essential psychological unit

1955   Corsini and Rosenberg, group classifications
1959   Knowles and Knowles, first group dynamics book
1960s   group dynamics enters college curricula
1961   Foulkes, group psychoanalysis
1968   Cartwright and Zander, definition of group
1975   Yalom, taxonomy of group
1985   Gazda, life skills training model

TERMS AND NAMES
TO REMEMBER

Terms

You should have an understanding of the following terms and be able to define them in your own words.

Adlerian
authoritarian
behavioral
cohesiveness
confidentiality
confrontation
consolidation
counselor
democratic
encounter
ethics
facilitator
feedback
gestalt
group-centered leader
group dynamics
group process
group roles
Hawthorne effect
hidden agendas
horizontal intervention
humanistic
informed consent
initial stage
in vivo

laissez-faire
life scripts
norms
open group
orientation
phenomenological
prevention
proaction
psychiatrist
psychodrama
psychologist
psychotherapy
reality testing
sensitivity group
sociogram
sociologist
teleological
termination
T-group
transactional analysis
transference
transition stage
values clarification
vertical intervention
working stage

Names

You should be familiar with these people and be aware of their contributions to the counseling profession with regard to group dynamics, process, and counseling.

Adler	Corey and Corey	Hill	Moreno
Bale	Corsini and Rosenberg	Janis	Rogers
Bandura	Foulkes	Johari	Slavson
Butler	Freud	LeBon	Triplett
Cattell	Gazda	Lewin	Yalom

FILL IN THE BLANKS

The following section reviews some of the major points in this content area. Check your knowledge of the area by filling in the appropriate name, term, or concept in each blank provided. Answer choices are found above, in the section containing terms and names to remember. You will find the correct answers at the end of the chapter.

(1) _____ leadership leaves all the group decision making up to the members of the group.

(2) The group's attractiveness to its members is known as _____ _____.

(3) One of the first thing a group needs to do is start developing standard rules of conduct, or _____, to govern group behavior.

(4) One of the basic techniques in transactional analysis is called _____ _____ analysis.

(5) Personal growth group leaders are referred to as _____ _____.

(6) _____ in counseling consists of the members of the group analyzing the group's functioning.

(7) In a(n) _____ members may join at any time during the life of the group.

(8) _____ is a direct expression of one's views and feelings in a conflict situation that also invites the opposition to do the same.

(9) One way groups are helpful is by providing members with _____ _____ or real-life situations where they can try out new behaviors.

(10) The _____ concludes that group members change their behavior as a result of observation.

(11) "What happens in the group stays in the group" is an underlying assumption of _____.

(12) According to Gazda, the stage linking exploration and action is the _____ stage.

(13) *Primary, secondary,* and *tertiary* refer to _____ _____.

(14) _____ define the expectations of the group concerning the behavior of group members.

(15) Counselors who focus on the group as a whole use _____ _____.

(16) _____ occurs when client's project onto the therapist feelings having to do with past relationships.

(17) _____ is a method of letting clients know ahead of time the nature, expectations, and goals of the group, especially in mandatory groups.

(18) Neurotic personalities are better handled in group _____ _____ than in group counseling.

(19) When group members give _____ to another group member, they are letting that person know how his or her behavior affects others.

(20) Established principles that guide counselors in the conscientious practice of their profession are known as _____.

(21) Another name for laboratory group is _____ _____ group.

(22) _____ is an action method of group therapy that was first developed in Vienna.

(23) A _____ has an M.D. degree, while a _____ has a Ph.D. degree.

(24) A diagram that depicts relationships within a group is called a _____ _____.

(25) An observation that can be scientifically described is said to be _____ _____.

MATCHING TEST

Match the names in the left-hand column with the appropriate concepts in the right-hand column.

___ (1) Adler

___ (2) Bale

___ (3) Bandura

___ (4) Benne and Sheats

___ (5) Cartwright and Zander

___ (6) Cattell

___ (7) Conyne

___ (8) Foulkes

___ (9) Freud

___ (10) Gazda

___ (11) Hill

___ (12) Janis

___ (13) LeBon

___ (14) Lewin

___ (15) Luft and Ingram

___ (16) Moreno

___ (17) Pratt

___ (18) Rogers

___ (19) Sherif

___ (20) Slavson

___ (21) Toseland and Rivas

___ (22) Triplett

___ (23) Tuckman and Jensen

___ (24) Wolf

___ (25) Yalom

(a) group pressure to conform

(b) psychodrama

(c) individual in group

(d) group level and purpose

(e) group as a whole

(f) curative factors

(g) first class for TB patients

(h) term: group dynamics

(i) roles: task, individual, maintenance

(j) social norms

(k) family group guidance

(l) guidance, counseling, psychotherapy

(m) first small intensive therapy group

(n) group mind

(o) group stages

(p) group centered

(q) group syntality

(r) psychoanalytic theory

(s) four areas of group dynamics

(t) groupthink

(u) Johari's window

(v) learning theory

(w) groups for schoolchildren

(x) interaction matrix

(y) interaction analysis

CASE STUDY

Ten members were present at a group session in a residential facility for chemical dependency. During a routine "check-in" at the beginning of group, Joe, Sue, Bob, Donna, John, and Mary all said they were "okay" or "doing fine" today. Ken, an alcoholic, stated that he didn't see why he was forced into treatment with a bunch of drug addicts and wanted to know why alcohol- and drug-addicted patients weren't treated in different groups. Karen, a six-months pregnant 20-year-old, complained of sleeplessness and bodily discomfort. Vicky, a divorced mother of three, briefly mentioned an argument she had with her mother over the phone relating to her mother's failure to bring her children to visit. When Thomas, the group leader, assured Vicky that the group would come back to her to work on her problem, Vicky stated, "I really don't want to talk about it." Mike, a cocaine addict who had been in residential treatment twice before, expressed fear concerning his upcoming discharge and the difficulty of remaining sober.

Thomas then invited those with special concerns to tell more about their situations. Vicky immediately went into a long, blow-by-blow account of her argument with her mother, talking nonstop for several minutes. Finally, Mary interrupted her, saying, "Vicky, I'm really tired of listening to you. Every day you go on and on about your mother, your kids, your ex-husband. Whatever anyone here suggests, you've already tried it, or you know it won't work, or some other negative comment. You said you don't want to talk about it, so don't talk about it. I'm here to work on my sobriety and I don't want you or anyone else wasting my time. You went for weeks on crack and couldn't care less about your kids. Now you expect your mother to drive 60 miles just so you can show them off at visiting time. You're just playing games with yourself and all the rest of us. Get real and stop wasting our time!" Most of the other group member chimed in with "Yeah," "That's right," and other affirmative comments.

Vicky was taken aback for a few moments, then got defensive, saying, "I'm not playing games, I'm just trying to get better like everyone else here." Thomas asked Vicky if she was willing to receive feedback from other members to see if they could provide some insight into the issue of game playing. Vicky replied, "Sure, why not, put me on the hot seat."

Many group members shared their perceptions about both personal and group encounters with Vicky. They gave concrete examples of how she often said one thing and did another; how she played up to certain people while they were around and then talked about them later. For the first time in her ten days in the group, Vicky seemed to really pay attention to what others had to say. She listened quietly, nodded her head a lot, and tears came to her eyes as Karen reminded her of how she offered so much motherly advice one day, and the next day told Karen she was unfit to bear a child, making Karen feel angry and worthless. When the group was finished with their feedback, Vicky thanked them and said, "I guess I really have been playing games. I'm so afraid to knock the barriers down. What if I don't get better, or what if I don't like myself?"

"What if you do let that barrier down just a little bit?" asked Thomas. "Who would you see?"

"I'd see a frightened little girl," Vicky sobbed, "and she needs help."

Thomas assured Vicky that the group, the treatment center, and Vicky's family truly wanted to help and support her. He asked if she would like to say anything more. She replied that she just wanted to think about what had happened and figure out how she could allow herself to ask for help in a straightforward rather than game-playing manner.

"Let's move on to you now, Ken," said Thomas. "We have 40 minutes of group time left . . . "

Analysis

(1) After reading the group therapy vignette above, write a brief analysis of the group process.

_____

_____

_____

_____

_____

_____

(2) Identify at least three norms you noticed operating in this group and briefly explain.

_____

_____

_____

_____

_____

_____

(3)   In which stage of development do you think this group is operating? Explain.

_____

_____

_____

_____

_____

_____

(4)   Briefly describe the quality and type of leadership you think Thomas displayed.

_____

_____

_____

_____

_____

_____

(5)   Choose two leader interventions and critique them. What do you think Thomas did right? What would you do or say differently?

_____

_____

_____

_____

_____

_____

MULTIPLE-CHOICE TEST

Check your understanding of this content area by responding to the following questions. You will find the answer key at the end of the chapter.

1. "Empty chair" is a group technique used by which type of group counselor?
   a. gestalt
   b. behavioral
   c. transactional analysis
   d. Adlerian

2. In a counseling group using the psychodrama technique, the group member whose problem is being addressed takes the role of
   a. stage hand
   b. auxiliary ego
   c. director
   d. protagonist

3. Johari's window is a technique used to indicate differences in
   a. cohesion
   b. orientation
   c. openness
   d. behavior

4. Which type of group counselor views people as basically positive and moving toward actualization?
   a. behavioral
   b. group centered
   c. Adlerian
   d. psychoanalytic

5. Group members who have personal goals that they believe are unknown to the rest of the group are operating with
   a. encounter
   b. group conflict
   c. confrontation
   d. hidden agendas

6. In a closed group
   a. there are certain "taboo" topics that may not be discussed
   b. no new members may join after the first session
   c. there are no women allowed
   d. the group goals have already been achieved

7. Effective communication happens in groups when
   a. message receivers do not speak
   b. message receivers hear "you" messages
   c. message senders use "I" messages
   d. message senders use third-person pronouns

8. Intellectualization occurs in the group when a member
   a. studies group counseling methods in class
   b. has an extremely high IQ
   c. corrects the grammar of other group members
   d. presents cognitive information without relating emotional content

9. Early in the life of the group
   a. norms are developed
   b. trust is developed
   c. cohesion takes place
   d. goals are achieved

10. Which of the following is not a leadership style?
    a. authoritarian
    b. dynamic
    c. laissez-faire
    d. democratic

11. Group therapy differs from group counseling in that it

    a. focuses more on the unconscious motivations of group members
    b. attempts to teach new behaviors to the members of the group
    c. takes place mainly within educational settings
    d. necessitates the use of coleaders

12. When members feel threatened by the group, they will most likely

    a. use intellectualization
    b. give useful feedback
    c. take over the group leadership
    d. respond in a defensive manner

13. Leaders use nonverbal attending behavior to

    a. demonstrate interest and caring
    b. end the monologue of a group member
    c. set group norms
    d. resolve conflict

14. Oral or written behavioral agreements in group counseling are referred to as

    a. trust
    b. issues
    c. contracts
    d. conclusions

15. Brainstorming is a process used by groups for problem solving. Which of these is not a characteristic of brainstorming?

    a. there is a time limit
    b. ideas are critically evaluated
    c. quantity of ideas is foremost
    d. creativity overrides practicality

16. Power and conflict in groups are closely related. In which of the following circumstances does conflict exist?

    a. one member wants the others to do something and has enough power to make them do it
    b. one member wants the others to do something they don't want to do and lacks power to force them to

    c. one member wants the others to do something and lacks the power to force them, but they want to do it
    d. one member wants the others to do something they want to do and has the power to force them

17. Which of these is not a goal in personal growth groups?

    a. self-enhancement
    b. self-actualization
    c. self-criticism
    d. interpersonal effectiveness

18. You are a counselor at a community mental health center. You run a substance abuse group for court-ordered DUI offenders. You might expect

    a. cohesion
    b. illiteracy
    c. incoherence
    d. resistance

19. In rational-emotive and cognitive-behavioral therapy groups the focus is more on thoughts than on feelings. These techniques help people become aware of their

    a. self-denial
    b. defenses
    c. self-talk
    d. depression

20. Self-disclosure involves

    a. "war stories"
    b. sharing self-knowledge with the group
    c. dumping negative feelings on the group
    d. "letting it all hang out"

21. When a group member projects feelings deriving from past relationships onto the therapist, it is called

    a. countertransference
    b. transference
    c. reframing
    d. confrontation

22. Which of these is not characteristic of the working stage?
    a. open communication
    b. high level of trust
    c. confrontation
    d. decreased intensity

23. Confidentiality may be breached by a counselor
    a. when ordered by the court
    b. when a member is no longer part of the group
    c. to the parents or spouse of the group members
    d. under no circumstances

24. Role playing is an effective technique used in group counseling. Which of the following is not a benefit of role playing?
    a. practicing new skills
    b. identifying effective and ineffective behaviors
    c. escaping from being oneself
    d. preparing for real-life situations

25. Conflict within the group setting
    a. should be avoided at all costs
    b. should be settled by those in power
    c. negates the progress of the group
    d. promotes group involvement

ANSWER KEY

Fill in the Blanks

(1) laissez-faire
(2) cohesiveness
(3) norms
(4) life script
(5) facilitators
(6) group process
(7) open group
(8) confrontation
(9) in vivo
(10) Hawthorne effect
(11) confidentiality
(12) transition
(13) prevention
(14) group roles
(15) horizontal intervention
(16) transference
(17) informed consent
(18) psychotherapy
(19) feedback
(20) ethics
(21) sensitivity
(22) psychodrama
(23) psychiatrist, psychologist
(24) sociogram
(25) phenomenological

Matching

(1) k
(2) y
(3) v
(4) i
(5) a
(6) q
(7) d
(8) e
(9) r
(10) l
(11) x
(12) t
(13) n
(14) h
(15) u
(16) b
(17) g
(18) p
(19) j
(20) m
(21) s
(22) w
(23) o
(24) c
(25) f

Multiple-Choice

1. a
2. c
3. c
4. b
5. d
6. b
7. c
8. d
9. a
10. b
11. a
12. d
13. a
14. c
15. a
16. b
17. c
18. d
19. c
20. b
21. b
22. d
23. a
24. c
25. d

CHAPTER 5

Life-Style and Career Development

SUMMARY	101
Information Processing	**101**
Sources of Information	101
Evaluation and Use of Information	102
Vocational Counseling Theory	**102**
Trait-and-Factor Theory	102
Decision-Making Theory	103
Personality Theories	103
Social Learning Theory	104
Developmental Theories	104
Vocational Counseling Practice	**105**
Vocational Guidance	106
Career Counseling	106
Appraisal	106
Related Counseling Theory and Practice	**107**
Women's Issues	107
Ethnic Minorities	107
Mid-Life Clients	107
Older Workers	107
Leisure	108
LEARNING OBJECTIVES	109
TIME LINE	110
TERMS AND NAMES TO REMEMBER	111
Terms	**111**
Names	**111**
FILL IN THE BLANKS	112

MATCHING TEST   114
CASE STUDY   115
   Analysis   **115**
MULTIPLE-CHOICE TEST   117
ANSWER KEY   120
   Fill in the Blanks   **120**
   Matching   **120**
   Multiple-Choice   **120**

SUMMARY

Life-style and career development include areas such as vocational choice theory, relationships between career choice and life-style, sources of occupational and educational information, approaches to career decision-making processes, and career development exploration techniques. (Loesch & Vacc, 1986, p. 13-14)

Information Processing

Information seeking is inherent in the process of life-style and career decision making. Because decisions made with accurate information are presumably better than those based on misconceptions or ignorance, all models of career counseling in some way address the issue of occupational information (Brooks, 1984). According to Isaacson (1985), individuals in the first phase of career development/education, the awareness stage, begin to develop insight and understanding of self, a broad comprehension of the structure of the work world, and how the system works. Individuals seeking career information also require educational, personal, social, and life-style information. They need to develop a clear picture of their own strengths and weaknesses as well as their aptitudes, interests, attitudes, and values toward work and learning in order to evaluate career and educational information accurately and make good career decisions (Herr & Cramer, 1988).

Sources of Information

Career development information can be disseminated in a group setting or individually. Depending upon the level of awareness of the client or students, a variety of methods may be employed to facilitate the information-gathering process.

When choosing methods appropriate to the setting, counselors might consider nine topics relevant to self-understanding in the choice process (Isaacson, 1985, p. 145):

(1) client's view of self
(2) client's characteristics, including ability, achievement, aptitude, interests, motivations, values
(3) client's view of the future, including aspirations, dreams, goals, hopes
(4) client's health and physical status
(5) client's family
(6) client's educational experience
(7) client's work experience
(8) significant individuals in the client's life
(9) significant experiences in the client's life

Information delivery systems. According to Herr and Cramer (1988), information on the above topics may be obtained through a wide variety of information delivery systems. They discuss ten such systems: (a) printed matter, (b) media approaches, (c) interview approaches, (d) simulation approaches, (e) field trips, (f) formal curriculum, (g) direct experience, (h) computers, (i) career centers, and (j) networks. Within these systems, knowledge about self, information about specific jobs or occupations, information regarding training and/or educational requirements and sources, and general and specific details of the world of work may be found.

The DOT. The *Dictionary of Occupational Titles* (DOT; U.S. Department of Labor, 1978), now in its fourth edition, is by far the most widely used printed resource. The DOT contains information about approximately 20,000 jobs in nine categories: (a) professional, technical, and managerial occupations; (b) clerical and sales occupations; (c) service occupations; (d) agricultural, fishery, forestry, and related occupations; (e) processing occupations; (f) machine trades occupations; (g) benchwork occupations; (h) structural work occupations; and (i) miscellaneous occupations. Each occupation is assigned a nine-digit code. The first digit gives the occupational category, while the next two

101

digits tell the division within the category. The middle three digits refer to worker traits needed in terms of interest and ability for working with data, people, and things, respectively. The last three digits specify the particular occupation within the six-digit group.

The OOH. Another primary source of printed information for career development is the *Occupational Outlook Handbook* (OOH; U.S. Department of Labor, 1980). This book lists over 800 of the most popular careers. It provides an overview of each career in terms of the nature of the work, earnings, training requirements, and employment outlook. It suggests places one can write to for further information. Other printed materials include books and guides on educational and job opportunities, and occupational filing systems and kits.

Media. Media in this case include films, filmstrips, cassettes, and other audiovisual materials that enhance the learning process, especially for unmotivated clients. Interviews, simulations, and field trips allow for active participation in the learning process, while direct experience helps individuals to get a more realistic view of the work world and to evaluate their interests and abilities in particular fields. Some aspects of career development are best presented through formal curriculum. The infusion of knowledge brought about in the structured teaching-learning experience not only educates students, but also increases their achievement (Herr & Cramer, 1988).

Computers. Computer programs to assist in the career development process are enjoying wide use. "They are especially useful for clients reluctant to peruse all 20,000 DOT listings" (G. Leddick, personal communication, 1989). Some of the more popular programs include DISCOVER, CHOICES, and SIGI. Often these programs are made available through career resource centers, where career-related information is acquired, stored, and disseminated to individuals by professionals. In addition to individual career centers located within educational institutions, agencies, and workplaces, several national networks have been set up to gather and disseminate occupational information. Two of the most prominent of these are the National Occupational Information Coordinating Committee (NOICC) and the Occupational Data Analysis System (ODAS). These systems attempt to consolidate occupational information efficiently and to seek expansion into the future (Herr & Cramer, 1988).

Evaluation and Use of Information

The acquisition of information alone is not enough to bring about a career decision. Effective counselors are competent in assisting clients in acquiring, processing, and applying information and skills needed to make career decisions, and in implementing career plans. According to Isaacson (1985), the task is twofold: first, to identify an array of occupations that meet the interests and abilities of the client; and second, to help the client evaluate and prioritize the options that match his or her interests, abilities, and goals.

Throughout the process, the client is constantly comparing the attributes and requirements of jobs with perceptions of self and situation until a final "tentative" choice is made. Herr and Cramer (1988) assert that readiness and motivation to satisfy a career-related need are requisite to effective use of occupational information at any point in life.

Vocational Counseling Theory

Although the field of career development, described by Borow (1961), is relatively new, unproven, and incomplete, the theories of career development offer guidelines for counselors whose clients are working on career issues. Each theory presents the viewpoint or position of its particular proponent. Counselors should evaluate each theory in view of its utility for working with clients as they develop their own personal theories (Isaacson, 1985). Theories may be classified in a number of ways, but in this text five categories will be briefly discussed: (a) trait-and-factor theory, (b) decision-making theory, (c) personality theory, (d) social learning theory, and (e) developmental theory.

Trait-and-Factor Theory

Frank Parsons, frequently referred to as the "father of guidance," is known for his early interest in the field of vocational guidance. In his book *Choosing a Vocation* (1909), Parsons presents a three-part model of career guidance that he terms "trait-and-factor." According to this theory, individuals must first gain a full understanding of their own personal attributes, strengths, and weaknesses (traits). Second, they must discover the conditions for success (factors) in a particular occupation, including compensation and mobility. Third, they must apply "true reasoning" to the information in order to make the best decision. This method requires a directive approach by the counselor.

Williamson (1950), one of the main promoters of this historic theory, lists six steps trait-and-factor counselors follow as they assist clients in resolving the present problem: (a) analysis, (b) synthesis, (c) diagnosis, (d) prognosis, (e) counseling, and (f) follow-up. Although trait-and-factor theory in its pure form is not often used by counselors today, its influence is evident in many current theories.

Decision-Making Theory

The second category, decision-making theory, has several proponents, including Tiedeman, Katz, and Gelatt.

Tiedeman's model. Tiedeman agreed with Super's developmental perspective but saw a lack of attention to personality and individual responsibility. To fill this void, Tiedeman and O'Hara (1963) presented a seven-step model of decision making. The first four steps represent the period of anticipation or preoccupation; they are (a) exploration, (b) crystallization, (c) choice, and (d) clarification. The last three steps represent the period of implementation or accommodation; these are (e) induction, (f) reformation, and (g) integration. Each stage represents a change in the dominant condition of the decision process as well as a qualitatively different psychological state (Herr & Cramer, 1988).

Tiedeman and his colleagues continually refined their work, which led to the conclusion that a decision-guided life is proactive, rather than reactive. To demonstrate this concept, Miller and Tiedeman (1972) presented a cubistic model of decision making that encompassed three basic conditions necessary for the deci-

sion-guided life: (a) problem condition, which includes problem forming, problem solving, and solution using; (b) psychological states involving exploration, clarification, and accommodation; and (c) self-comprehension, including learning about, doing, and doing with awareness. The cubistic model was simplified into a pyramid containing the same basic concepts. Tiedeman and Miller-Tiedeman (1984) continue to refine their theory, focusing on self-empowerment and the utilization of "I" power to unite ego and values developments through further comprehension of decision making.

Katz's model. Katz (1973) stressed the importance of identifying and clarifying values before going on to consider alternatives, information, or probabilities. Katz's (1973, 1980) work is important because he has used it as a basis for developing a computer-based career development tool, the System of Interactive Guidance and Information (SIGI), geared particularly to the junior college level. This system helps students to examine their values, explore options, and then go on to obtain information relative to their values, thus increasing their competence in decision making (Herr & Cramer, 1988).

Gelatt's model. Gelatt (1962) focuses on information processing as the basis for decision making. The decision requires three systems: (a) a predictive system to assess alternatives, possible outcomes, and probabilities; (b) a value system to analyze the preference of various outcomes; and (c) a decision system to integrate information and select appropriate action. This approach suggests that the individual is better able to direct self-development toward desirable outcomes by understanding the possible sequences of experiences that lie ahead (Isaacson, 1985). *Positive Uncertainty*

Personality Theories

Two of the major proponents of career development theories based on personality are Anne Roe and John Holland.

Roe's theory. Roe's theory is based on Maslow's (1954) concept of needs. She suggests that experiences that occur in early childhood either reinforce or weaken higher-order needs that later influence career. Roe (1957) presents five propositions on the origin of interest and needs: (a) genetic inheritance, (b) sociocultural background, (c) relations between personality and perception, (d) psychic energies as the major determinant of interests, and (e) need intensity and satisfaction as determinants of motivation. Although much of Roe's work has not been supported by empirical research, many of her ideas are still relevant. She was the first to categorize jobs, and her booklet that classifies occupations into eight groups (service, business contact, organization, technology, outdoor, science, general culture, and arts and entertainment) with six levels (professional and managerial 1 and 2, semiprofessional and small business, skilled, semiskilled, unskilled) is still widely used (Roe, 1976).

Holland's theory. Holland (1973) asserts that vocational interests are an aspect of personality. His theory is based upon four assumptions: (a) People can be categorized as one of six personality types—realistic, investigative, artistic, social, enterprising, conventional; (b) there are six kinds of environments that correspond to the personality types; (c) people seek out environments that match their type; and (d) behavior is determined by the interaction of personality and environment. Holland presents the six types and their correlations in a hexagonal model that has been widely used and frequently researched.

Holland has also developed three devices that are useful for career counseling: (a) the Vocational Preference Inventory (VPI; 1953), (b) the Self-Directed Search (SDS; 1977), and (c) the Vocational Exploration and Insight Kit (VEIK; 1980). Critics of Holland's theory contend that the typology approach is too simplistic, that the theory is too sexist, and that it fails to deal with how people develop their personality types. Despite these criticisms, Holland's theory has had a great impact on the field.

Social Learning Theory

Krumboltz, Mitchell, and Jones (1976) based their career decision theory on social learning theory. They identified four factors that influence career decisions: (a) genetic endowment and special abilities, (b) environmental conditions and events, (c) learning experiences, and (d) task approach skills. The career path in this

theory is not deterministic; there are always alternatives. Genetic and environment factors are largely out of the control of the individual and to some extent influence the type of learning experiences available to each individual. To promote maximal career development of all individuals, all must have the opportunity to be exposed to the widest possible array of learning experiences, regardless of race, gender, or ethnic origin (Mitchell & Krumboltz, 1984).

The learning experiences have four possible outcomes that determine the career decision-making behavior of individuals: (a) self-observation generalizations, (b) worldview generalizations, (c) task approach skills, and (d) actions. Problems in any of these areas may lead to difficulty in career decision making. In this case counselors can employ a wide array of techniques, including paper-and-pencil tests, interviews, simulations, and career kits to assess the problem area and help clients move forward in the career decision process.

Developmental Theories

Several theorists support a developmental approach to career development. Some of these are Ginzberg, Super, Havighurst, and Schlossberg.

Ginzberg's theory. The theory of Ginzberg, Ginsburg, Axelrod, and Herma was presented in the volume *Occupational Choice: An Approach to a General Theory* (1951). Through an interview process with well-to-do young men, these researchers distinguished three major periods in the career choice process: fantasy, tentative, and realistic. The tentative period (ages 11-18) is further divided into four stages known as interest, capacity, value, and transition. The realistic period (from age 18 into the 20s) consists of three stages: exploration, crystallization, and specification. From this study emerge three basic elements of the theory: (a) Occupational choice is a process; (b) this process is largely irreversible; and (c) compromise is an essential aspect of every choice.

With further research, over time the theory has been modified and reformulated to state that occupational choice is a lifelong process of decision making for those who seek major satisfactions from their work. This leads such people to reassess repeatedly how they can improve the fit between their changing career goals and the realities of the world of work (Ginzberg, 1984). Although Ginzberg's theory lacks comprehensiveness, definition and elaboration of explanatory constructs, and integration of propositions, it has stimulated research and theorizing, and it illuminates the importance of the economy and socioeconomic variables that influence career development (Brown, 1984).

Super's theory. Super (1969) has referred to his model as a loosely unified set of theories dealing with specific aspects of career development taken from developmental, differential, phenomenological, and social psychology and held together by self-concept or personal construct theory. Super's career model presents a longitudinal, developmental approach rather than a one-time choice. His research focuses upon career or vocational maturity (Crites, 1973) assessed through his longitudinal Career Pattern Study.

Super (1980) depicts life-span, life-space career development through the life-career rainbow, which presents six life roles (child, student, leisurite, citizen, worker, and homemaker) and five life stages (growth, exploration, establishment, maintenance, and decline). These roles are played out at home and in the community, school, and workplace. The roles, stages, and situations interact to form the individual's career. The combination of life-style, life space, and life cycle form the individual's career pattern.

Havighurst's theory. Havighurst (1964) explains career development as a six-stage life-long process. One must successfully complete the tasks of one stage before moving on to the next. Havighurst's six developmental stages are as follows: (a) identification with a worker, ages 5-10; (b) acquiring the basic habits of industry, ages 10-15; (c) acquiring identity as a worker in the occupational structure, ages 15-25; (d) becoming a productive person, ages 25-40; (e) maintaining a productive society, ages 40-70; and (f) contemplating a productive and responsible life, age 70 and older.

Schlossberg's theory. In addition to her own contribution, Schlossberg (1984), an adult development specialist, has synthesized the work of other adult theorists and applied them to career development. The result of this work is a list of five propositions about adult development: (a) Behavior in adulthood is determined by social rather than by biological clocks. (b) Behavior is at times a function of life stage, at other times of age. (c) Sex differences are greater than either age or stage differences. (d) Adults continually experience transitions requiring adaptations and reassessment of the self. (e) The recurrent themes of adulthood are identity, intimacy, and generativity. These propositions have been explored with respect to helping adults in transition. Schlossberg suggests looking at transitions in terms of their type, context, and impact. Her work is particularly applicable to career because so many adults undergo career transitions one or more times in their lives.

Vocational Counseling Practice

Because career and work concerns represent underlying, if not presenting, problems in the majority of counseling cases, it is important for counselors to have a clear understanding of the terminology and meanings related to career development and its effect on life-style. As the interaction of life-style and career becomes more evident, more attention must be given to the integration of work, family, community, and leisure roles.

Counselors who engage in vocational counseling practice may operate in a variety of settings, including schools, community agencies, workplaces, and private practice. Effective counselors will possess the competencies put forth by the National Career Development Association (NCDA), formerly called the National Vocational Guidance Association (NVGA) (National Vocational Guidance Association, Board of Directors, 1982). In this position paper, the NVGA Board of Directors states, "Vocational/career counseling consists of those activities performed and coordinated by individuals who have the professional credentials to work with and counsel other individuals or groups of individuals about occupations, career, life/career, career decision making, career planning, career pathing, or other career development related questions or conflicts." Professional credentials include demonstrated competency in six areas designated by NVGA: (a) general counseling, (b) information, (c) individual/group assessment, (d) management/administration, (e) implementation, and (f) consultation. No matter what the setting, in practice, counselors will utilize all six competencies to a greater or lesser degree.

Vocational Guidance

Because all individuals must undergo career and life-style development, career guidance and counseling provide opportunities for intervention that may improve career behavior and prevent problems in the work arena. *Vocational guidance* has been identified with schools and serves an educative function, whereas *career counseling* purports to serve a therapeutic function and is usually associated with nonschool settings and service to adults. Gibson and Mitchell (1986) note that because vocational guidance in schools is "primarily a developmental and educational process, it provides counselors with the opportunity to function in a developmental, and, in a sense, preventive capacity" (p. 301). It usually takes the form of an organized program to promote self-understanding, understanding of work and society changes, leisure awareness, understanding of the multifaceted nature of career planning, and recognition of information and skills for self-fulfillment.

Career Counseling

Career counseling in nonschool settings has recently begun to focus on adults as well as youth. Rapid technological and social changes have presented adults with increasing challenges and opportunities in the world of work. No longer do Americans enter one job at the age of 18 and retire from the same job at the age of 65. The majority of adults experience one or more career changes during the life span and often require the assistance of career counseling as they make transitions. According to Brooks (1984), career counselors attempt to help clients make some choices or decisions that will bring satisfaction or fulfillment. She lists three goals

of career counseling: (a) facilitating development, (b) building decision-making skills, and (c) making career-related choices.

Herr and Cramer (1988) discuss the role of career development specialists practicing in the workplace. Some of the services these counselors must be prepared to provide include, but are not limited to, working with plateaued workers, training and education programs, mentoring, career ladders, wellness programs, outplacement counseling, retirement planning, employee assistance programs, and occupational stress management. Because this is relatively new territory for counselors, there is little research to support particular practices or interventions.

Appraisal

An important aspect of career development in any setting is appraisal. Clients in need of career counseling are unable to make career decisions on their own due to lack of self-knowledge and/or lack of knowledge about the world of work. According to Isaacson (1985), counselors can employ a variety of appraisal instruments in order to develop a complete picture of the individual. Some of these instruments include questionnaires, sociometric information, rating scales, case studies, and autobiographies. The purpose of these tests may be predictive, as in aptitude or ability tests, or it may be diagnostic, as in interest inventories and personality tests that identify strengths, weaknesses, and personal characteristics. Instruments such as achievement tests may also be used to monitor client progress and to evaluate skill acquisition. Tests should not be use indiscriminately for career counseling, but only when counselor and client agree that tests can provide needed information that is not available any other way.

Isaacson (1985) discusses numerous appraisal instruments available to career counselors. Some of the more widely used types of instruments include career maturity measures, interest inventories, ability and aptitude tests, and personality, temperament, and values instruments. Interpretation of test results should focus on the goal of obtaining information to help the client answer questions about him- or herself. The counselor should refer to the questions that led to the use of the test to help the client gain insight and self-understanding.

Related Counseling Theory and Practice

Because much of the research on career development has been conducted with white, middle-class males, much of the theory and practice of career counseling has focused on this group. Counselors are becoming sensitized to the special needs of other groups in the world of work, such as women, ethnic minorities, people making mid-life career changes, and older workers. Due to the rapid pace of life, a number of life problems and issues find their way into the workplace. Some of these issues include marriage and family problems, retirement concerns, and leisure concerns. As counselors become more involved with adults in the work force, they need to familiarize themselves with theories of adult development and aging, as well as adult learning theory. Counselors must be prepared to assist diverse populations with a multitude of concerns. They must be aware of their own limitations in handling some of these special groups and issues, and they must be willing to refer clients to other sources in order to solve problems that are beyond the scope of career counseling.

Women's Issues

Herr and Cramer (1988) name three characteristics of the adult population that should be considered in the career counseling of adult clients: (a) changing marital patterns, (b) changing childbearing and child-rearing patterns, and (c) changing occupational patterns. These changes account for the growing needs of women in the workplace. The growing divorce rate and the declining birthrate have sent more women into the workplace, often underskilled as well as underprepared for the harassment and discrimination to which they might be subjected. In addition to responsibilities on the job, these women often face financial difficulties, inadequate child-care facilities, and role conflicts. Career counselors working with

women need to understand marriage and family dynamics to be most effective with this population.

Ethnic Minorities

Effective career counseling with ethnic minorities requires sensitivity to the limitations of traditional theories and methods. It also requires counselors to be sensitive to their own biases and prejudices. They must be skilled in using special strategies with individual clients to help them overcome limited opportunities, racism, and societally imposed negative self-attitudes. Counselors must take it upon themselves to gain the knowledge, attitudes, and skills they need to work effectively with culturally different clients (Brooks, 1984).

Mid-Life Clients

Mid-life career change is a process in which an adult, usually between the ages of 35 and 45, enters a new occupation that may require adjustments in training or experience (Brown, 1984). The mid-life career shift can be a period of growth and challenge for the individual, who may require professional assistance in career planning. Counselors can help mid-life career changers by concentrating on five major themes: abilities, interests, values, confinements, and environment (Herr & Cramer, 1988). They can assist these adults through self-help groups, informational models, job information seminars, occupational libraries, and developmental and structured group models (Brown, 1981).

Older Workers

As the mean age of the population increases, and as the mandatory age of retirement is raised, more older workers will need the services of career counselors. Herr and Cramer (1988) name several factors with which displaced older workers must contend: (a) Physical decline makes performance of certain tasks more difficult and slow; (b) employers with negative attitudes toward older workers will hire cheaper labor; and (c) lack of mobility, flexibility, and up-to-date knowledge and skill, referred to as obsolescence, make older workers less desirable to employers. For these clients, counselors can provide support, accurate assessment of the client and the situation, job-seeking skills, placement, and follow-up. They can also assist clients in preretirement and retirement planning.

Leisure

Because career and work play a paramount role in adult life and because work is fundamental to self-concept, work life largely determines life-style. The knowledge explosion, changing social values, movement to corporate hierarchies, occupational and geographic mobility, new housing patterns, and changes in occupational patterns and economic base affect virtually every occupational group (Herr & Cramer, 1988). Some of these changes have reduced the time spent on jobs and have freed people to enjoy more leisure time. As they address career issues, counselors cannot overlook the dynamic relationship between career and leisure. Within the career counseling process some attention should be paid to clients' leisure needs, interests, and attitudes as counselors assist them in developing balanced and satisfying lives.

LEARNING OBJECTIVES

After studying the material in this chapter, you should be able to do the following:

(1) Discuss the role of information processing in career development.

(2) Name several widely used career information sources.

(3) Discuss the use of computerized career information.

(4) Classify career theories as trait-and-factor, decision making, personality, social learning, or developmental.

(5) Define the terms *life-style, career development, career guidance,* and *career counseling.*

(6) Discuss several methods of appraisal that are used in career counseling.

(7) Name several specialized populations that career counselors may need to assist.

(8) Discuss the unique issues of these specialized populations.

(9) Explain the dynamic interaction of work and leisure.

TIME LINE

You should be aware of important developments in the evolution of life-style and career development.

1909	Parsons, trait-and-factor theory		1975	APGA position paper on career guidance, counseling
1951	Ginzberg, life-style development theory		1976	Krumboltz, social learning in career development
1956	Roe, first personality approach		1976	ACES position paper, counselor preparation for career development
1957	Super, life stage development/tasks			
1961	Borow, definition of career development		1978	Schlossberg, adult career and life-style issues
1962	Gelatt, decision model		1980	APGA study of school counselor in career education
1963	Katz, decision-making approach			
1963	Tiedeman and O'Hara, career choice		1981	NVGA position paper, career counseling competency
1964	Havighurst, stages of vocational development		1984	ASCA statement, school counselor/ career guidance
1966	Holland, typology of personality			
1973	Crites, career maturity concept			
1973	NVGA position paper on career development			

TERMS AND NAMES
TO REMEMBER

Terms

You should have an understanding of the following terms and be able to define them in your own words.

anticipation
appraisal
aptitude
career
career counseling
career decision
career development
career guidance
career rainbow
career resource center
CHOICES
clarification
conventional
crystallization
data, people, and things
developmental stages
DOT
DISCOVER
enterprising
exploration stage

fantasy period
implementation
investigative
leisure
life-style
obsolescence
Occupational Outlook Handbook
realistic period
self-observation generalization
SIGI
simulation
social
specification
task approach skills
tentative period
trait-and-factor
transitions
values
worldview generalizations

Names

You should be familiar with these people and be aware of their contributions to the counseling profession with regard to life-style and career development.

Borow
Crites
Gelatt
Ginzberg
Havighurst
Herr and Cramer
Holland
Katz
Krumboltz

Maslow
Miller-Tiedeman
Parsons
Roe
Schlossberg
Super
Tiedeman and O'Hara
Williamson

FILL IN THE BLANKS

The following section reviews some of the major points in this content area. Check your knowledge of the area by filling in the appropriate name, term, or concept in each blank provided. Answer choices are found above, in the section containing terms and names to remember. You will find the correct answers at the end of the chapter.

(1)   The matching approach to career development is known as _____ _____.

(2)   To help counselees gain more realistic information about the training needs for various occupations, counselors can refer them to _____ _____.

(3)   Role playing is a form of the career development approach known as _____.

(4)   _____'s theory of career development uses the hierarchy of needs developed by Maslow.

(5)   The *Dictionary of Occupational Titles* codes occupations according to field and gives reference to_____.

(6)   According to Holland, one who likes to observe, analyze, and evaluate has a(n)_____ personality type.

(7)   _____ emphasized that occupational choice is a process.

(8)   Super's _____ graphically depicts the life span.

(9)   As a result of learning experiences, individuals make _____ _____ about their attitudes and skills.

(10) _____ conceptualized the idea of self-empowerment in career, or "I" power.

(11) _____ is an educative process.

(12) Schlossberg believes that adults experience a series of changes called _____.

(13) _____ can be defined as a sequence of occupations and other life roles that people pursue.

(14) The Strong-Campbell Interest Inventory is a form of _____ _____.

(15)   The first four of Tiedeman's steps represent the period of anticipation, while the last three steps represent _____ _____.

(16)   According to Ginzberg, a 12-year-old is in the _____ _____ of career development.

(17)   _____'s model is a six-stage lifelong process.

(18)   A _____ may disseminate information about various careers, provide career counseling, and house computers for career exploration.

(19)   A concern of older workers in our society is _____ _____.

(20)   _____ occurs when one chooses an occupational field.

(21)   The _____ system incorporates Super's stages, Tiedeman and O'Hara's decision-making model, and Holland's personality categories.

(22)   A _____ personality type enjoys working with people and helping others.

(23)   The Vocational Preference Inventory was developed by _____ _____.

(24)   _____ is usually a one-on-one activity done with adults.

(25)   People make _____ as they make observations about their environment and use these to predict what will occur in the future and in other environments.

MATCHING TEST

Match the names in the left-hand column with the appropriate concepts in the right-hand column.

___	(1) Borow	(a) father of vocational guidance
___	(2) CHOICES	(b) anticipation/implementation
___	(3) Crites	(c) SIGI
___	(4) DOT	(d) decisions and outcomes
___	(5) Gelatt	(e) needs, genetic endowment
___	(6) Ginzberg	(f) Self-Directed Search
___	(7) Havighurst	(g) social learning
___	(8) Herr	(h) fantasy/realistic/tentative
___	(9) Holland	(i) Career Development Inventory
___	(10) Katz	(j) 6 developmental stages
___	(11) Krumboltz	(k) adult development
___	(12) Maslow	(l) Career Maturity Inventory
___	(13) Miller-Tiedeman	(m) life-span approach
___	(14) ODAS	(n) self-empowerment
___	(15) OOH	(o) hierarchy of needs
___	(16) Parsons	(p) occupational classification system
___	(17) Roe	(q) employment outlook information
___	(18) Schlossberg	(r) initiated career development
___	(19) Super	(s) computerized career information
___	(20) Tiedeman	(t) career information system

CASE STUDY

Brian is a third-year high school student who is seeking help to identify career choices for exploration. Brian enjoys working with his hands and seems to have a knack for using tools. Though not particularly fond of school, he does enjoys subjects that give him a chance to evaluate information and make decisions. Even though his IQ is slightly above average, his grades run below average. He performs poorly on standardized tests and has an aversion to test taking in general. Brian's teachers view him as likable although they report that he socializes too much and tends to disrupt classes with his constant stream of wisecracks. Brian would be willing to continue his education beyond high school. He expresses a need to earn at least $20,000 per year upon entering the work force full-time.

Analysis

(1) If Brian came to you for career counseling, what approach would you take in working with him?

_____

_____

_____

_____

(2) Which theories would be most helpful to you in your effort to help Brian with his career decision? How would you apply the theory to this case?

theory:

_____

application:

_____

_____

theory:

_____

application:

_____

_____

(3)   Which appraisal instruments do you think would be most appropriate for use in this case?

_____

_____

(4)   What kind of information would you hope to gain by using these particular instruments?

_____

_____

_____

(5)   How will you handle Brian's negative attitude toward testing?

_____

_____

_____

(6)   What other career exploration activities will you suggest for Brian?

_____

_____

_____

MULTIPLE-CHOICE TEST

Check your understanding of this content area by responding to the following questions. You will find the answer key at the end of the chapter.

1. Decision-making models are useful for career development in that they
   a. lead to the "right" career choice
   b. give the counselor control over the situation
   c. help one generate and evaluate several alternatives
   d. define training needs

2. Counselors can best prepare clients for occupational placement by
   a. teaching job-seeking and job-getting skills
   b. enrolling them in training programs
   c. administering a battery of tests
   d. arranging employment interviews for clients

3. The trait-and-factor approach emphasizes
   a. crystallization
   b. development
   c. skills
   d. matching

4. Ginzberg and associates designate three stages of career development; these are
   a. realistic, conventional, fantasy
   b. child, employment, retirement
   c. fantasy, tentative, realistic
   d. investigation, socialization, realization

5. The life-career rainbow was introduced by
   a. Roe
   b. Super
   c. Holland
   d. Ginzberg

6. Roe's theory is based on
   a. motivation
   b. information
   c. competencies
   d. needs

7. A good source of information regarding pay scales for various occupations would be
   a. *Occupational Outlook Handbook*
   b. *Career Development Quarterly*
   c. *Dictionary of Occupational Titles*
   d. *Occupational Encyclopedia*

8. According to Holland, congruence occurs when
   a. the person's personality types occur close on the hexagon
   b. one personality type is high and the other five are low
   c. when all six personality types are relatively equal
   d. individuals work or live in environments of the type identical or similar to their own

9. According to Krumboltz, instrumental and associative learning experiences occur through
   a. self-observation generalizations
   b. direct experience with reinforcement or punishment
   c. environmental conditions and events
   d. vicarious experience

10. A junior college student comes to the career resource center for help in deciding upon an educational or training program. Her Holland code is determined to be REA. According to Holland, this student is
    a. uncrystallized
    b. undifferentiated
    c. inconsistent
    d. incongruous

11. Some career theorists emphasize classification of occupations. Holland uses a hexagonal model of personality type. Roe uses a

    a. conical model of levels and groups
    b. semicircular model of roles and stages
    c. paradigm of steps over time
    d. cubistic model of problem, psychological state, self-comprehension

12. In career counseling a person's stated interests

    a. are a good indicator of career choice
    b. are part of the fantasy stage
    c. should match parental occupations
    d. should match their skills

13. Super's life-span, life-space approach to career development attempts to bring together the theoretical constructs of

    a. personality traits and job dimensions
    b. life stage and role theory
    c. needs theory and job satisfaction
    d. learning theory and self-concept theory

14. According to Tiedeman and O'Hara, the earliest stage of career development is called

    a. gathering
    b. generalization
    c. planning
    d. exploration

15. A medical student seeks help from the university career counseling center. She needs help in determining whether to specialize in oncology or cardiology. According to Ginzberg's stage theory, she is in a stage of the realistic period called

    a. exploration
    b. crystallization
    c. specification
    d. integration

16. According to Roe, a significant determinant of career choice is

    a. genetic endowment
    b. early home climate

    c. worldview
    d. school environment

17. A career development intervention based on Gelatt's paradigm would focus on which skills?

    a. job-seeking skills
    b. decision-making skills
    c. problem-solving skills
    d. information-processing skills

18. Katz has designed a computer-based instrument used for values clarification in career development. This system is known as

    a. CHOICES
    b. NVGA
    c. SIGI
    d. VPI

19. Vocational counseling differs from vocational guidance in that it is mainly

    a. a therapeutic process
    b. an educational process
    c. a group process
    d. an internal process

20. The DOT organizes thousands of jobs into nine categories. Part of the code assigned to each job refers to

    a. skilled, semiskilled, or unskilled
    b. traits, interests, and abilities
    c. professional, technical, or managerial
    d. data, people, and things

21. According to Ginzberg, a major task of 18- to 22-year-olds is

    a. clarification of values
    b. identification of interest
    c. realization of skills
    d. crystallization of career choice

22. Schlossberg believes the greatest differences from adult to adult are in

    a. age
    b. stage
    c. sex
    d. ability

23. The National Vocational Guidance
    Association asserts that career
    counselors should possess competency in

    a. management/administration
    b. consultation
    c. general counseling
    d. all of the above

24. In career counseling appraisal
    instruments should be used

    a. with discretion
    b. as a general rule
    c. for all mid-life career changers
    d. only with youth

25. You are employed as a career counselor
    in a large corporation. One of your
    clients, an employee of the company,
    exhibits psychotic behavior that makes
    career counseling all but impossible.
    Your best course of action would be to

    a. find appropriate placement for the
       client within the company
    b. refer the client for psychological help
    c. recommend that the company
       terminate the employee
    d. substitute psychotherapy for career
       counseling

ANSWER KEY

Fill in the Blanks

(1) trait-and-factor
(2) *Occupational Outlook Handbook*
(3) simulation
(4) Roe
(5) data, people, and things
(6) investigative
(7) Ginzberg
(8) life-career rainbow
(9) self-observation generalizations
(10) Miller-Tiedeman
(11) career guidance
(12) transitions
(13) career
(14) appraisal
(15) implementation
(16) tentative period
(17) Havighurst
(18) career resource center
(19) obsolescence
(20) crystallization
(21) DISCOVER
(22) social
(23) Holland
(24) career counseling
(25) worldview generalizations

Matching

(1) r
(2) s
(3) l
(4) p
(5) d
(6) h
(7) j
(8) m
(9) f
(10) c
(11) g
(12) o
(13) n
(14) t
(15) q
(16) a
(17) e
(18) k
(19) i
(20) b

Multiple-Choice

1. c
2. a
3. d
4. c
5. b
6. d
7. a
8. d
9. b
10. c
11. a
12. a
13. b
14. d
15. c
16. b
17. b
18. c
19. a
20. d
21. d
22. c
23. d
24. a
25. b

CHAPTER 6

Appraisal of the Individual

SUMMARY	123
Factors Influencing Assessment	**123**
Purpose of Testing	123
Qualifications of Test Users	123
Setting and Conditions of Test Use	124
Assessment Theory	**124**
Historical Background	124
Phases of Development	124
Assessment Practices	**124**
Test Selection	125
Test Categories and Types	125
Resources	126
Test Scoring	126
Ethical Considerations	127
Interpretation of Assessments	**127**
Administration and Scoring	127
Scores, Norms, and Related Technical Features	127
Communication of Results	128
LEARNING OBJECTIVES	130
TIME LINE	131
TERMS AND NAMES TO REMEMBER	132
Terms	**132**
Names	**132**
FILL IN THE BLANKS	133
MATCHING TEST	135

CASE STUDY   136
   Analysis   **137**
MULTIPLE-CHOICE TEST   140
ANSWER KEY   143
   Fill in the Blanks   **143**
   Matching   **143**
   Multiple-Choice   **143**

SUMMARY

Appraisal of the individual includes development of a framework for understanding the individual, including methods of data gathering and interpretation, individual and group testing, case-study approaches, and the study of the individual differences. Ethnic, cultural, and sex factors are also considered. (Loesch & Vacc, 1986)

Factors Influencing Assessment

The assessment process is influenced by the user's purpose in testing and the qualifications of the user, as well as the setting and conditions of test use. School and mental health personnel are concerned with human behavior that indicates personal growth and development or learning. Just as measurements have been used in a variety of other settings throughout history, measurement or assessment of individual learning and behavior is becoming an increasingly important aspect of education and counseling.

Purpose of Testing

Use of appraisal in these settings has expanded to include not only educational and vocational guidance, but also enhancement of emotional well-being, self-understanding, and personal development; increase in effective interpersonal relations; and assistance with the problem-solving/decision-making process (Anastasi, 1988). According to Litwack (1986), appraisal techniques are useful in counseling because they provide some of the answers in a variety of areas concerning the client:

(1) *placement:* Where does this client fit into the system?

(2) *admissions:* Should this client be allowed into the system?

(3) *diagnosis:* What are the client's strengths and weaknesses?

(4) *counseling:* How can the counselor help the client work toward goals?

(5) *educational planning:* What are group strengths, weaknesses, curriculum needs?

(6) *licensure/certification:* Is this person qualified to practice this profession?

(7) *self-understanding:* How can the client gain self-acceptance?

(8) *time saving:* What areas need attention?

Qualifications of Test Users

Professional counselors need to be aware of their own limits in the field of appraisal. While most graduate-level counselors have received training in the administration and interpretation of educational and psychological tests, they are responsible for assessing their own competence in each testing situation and for performing only those functions for which they are prepared (NBCC Code of Ethics, 1982, amended 1987; see Appendix A). Professional counselors are responsible for obtaining proper training, assistance, and supervision when they are involved in appraisal.

The requisite qualifications for test users depends on four factors: (a) the particular role of the user, (b) the setting in which the use takes place, (c) the nature of the test, and (d) the purpose of the testing (American Personnel and Guidance Association, 1978; see Appendix C).

Though counselors are trained in appraisal techniques, in some settings psychologists may be responsible for more clinically oriented assessments. In school settings teachers often administer tests and report the results, while school administrators usually make decisions for the institution based upon group test performance. Reasons for appraisal vary but are always affected by the skills of the examiner, the needs of the agency or institution, and the needs of the individuals being tested (Litwack, 1986).

124

Setting and Conditions of Test Use

The setting and conditions of test use greatly influence the validity of test results. Variations from the standard procedure, as well as unusual influences specific to a particular test situation, contribute to error variance and reduce the generalizability of the results. Therefore, administrators of standardized tests must pay careful attention to directions, timing, sequence, and presentation of testing materials in order to assure validity.

Test administrators should be aware of conditions and reactions of individuals taking the test. They should be easily understood, empathic, and unbiased. They are responsible for seeing that physical conditions (such as heat and lighting) are conducive to comfortable test taking. They should note any deviation from standard procedure, any unusual behavior of examinees, and any unique circumstances that may affect test outcome, and they should provide a written record of these observations so that invalid or questionable scores are identified as such. Finally, administrators should secure qualified help to provide uniform conditions when large groups are being tested (American Personnel and Guidance Association, 1978).

Assessment Theory

The use of assessment techniques has contributed to the development of educational and psychological theory. Testing promotes a better understanding of human growth and development, aids in the comprehension of individual differences, and advances the science of measurement called psychometrics. According to Thorndike and Hagen (1977), assessment theory is based on the assumption that the more we know about people and the more accurately we know it, the more likely we are to arrive at sound decisions about them or wise plans of action for them.

Historical Background

Prior to 1850, virtually all educational and psychological assessment was done orally. Sparked by Darwin's *Origin of Species* (1859), a number of scholars began to study individual differences. Sir Francis Galton demonstrated both by ingenious tests and by statistical methods that individuals differ in physical, sensorimotor, and personality traits. He also laid the groundwork for modern statistical methods that assured the progress of educational measurement, especially standardized tests (Noll & Scannell, 1972).

Another investigator, Cattell, having studied in Europe, then began investigating individual differences in the United States. He used sensory and motor performance tests and studied the relationship between these tests and academic performance. This trend continued, and, as Thorndike advanced the development and use of standardized tests and Terman translated the Binet intelligence scales into English, the testing movement was under way.

Phases of Development

Thorndike and Hagen (1977) identify three phases in the development of assessment theory and practice: (a) the pioneering phase (1900-1915), marked by experimentation with intelligence testing (Binet, Otis) and achievement testing (Stone, Buckingham, Thorndike); (b) the boom period (1915-1930), characterized by an onslaught of intelligence and achievement tests and the emergence of personality questionnaires and inventories, many of which were administered and interpreted uncritically and unethically; (c) the period of critical evaluation (from 1930 on), concerned with broadening techniques, limiting interpretations, and seeking a balanced approach to the appraisal of human behavior. As tests come into wider use, tempered by critical attention to reliability, validity, and interpretation, the theoretical basis for understanding human growth and development increases, and the science of measurement itself becomes more precise.

Assessment Practices

In choosing methods of formal appraisal, counselors need to be aware of the distinguishing characteristics of a wide variety of assessment techniques and to choose those that are best suited to the client or group being tested. Several dichotomies inherent in assessment procedures must be considered in deciding which type of test to administer: group versus individual, power versus speed, spiral versus cyclical, vertical versus horizontal, special versus general, structured versus unstructured, and paper-and-pencil versus oral or performance testing, for example.

Test Selection

Sax (1980) lists a number of practical and technical considerations in test selection. Practical considerations include cost, time limits, ease of administration, format, availability of alternate format, multiple-level exams, availability of answer sheets and simple scoring procedures, and ease of interpretation. Technical considerations include dissemination of information, aids to interpretation, directions for administration and scoring, norms and scales, validity, reliability and measurement error, qualifications and concerns of users, choice or development of test or method, administration and scoring, and interpretation of scores.

Test Categories and Types

With due consideration to practical and technical considerations, the test user may choose from five categories of standardized tests: (a) achievement; (b) aptitude; (c) intelligence; (d) interest, attitudes, and values; and (e) personality.

Achievement tests. Achievement tests are designed to measure skills or knowledge learned as a result of instruction. Content validity is important here because achievement tests should be designed to measure the attainment of behavioral objectives or learning goals after instruction takes place. Achievement tests may be either teacher-made or standardized. Standardized achievement batteries are designed to measure general academic achievement in a number of content areas common to most academic settings. Students taking these tests may be compared horizontally, in terms of the normative sample, or vertically, in terms of students' progress in a particular area from grade to grade. Some well-known standard-

ized achievement tests are the California Achievement Test (CAT), the Comprehensive Test of Basic Skills, the Metropolitan Achievement Test (MET), and the Iowa Tests of Basic Skills.

Aptitude tests. Aptitude tests are used to predict abilities and behaviors prior to instruction. Because aptitude tests are used for selection and placement, it is important that they have high predictive validity. Aptitude tests may predict success in one specific area, such as clerical, musical, or artistic, or they may be differential, consisting of a number of subtests. In the differential type, subtests should correlate highly with particular criteria, such as verbal or numeric, and have low correlations with each other. Some types of aptitude tests include readiness tests at the primary level, the Differential Aptitude Test at the high school level and above, the ACT Assessment Program and the Scholastic Aptitude Test (SAT) to predict college success, and the Graduate Record Exam and the Miller Analogies Test at the graduate school level.

Intelligence tests. Intelligence tests measure general mental abilities. Intelligence test results are usually reported in terms of IQ scores, but they may also yield mental age and grade equivalent norms. The traditional IQ is the ratio of mental age to chronological age times 100. Newer intelligence tests report deviation IQ scores, which are standard scores with a mean of 100 and a standard deviation of 15. The first intelligence test was developed by Alfred Binet in France and was translated into English by Dr. Lewis M. Terman of Stanford University, resulting in the Stanford-Binet Intelligence Scale. Other leaders in the field of intelligence include Spearman, with his general factor theory of intelligence (g factor); Thorndike, with his stimulus-response theory of learning, "connectionism"; Thurstone, with his theory of primary mental abilities; and Guilford, with his structure of intellect theory composed of operations, products, and content.

Both individual and group intelligence tests are used. Wechsler and Stanford-Binet are the two most widely used individual intelligence tests. Wechsler has developed individual intelligence tests for adults (WAIS-R), for children (WISC-R), and for preschoolers (WPPSI-R).

"Research shows the Wechsler a better measure for the average range, while the Stanford-Binet is better at measuring extremes of intelligence" (G. Leddick, personal communication, 1989). Some examples of group intelligence tests include the Otis-Lennon Mental Ability Test, the Cognitive Abilities Test, and the California Test of Mental Abilities. Ongoing debates concerning intelligence tests focus on cultural bias and heredity versus environment (Sax, 1980).

Interests, attitudes, and values tests. Measures of interest, attitudes, and values are grouped into one category, but it is necessary to differentiate among the three. Interest has to do with preference for one activity over another; attitudes are preferences for groups, institutions, or objects; and values represent degrees of commitment to ideas or principles (Sax, 1980). These types of tests are most effective with older adolescents and adults. They may be helpful in vocational and educational planning because they provide a wide variety of alternatives.

Though interest inventories may be used for placement purposes, according to Litwack (1986) they are not reliable for selection for several reasons: (a) It is easy for respondents to fake their responses when they believe it is advantageous to answer in a particular way; (b) individuals tend to respond in socially desirable ways and to agree when in doubt; and (c) many inventories emphasize professional roles while ignoring skilled or semiskilled occupations.

Some inventories that measure interests are the Strong-Campbell Interest Inventory, the Kuder General Interest Survey, and the Minnesota Vocational Interest Inventory. Some attitude measures are the Minnesota School Attitude Survey and the Attitudes Toward Women Scale. Values can be assessed by the Survey of Personal Values, the Survey of Interpersonal Values, and the Work Values Inventory.

Personality tests. Personality tests measure personal qualities or traits and emotional and motivational characteristics. Some of these tests are self-report inventories, while others use projective techniques, such as unstructured tasks observed and interpreted by a clinician. Personality assessments are limited by susceptibility to faking, low reliability and validity, and subjective interpretation.

Sax (1980) notes three types of response bias inherent in personality assessment: (a) acquiescence, the tendency to respond positively, as in "agree" or "true"; (b) social desirability, the tendency to respond in such a way as to make oneself appear more acceptable; and (c) deviant responses, choices made by atypical persons that set them apart from the norm.

Some examples of self-report inventories are the Minnesota Multiphasic Personality Inventory (MMPI), the Myers-Briggs Type Indicator, and the Jackson Personality Inventory. Projective techniques may be verbal, as in the Kent-Rosanoff Free Association Test; pictorial, as in the Thematic Apperception Test (TAT); or expressive, as in the Manchover Draw-a-Person Test. Performance tests, situational tests, observer reports, and biographical reports are other types of personality measures.

Informal assessment. Besides formal testing, there are a number of informal methods of assessment that can be used to supplement test results in order to provide a total picture of the individual. These include systematic and formal observation, anecdotal notes, rating scales and checklists, self-reports, sociometric approaches, previous records, structured or open-ended interviews, conferences, and case conferences. The more data gathered, the more reliable the appraisal.

Resources

There are a number of resources available to keep counselors aware of developments in the area of tests and measurement. Books such as *Mental Measurement Yearbook* and *Tests in Print* provide information about current published standardized tests. Background material on test procedures, principles, and other general information comes from textbooks, while information about current research and practice, as well as reviews of new tests, can be found in testing and counseling journals. The test materials themselves, their manuals and reports, provide information specific to those tests.

Test Scoring

It is the responsibility of test administrators to guard against errors in scoring and recording test results. The administrators should routinely check for accuracy and consistency in machine as well as manual scoring by checking for inappropriate or impossible scores. They should check for appropriate use of scoring rules and normative conversions, and verify the accuracy of the conversion of raw scores to normative or descriptive scores. They should include records of unusual behavioral observations and test conditions that influence test scores as part of the test results that are recorded. Finally, test administrators should label the scores that are reported and note the date of administration (American Personnel and Guidance Association, 1978).

Ethical Considerations

Counselors must adhere to a strict code of ethics in the use of tests and measurements. They should keep in mind that the purpose of appraisal is to provide an assessment of the individual in either comparative or absolute terms for the benefit of that individual. It is the counselor's responsibility to be thoroughly familiar with the test materials, to avoid general assessments drawn from single scores, and to base assessment on the present state of the client rather than on past performance. Counselors must keep personal bias under control and should refrain from imposing solutions on clients. They should give useful interpretations to clients, keeping in mind that tests are only one indicator of the client's condition.

Interpretation of Assessments

According to the *Responsibilities of Users of Standardized Tests* (American Personnel and Guidance Association, 1978), counselors who interpret assessment materials must be well versed in administration and scoring. They must have adequate understanding of scores, norms, and related technical features, including, but not limited to, reliability and validity. They must act responsibly and ethically in the communication of test results.

Administration and Scoring

Before interpreting test results, it is the responsibility of the interpreters to obtain background information about the test circumstances. They should examine all test materials,

including both the scores and any written reports submitted by the administrators or proctors of the test. They should have full knowledge of the test situation in question and should take into account any factors such as ethnic, cultural, or socioeconomic background that may influence the outcome.

Scores, Norms, and Related Technical Features

Interpreters of test results should have a working knowledge of the statistical procedures involved in scoring and reporting the results. They should become familiar with the test manuals, handbooks, and guides that provide information about norms, reliability, and validity of test scores. They should understand various methods of reporting test data, such as frequency distributions, tables, graphs, histograms, and pie charts.

Central tendency and variability. In order to interpret test results accurately, the professional needs to understand the measures of central tendency and variability. The *mean* is the arithmetic average of the scores; the *median* is the midpoint on an ordered distribution; and the *mode* is the most frequently occurring score and the least stable measure of central tendency. *Range* refers to the variability or difference between the highest score and the lowest score in a given distribution. *Standard deviation* is a variability measure that uses the mean as a reference point. The more scores vary around the mean, the greater the standard deviation. *Variance* is the standard deviation squared, and refers to an area rather than a distance.

Standard scores. An understanding of standard scores is mandatory for the interpretation of test results. Raw scores can be converted to standard scores such a Z scores and t scores. The Z score always has a mean of 0 and a standard deviation of 1. Since Z scores can be both negative and fractional, it is sometimes desirable to convert them to t scores, which are always positive whole numbers and are therefore easier to understand and compare. A t score is obtained by multiplying the Z score by 10 and adding 50 to that product, resulting in a mean of 50 and a standard deviation of 10.

Other standard scores to know are Educational Testing Service (ETS) scores and deviation IQ scores. ETS scores are obtained by multiplying the Z score by 100 and adding 500 to that product, resulting in a mean of 500 and a standard deviation of 100. Deviation IQ is obtained by multiplying the Z score by 15 and adding 100 to that product. The resulting scores have a mean of 100 and a standard deviation of 15.

Normal curve. The most commonly occurring distribution in human appraisal is the normal curve, or bell-shaped curve. In this distribution the majority of scores fall in the middle range, with few scores at either extreme. To obtain stanines, the normal curve is divided into nine equal parts so that a single-digit score can be assigned.

Correlations. A correlation can be used to show a relationship between two sets of scores. Correlations are the average product of Z scores. A positive correlation indicates that a positive or negative Z score on one measure would correspond to a Z score of the same sign on the other measure. A negative correlation indicates that an individual scoring a positive Z score on one variable would score negative on the other variable, and vice versa. Sax (1980) recommends some cautions in the interpretation of correlations. Correlations are not percentages but ordinal indices. Correlations do not necessarily imply causal relationships. Correlations indicate relationships between variables when those variables are best represented by a straight regression line.

Reliability. An interpreter of tests must also be able to evaluate the reliability and validity of the assessment instrument. The reliability of measurements is the extent to which they can be depended upon to provide consistent, unambiguous information. Reliability can be estimated by looking at stability, which tells whether the set of measurements corresponds with itself over time; equivalence, which tells the correlation between scores on two or more sets of measurements presumed to measure the same universe of items, with no time interval in between; stability and equivalence, which correlates two or more sets of measurements over different periods of time; and internal consistency or homogeneity, which determines the extent to which measurements on a single form are intercorrelated using split-half, Spearman-Brown, or Kuder-Richardson formulas.

Validity. Validity is the extent to which measurements correspond with criteria. That is, how useful are they in making decisions relevant to a particular purpose? Content validity is concerned with the relationship between the test items and the objectives. Criterion-related validity is concurrent if it refers to measurements that correlate with a criteria when both are obtained at the same time; it is predictive if it refers to the correlation between test scores and performance on a criterion when there is a time lapse. Construct validity tells the extent to which measurements justify or support the existence of a psychological attribute, trait, or ability. Convergent validity is used to gain evidence in support of construct validity, while discriminant validity is used to gain evidence showing lack of correlation between two variables. Responsible interpretation requires the application of knowledge about validity in order to make sound judgments concerning placement/selection, description/diagnosis, and growth/change.

Communication of Results

Once professionals have interpreted test results to their own understanding, they must be careful in the communication of those results to others. They should be confident in their use of the information contained in the test manual and be able to explain technical terms such as percentile and stanine in such a way that they can be clearly understood by anyone receiving the results. They need to decide whether to communicate the results in narrative form or in face-to-face meetings.

It is necessary to obtain informed consent of those tested before releasing test information to outside parties. Clients' right to privacy must always be respected. Attention must be given to cultural, ethnic, and/or gender bias that may affect the outcome of some tests. Because test results affect the individual tested as well as the professional position of the examiner, test interpreters must be familiar with procedures for testing minority group members and disabled persons. Test results have an impact on individuals' self-esteem and can influence their life changes and engage their heartfelt political and social attitudes (Brimm, 1965). Systematic bias due to the examiner's lack of sensitivity to minority group needs is unethical and could subject such an examiner to prosecution (G. Leddick, personal communication, 1989).

Test results must not be used indiscriminately; their use should be tempered with sound professional judgment and guided by the best interests of the client. Test results should always be communicated in an understandable manner, with due respect for confidentiality. While the Buckley Amendment protects the confidentiality of all records, Public Law 94-142 specifically protects student records. It prohibits unauthorized release of student records by schools while allowing parents and students over the age of 18 access to them. Finally, to put test results in their proper perspective, it should be stressed that test results are only one part in the overall appraisal of an individual.

LEARNING OBJECTIVES

After studying the material in this chapter, you should be able to do the following:

(1) Understand the purposes for using appraisal techniques as part of the counseling process.

(2) Be aware of the development of assessment theories and how they affect the understanding of human growth and development.

(3) Define technical terms used in tests and measurement, such as *reliability* and *validity.*

(4) List the five major categories of standardized tests and group various tests according to category.

(5) Explain various methods of formal appraisal.

(6) Describe various methods of informal appraisal.

(7) Identify several factors influencing assessment.

(8) Be aware of the responsibilities of standardized test users.

(9) Explain the process of interpreting assessments and communicating the results.

(10) Be aware of ethical issues in appraisal practice.

(11) Recognize the names of the major contributors to the field of appraisal.

TIME LINE

You should be aware of important developments in the evolution of the appraisal process.

1900	Translation of Binet-Simon Scale into English	1942	Iowa Tests of Educational Development
1918	Thorndike, "father of educational measurement"	1943	MMPI
1920	Otis Scales and Otis Quick Scoring Test of Mental Ability	1944	Cattell Culture Fair Intelligence Test
		1947	formation of Educational Testing Service
1922	Stanford Achievement Test	1947	Differential Aptitude Test
1923	Koh's Block Design Test: first performance test to measure intelligence	1949	WISC
		1955	WAIS
1927	Strong Interest Inventory	1967	WPPSI
1929	first statewide testing program in Iowa	1970	General Aptitude Test Battery
1930	formation of College Entrance Examination Board	1970	Armed Services Vocational Aptitude Battery
1931	Bernreuter Personality Inventory	1974	APGA Standards for Educational and Psychological Testing
1934	Bell Adjustment Inventory		
1939	Kuder Personal Preference Record	1978	AACD Responsibilities of Users of Standardized Tests
1940	Iowa Tests of Basic Skills		
1941	Chicago Tests of Primary Mental Abilities: first multiple aptitude battery	1980s	computerized testing trend

TERMS AND NAMES
TO REMEMBER

Terms

You should have an understanding of the following terms and be able to define them in your own words.

achievement test
anecdotal report
aptitude battery
attitude tests
behavioral objective
central tendency
coefficient of determination
College Board score
criterion-referenced test
concurrent validity
construct validity
content validity
deviation IQ
diagnostic test
grade placement score
halo effect
Hawthorne effect
intelligence tests
interest inventory
isolate
local norms
mean of group
median
Mental Measurement Yearbook

mode
normal distribution
norm-referenced test
norms
percentile
predictive validity
proficiency tests
projective inventory
psychometric instrument
ratio IQ score
regression effect
reliability
shared variance
skewed distribution
specimen set
standard deviation
standardized tests
survey test
t score
Tests in Print
validity
variability
WAIS-R
WISC-R

Names

You should be familiar with these people and be aware of their contributions to the counseling profession with regard to the appraisal process.

Allport	Cattell	Kuder	Strong
Bernreuter	Edwards	Myers-Briggs	Terman
Binet	Galton	Otis	Thorndike
Buros	Guilford	Rorschach	Thurstone
Campbell	Holland	Spearman	Wechsler

FILL IN THE BLANKS

The following section reviews some of the major points in this content area. Check your knowledge of the area by filling in the appropriate name, term, or concept in each blank provided. Answer choices are found above, in the section containing terms and names to remember. You will find the correct answers at the end of the chapter.

(1)   Intelligence tests use a mean, or average score of _____ _____.

(2)   _____ tests measure information acquisition or skill mastery.

(3)   IQ is a measure of _____.

(4)   Most _____ tests given in schools are paper-and-pencil tests.

(5)   If a test has high _____, we can assume the test actually measures what it claims to measure.

(6)   Achievement tests may be used for _____ _____ and remediation.

(7)   _____ refers to average performance considering the mean, median, and mode.

(8)   A _____ describes what a student needs to do to attain a certain goal.

(9)   Ratio IQ equals the ratio of _____ age to _____ age times 100.

(10) Kuder-Richardson Formula 20 is a mathematical formula used to estimate _____ reliability.

(11) In a sociogram, an unselected individual is referred to as an _____.

(12) The most frequently occurring score in a given distribution is the _____.

(13) If scores pile up at one end of the distribution or the other, it is said to be a _____ distribution.

(14) _____ are normal scores with a mean of 50 and a standard deviation of 10.

(15) _____ tests measure a person's capacity or potential in a given area.

(16) A typing test is an example of a _____
      test.

(17) Unstructured or ambiguous tasks used to assess personality are called

      _____.

(18) Of the several types of validity, _____
      refers to the extent to which measurements correlate with a particular
      criterion when both are measured at the same time, while _____
      _____ refers to the correlation between
      test scores on a particular criterion and later performance on the same
      criterion.

(19) _____ are often used in career, or
      vocational, counseling.

(20) Informal observations of pupil behaviors recorded by teachers in a clear
      and factual manner are called _____.

(21) The tendency for an individual's score to move closer to the mean on
      subsequent testing is known as _____.

(22) The degree to which scores in one distribution explain scores in another
      distribution is referred to as _____.

(23) The _____, a common rating error,
      causes the rater to evaluate a subject based on an overall impression,
      rather than on the particular trait in question.

(24) A _____ of 4.2 means the student is
      doing as well as the average child in the second month of grade 4.

(25) _____ are ordinal measures that tell the
      point on the distribution before which a given percentage of individuals
      fall.

MATCHING TEST

Fill in each blank in the left-hand column with the letter of the corresponding type of test from the right-hand column.

____ (1) Stanford-Binet

____ (2) Kuder

____ (3) NBCC Exam

____ (4) Occupational Interest Survey

____ (5) GRE

____ (6) Otis-Lennon

____ (7) GRE Advanced Tests

____ (8) Rorschach inkblot test

____ (9) Tests of General Ability

____ (10) Thematic Apperception Test

____ (11) School and College Ability Test

____ (12) Metropolitan

____ (13) Manchover Draw-a-Person Test

____ (14) Strong-Campbell

____ (15) NMHCC Exam

____ (16) WAIS

____ (17) MMPI

____ (18) ASVAB

____ (19) CAT

____ (20) Myers-Briggs

____ (21) Kaufman Assessment Battery for Children

____ (22) Teacher-made unit test

____ (23) Locus of Control Scales

____ (24) Self-Directed Search

____ (25) Miller Analogies Test

(a) achievement

(b) aptitude

(c) intelligence

(d) interest

(e) personality

CASE STUDY

Maureen Walsh is a Ph.D. candidate interning in the college counseling center. At a recent session of group supervision, Maureen presented the following case.

Barbara Burns is a second-year student. She came to the college counseling center for academic, as well as life, planning. She lives alone in an off-campus studio apartment. Her tuition and living expenses are paid by her parents, and she works part-time at the campus bookstore to earn spending money for herself.

Barbara is enrolled in the general studies program, but cannot seem to choose a major. Having completed 24 credit hours out of 33 attempted, she has a grade point average of 2.85. She stated that she dropped a math class in her first semester because she was unable to understand the professor; she dropped geography the second semester because it was "boring" and she scored a C– on the first test; and she dropped a summer class in art history because she said it interfered with her favorite TV program.

Barbara is the second of three girls in her family. The oldest daughter is a nursing student at another state university. Barbara's father is a foreman in the water department of a large midwestern city about 350 miles from the college. Her mother "stayed home to raise the children" until two years ago, when Barbara's younger sister entered high school. Her mother now works part-time "to help put the girls through college." Her parents are not particular about Barbara's choice of major as long as she "gets the college education they were never able to have" and marries a "professional." At present Barbara communicates with her parents about once a month when they send her check.

Barbara states that she feels isolated. She hasn't found anyone "to relate to" in her apartment complex. Her classes hold little interest for her, as she feels a lack of direction in her studies. She has always been a good student, earning a place on the honor roll nearly every semester in high school. She had also been very active in her church youth group during high school. She states that she "didn't have much feeling for the religion" but stayed involved mainly to please her parents, whom she considers to be very religious.

Socially, Barbara is something of a loner. She states that most of her high school friends went to work or opted to live at home and attend community college. She occasionally goes to a movie or out to eat with a few girls she met in the dorm during her freshman year. Once in a while she goes out on a date, but she states that all her dates have gotten very "forward" the first or second time out and so she has "sworn off men—at least for now."

Because she expressed some urgency about declaring a major, Barbara was given the Strong-Campbell Interest Inventory. Barbara also took the Myers-Briggs and the Edwards Personal Preference Schedule to aid in personality exploration. She signed a release allowing admissions to send a copy of her high school test results to the counseling center. A summary of her test and interview information follows.

Subject: Barbara Burns   Age: 20
Race: White   Sex: Female
Health: Good
SAT (grade 11): Verbal = 695, Quantitative = 585, Total = 1280
GATB (grade 10):
            General = 140   Clerical Perception = 120
            Verbal = 145   Motor Coordination = 100
            Numeric = 135   Finger Dexterity = 100
            Spatial = 120   Manual Dexterity = 102
            Form Perception = 110
Edwards Personal Preference Schedule (percentiles):
            Achievement = 92   Affiliation = 95   Nurturance = 80
            Deference = 40   Intraception = 80   Change = 75
            Order = 70   Succorance = 70   Endurance = 70
            Exhibition = 35   Dominance = 15   Heterosexuality = 80
            Autonomy = 75   Abasement = 10   Aggression = 25
Myers-Briggs Personality Type: INTP (introverted, intuitive, thinking, perceptive)
Strong-Campbell Interest Inventory: Holland Code = IRE
            Realistic = High   Investigative = Moderately High
            Artistic = Moderately Low   Social = Low
            Enterprising = Moderately High   Conventional = Moderately Low
Characteristics of high-interest occupations:
            high relationship to things
            average relationship to data
            low relationship to people
High-interest occupations require:
            very high learning ability
            very high numeric skill and ability
            above-average verbal ability
Highest Basic Interest Scales:
            Science, Adventure, Medical Service
Highest Occupational Scales:
            Anthropologist, Systems Analyst, Pathologist

Analysis

(1)   Given the information above, write a brief analysis of the case. State facts supported by data.

_____

_____

(2) Using your judgment as a counselor, state your opinions or speculations about Barbara's situation.

_____

_____

_____

_____

_____

_____

(3) Do the results of the appraisal instruments/personal data information indicate any conflicts? What might be done to help the client resolve conflicts?

_____

_____

_____

_____

_____

_____

(4) Indicate your recommendations for the client in terms of career needs and personal needs. Are these needs being met? If not, what are some alternatives the client might consider? Each recommendation should include rationale, goal, method of implementation, and expected outcome.

_____

_____

_____

_____

_____

_____

_____

(5)   What other test or assessment materials might be appropriate for use in this case? Why?

_____

_____

_____

_____

_____

_____

Notes

_____

_____

_____

_____

_____

_____

_____

_____

_____

_____

_____

_____

_____

_____

_____

MULTIPLE-CHOICE TEST

Check your understanding of this content area by responding to the following questions. You will find the answer key at the end of the chapter.

1. In a normal distribution, what percentage of scores falls within the range of +2 to −2 standard deviations from the mean?
   a. 14
   b. 34
   c. 68
   d. 96

2. In order for a test to be standardized there must be
   a. a 68% pass rate
   b. uniform procedures in administering and scoring the test
   c. an equal number of questions in each test section
   d. computerized answer sheets

3. An interest inventory is useful for indicating
   a. likes and dislikes
   b. personality traits
   c. skills and abilities
   d. likelihood of success

4. Which of the following would not be an appropriate reference source for a counselor seeking information to help determine the testing needs of clients?
   a. *Tests in Print*
   b. *Mental Measurements Yearbook*
   c. *Psychology Today*
   d. test materials and reports

5. Z scores and *t* scores are examples of
   a. alphanumeric scores
   b. standard scores
   c. deviation scores
   d. raw scores

6. Which of these is not an informal appraisal technique?
   a. anecdotal report
   b. personality inventory
   c. rating scales
   d. checklists

7. A standard score with a mean of 50 and a standard deviation of 10 points is called
   a. true score
   b. IQ score
   c. Z score
   d. *t* score

8. Which of the following is not a measure of central tendency?
   a. median
   b. mode
   c. stanine
   d. mean

9. Local norms are derived from
   a. data obtained in a particular setting
   b. data relating to a subtest
   c. the total population
   d. a random sample

10. In choosing an aptitude test for a client, the counselor should be most concerned with
    a. construct validity
    b. predictive validity
    c. face validity
    d. content validity

11. An 18-year-old freshman student came to the college counseling center for help in determining a major and completed an interest inventory. The student's highest score was in agriculture. The counselor can rightly conclude from this that the student

   a. grew up on a farm
   b. should major in agriculture
   c. will get high grades in agriculture classes
   d. is attracted to the field of agriculture

12. An observation instrument that focuses on the existence or absence of a particular characteristic is known as a

   a. checklist
   b. rating scale
   c. sociogram
   d. tally sheet

13. If a test has a mean of 100 and a standard deviation of 15, we know

   a. 50% of the respondents scored between 100 and 115
   b. 68% of the respondents scored above 85
   c. 50% of the respondents scored between 85 and 115
   d. 96% of the respondents scored between 70 and 130

14. Of the several types of reliability to be considered, which is the most desirable?

   a. internal consistency
   b. equivalency
   c. stability
   d. equivalency and stability

15. If counselors are interested in the variability in a set of test data, they will look at

   a. central tendency
   b. confidence intervals
   c. standard deviation
   d. correlation coefficients

16. Which word describes the following distribution of scores? Scores = 4, 6, 7, 7, 9, 9, 11, 13, 14.

   a. bimodal
   b. skewed
   c. variable
   d. average

17. When possible, the counselor should involve the client in test selection to

   a. minimize the effect of testing
   b. shift responsibility to the client
   c. reduce client resistance
   d. maximize test interpretation

18. A counselor administers a test to the same group of students on two different occasions. On the second occasion the counselor notices that many students who scored high on the first occasion had lower scores on the second occasion, while many who scored low the first time scored higher on the second occasion. This phenomenon is known as

   a. effect of learning
   b. effect of error
   c. maturation effect
   d. regression effect

19. In a particular testing situation, if the standard deviation = 0, we know that

   a. everyone received the same score on the test
   b. nobody passed the test
   c. everyone passed the test
   d. nobody took the test

20. If a teacher administers two standardized reading tests to her class and the correlation turns out to be –.83, we know that

   a. over 80% of the students did poorly on both tests
   b. achieving a high score on one test was related to achieving a low grade on the other
   c. on average, students answered 17% of the items incorrectly
   d. achieving a low score on one test predicted a low score on the other test

21. Which of the following is not a standard score?
    a. ETS score
    b. Z score
    c. ratio IQ
    d. deviation IQ

22. An aptitude test is an indication of
    a. unconscious desires
    b. general mental capacity
    c. previous experience in a given area
    d. potential for success in a given area

23. Item analysis is an integral part of the testing procedure. It is especially important in diagnostic testing because it
    a. emphasizes key points
    b. identifies areas of student weakness
    c. reinforces important content areas
    d. forces students to study harder

24. Personality assessment is fraught with error, or response bias. Which of these is not an example of response bias?
    a. defensive response
    b. acquiescence
    c. social desirability
    d. deviant response

25. If a distribution is positively skewed,
    a. mean and mode are equal
    b. mean is larger than median or mode
    c. median and mode are equal
    d. mean is less than median or mode

ANSWER KEY

Fill in the Blanks

(1) 100
(2) achievement
(3) intelligence
(4) standardized
(5) validity
(6) diagnosis
(7) central tendency
(8) behavioral objective
(9) mental, chronological
(10) internal consistency
(11) isolate
(12) mode
(13) skewed

(14) *t* scores
(15) aptitude
(16) proficiency test
(17) projective tests
(18) concurrent, predictive
(19) interest inventories
(20) anecdotal reports
(21) regression effect
(22) shared variance
(23) halo effect
(24) grade placement score
(25) percentiles

Matching

(1) c
(2) d
(3) a
(4) d
(5) b
(6) c
(7) a
(8) e
(9) c

(10) e
(11) b
(12) a
(13) e
(14) d
(15) a
(16) c
(17) e

(18) b
(19) a
(20) e
(21) c
(22) a
(23) e
(24) d
(25) b

Multiple-Choice

1. d
2. b
3. a
4. c
5. b
6. b
7. d
8. c
9. a

10. b
11. d
12. a
13. d
14. a
15. c
16. a
17. c

18. d
19. a
20. b
21. c
22. d
23. b
24. a
25. b

CHAPTER 7

Research and Evaluation

SUMMARY   145
  Statistics   **145**
    Types of Measurement   145
    Descriptive Statistics   146
    Inferential Statistics   146
    Statistical Procedures   147
  Research Methods and Practices   **147**
    Planning the Study   147
    Research Designs   149
    Observation and Data Collection 150
    Communicating Results   151
  Research Theory and Issues   **151**
    Research Theory   151
    Research Issues   151
LEARNING OBJECTIVES   153
TERMS AND NAMES TO REMEMBER   154
  Terms   **154**
  Names   **154**
FILL IN THE BLANKS   155
MATCHING TEST   157
CASE STUDY   158
  Analysis   **158**
MULTIPLE-CHOICE TEST   162
ANSWER KEY   165
  Fill in the Blanks   **165**
  Matching   **165**
  Multiple-Choice   **165**

SUMMARY

Research and evaluation includes areas such as statistics, research design, and development of research and demonstration proposals. It also includes understanding legislation relating to the development of research, program development, and demonstration proposals, as well as the development and evaluation of program objectives. (Loesch & Vacc, 1986, p. 14)

Statistics

As a science, statistics is concerned with the presentation, analysis, and interpretation of data obtained from samples of observations. Kerlinger (1986) suggests four purposes for the use of statistics: (a) to reduce large quantities of data to manageable and understandable form, (b) to aid in the study of populations and samples, (c) to aid in decision making, and (d) to aid in making reliable inferences from observational data, that is, in making decisions among hypotheses. Statistics may be obtained from several different types of measurement.

Types of Measurement

The measurements from which statistics may be gathered may be either qualitative, such as classifying students as bright or slow, or quantitative, such as the number of hours a student spends studying each day. In either case, scales of measurement have three common characteristics: (a) A measurement scale must consist of at least two different possible values; (b) the set of possible measures must be complete or exhaustive; and (c) the measures defined along the scale should be mutually exclusive (Saslow, 1982).

Measurement scales. Scales of measure may be interval, ratio, nominal, or ordinal. Interval scales consist of ordered categories that are equidistant from each other and have an arbitrary zero point (temperature, for example). Ratio scales are simply interval scales with absolute, rather than arbitrary, zero points (percentage scores on tests). Nominal, or categori-

cal, scales present information in the form of mutually exclusive groups with no inherent order (male or female, for example); ordinal data consist of categories with a natural order or continuum (agree, neutral, or disagree, for example). Interval and ratio data are quantitative, whereas nominal and ordinal data are qualitative.

Appraisal instruments. In educational research the measures used are often tests (see Chapter 6). Tests, or appraisal instruments, such as measures of achievement, intelligence, and aptitude, are generally scored on interval or ratio scales. Some appraisal instruments measure personality by means of inventories and projective techniques; others measure attitudes, beliefs, and values by means of nominal and ordinal scales. Ary, Jacobs, and Razavieh (1985) list four main types of attitude scales: (a) summated rating scales (Likert scales), (b) equal-appearing interval scales (Thurstone scales), (c) cumulative scales (Gutman scales), and (d) semantic differential scales.

Likert scales. One of the most widely used and successful techniques for measuring attitudes was developed by Likert (1932). A Likert scale consists of a number of statements about a particular object or topic accompanied by response categories (usually five) along a continuum such as strongly agree, agree, undecided, disagree, strongly disagree. For scoring purposes the response scales are weighted 5, 4, 3, 2, 1, respectively, for positive statements beginning at the favorable end; for negative statements, the opposite weights are assigned.

Thurstone scales. Unlike Likert scales, which weight responses, Thurstone scales assign values to the attitude items (see Thurstone & Chave, 1929). The responses are weighted by judges on a continuum from A to K (i.e., 1 to 11), with A being most favorable, F being neutral, and K being most unfavorable. The judges' responses are averaged and a numerical value is assigned to each item. Respondents' scores consist of the mean value for those statements with which they agree. A score of less than 6 is considered favorable, while more than 6 is unfavorable. Although both types of scales are used for a wide variety of topics, Thurstone scales afford a more absolute interpretation of the scale scores than do Likert scales, while Likert scales are much less difficult to construct.

Other scales. Two less widely used scales are Guttman scales and semantic differential scales (Osgood, Suci, & Tannenbaum, 1957). Guttman scales, which attempt to determine if the attitude being studied is unidimensional by analyzing each item for reproducibility, are difficult to produce and impractical to use (Ary et al., 1985). Semantic differential scales attempt to measure attitudes toward certain objects by presenting a set of bipolar adjectives, such as good-bad, along with seven response scale categories. The respondent marks one of the seven spaces to indicate the extent to which each adjective describes the object.

Descriptive Statistics

Once the measures have been taken, statistical procedures can be applied to answer the research questions. Those procedures that organize, summarize, and describe the data are called *descriptive* statistics, while those used to imply relationships between the treatment and the outcome are called *inferential* statistics. Descriptive statistics include measures of central tendency and measures of variability as well as correlations.

Measures of central tendency. The three most frequently used measures of central tendency are the mean, the median, and the mode. The mean is simply the arithmetic average of the scores. Although the mean is more stable than the median or mode, it is sensitive to extreme scores, or outliers, which can skew the distribution. In a skewed distribution the mean will be pulled toward the extreme scores (Huck, Cormier, & Bounds, 1974). The median represents the midpoint in the distribution of scores, with half the scores below it and half above it. The mode is the most frequently occurring score in the distribution. If two or more scores appear more frequently, the distribution is bimodal or multimodal.

Measures of variability. Measures of variability or dispersion tell how spread out the scores are. The most commonly used measures of variability are range, quartile deviation, variance, and standard deviation. Range is somewhat unstable because it refers to only two scores in the distribution, the highest and the lowest. Quartile deviation, or semi-interquartile range, is derived by dividing the distribution into four parts, with 25% of the scores in each. The quartile deviation refers to the 50% of the scores lying between the first and fourth quartile. To determine variance, one must find out how much each score deviates from the mean and apply a mathematical formula. To get the standard deviation, one takes the square root of the variance. Because variance and standard deviation are based upon all the scores in the group, they are better indicators of variability than are some other measures.

Correlations. Although central tendency and variability measures describe only one variable, correlations can be used to describe the relationship between two variables. Correlations tell the direction and the strength of the relationship. Correlations range from -1.00, a perfect negative or inverse relationship, to $+1.00$, a perfect positive relationship. The closer to 1, the stronger the correlation. The two most widely used correlations are the Pearson product-moment correlation (Pearson r), used for interval or ratio measures, and the Spearman rho, used for ordinal data (Ary et al., 1985).

Inferential Statistics

When descriptive statistics are inadequate for the purpose of the research, inferential statistics may be employed to estimate parameters (i.e., the characteristics of a larger group, the population) from statistics (i.e., the characteristics of a smaller group, the sample). The accuracy of the inference depends upon how representative the sample is of the population (Huck et al., 1974).

Sampling. In probability sampling the elements are chosen by chance, and each member of the population has a possibility of being chosen. Nonprobability, or nonchance, procedures are used when enumeration of the population elements is difficult if not impossible. Probability sampling includes simple random sampling, stratified sampling, cluster sampling, and systematic sampling. Some types of nonprobability sampling are (a) accidental,

(b) purposive, and (c) quota sampling (Ary et al., 1985).

Hypothesis testing. Inferential statistics may be used to compare two or more groups to see whether or not their populations are similar. Huck et al. (1974) outline five steps used in the hypothesis testing procedure:

(1) State the null hypothesis (i.e., there is no difference between the populations being compared). The results of the statistical test are stated in terms of the probability that the null hypothesis is false.

(2) Select the level of significance (i.e., how likely it is that the results are due to chance rather treatment). Usually the .01 or .05 level is used. The .95 level of confidence corresponds to the .05 level of significance and means the results of the study would be due to chance only 5 or fewer times out of 100.

(3) Compute the calculated value, t. Or F, appropriate to the data.

(4) Obtain the critical value from the appropriate statistical table. One must know the level of significance and degrees of freedom to use the tables.

(5) Reject or fail to reject the null hypothesis. If the critical value is greater than the calculated value, fail to reject the null hypothesis (i.e., there is no significant difference between the groups being compared). If the critical value is less than the obtained value, reject the null hypothesis (i.e., there is a significant difference).

Statistical Procedures

A number of statistical procedures may be applied to test the null hypothesis. Among the most widely used are the t test, analysis of variance, and the chi-square test (Ary et al., 1985). The t test for independent samples compares the means of the two conditions, usually treatment and control, to see if there is a statistically significant difference. The t test for non-independent samples can be used to compare the treatment effect for each subject as in repeated measures or pretest-posttest designs, or to estimate the effect of treatment for each pair in matched-group designs.

Analyzing variance. Analysis of variance (ANOVA) can test the difference between two or more means. ANOVA analyzes the data into two sources, variance between groups and variance within groups, which are incorporated into the F ratio. The F test is used to determine if there are significant differences. If significant differences exist, other procedures, such as Tukey's and Scheffé's, can be used to determine differences between specific groups. Multifactor analysis of variance (MANOVA) can be used to test the effect of more than one independent variable and also the interaction effects of such variables.

Chi-square analysis. The chi-square test can be used to find the significance of differences between proportions of subjects, objects, and so on in different categories. The observations, which are measured as frequencies, must be independent and the categories must be mutually exclusive. Many more sophisticated statistical procedures are available, but they are beyond the scope of this volume.

Research Methods and Practices

In order to carry out a successful research project the researcher must take care in planning the study, choosing the most effective research design, observing and accurately recording the data, and communicating the results of the study in a professional manner.

Planning the Study

Isaac and Michael (1981) suggest ten basic steps in the planning and conduct of research. First, the researcher must determine an area of interest or general question. Second, the researcher must conduct a review of the related literature. This review will help the researcher to formulate a researchable question and will also prevent unnecessary repetition of work that has already been done (Saslow, 1982). The literature often suggests the next logical question to be explored in the area. Third, with this information in hand, the researcher can define the actual problem to be investigated in clear, specific terms. Fourth, the researcher needs to reword the question into a testable hypothesis, defining its basic concepts and variables.

Variables of interest. Variables to be considered are independent, dependent, and control variables. The independent variable is manipulated in such a way as to cause, influence, or affect the outcome. The dependent variables, or outcome variables, depend on how the independent variables are manipulated. Control variables, such as demographic or background information, need to be held constant so that their effects are canceled out or controlled for.

Once the researcher has defined the variables, he or she should state the underlying assumptions about the nature and conditions of the behavior being studied, and should describe the methods, the measurements, and the relationship of this study to others. Next, he or she must construct the research design to maximize internal and external validity.

Internal validity. Campbell and Stanley (1966) have identified eight threats to the internal validity of research designs. If these variables are not controlled, their effects might be confounded with the treatment effects.

(1) *History*: Besides the experimental variable, other specific events over which the researcher has no control may occur between the first and second measurements.

(2) *Maturation*: Processes operating within the subjects simply as a function of the passage of time (e.g., aging, hunger, fatigue) may affect performance.

(3) *Testing*: Exposure to the pretest may affect performance on subsequent tests.

(4) *Instrumentation*: Changes in the measuring instrument, in observers, or in scorers may account for differences in scores.

(5) *Statistical regression*: With groups selected on the basis of extreme scores there is a tendency to move toward the common mean on subsequent measures.

(6) *Selection*: Between-group differences that are present before the experimental treatment may affect performance on the dependent variable measure.

(7) *Experimental mortality*: The differential loss of subjects from the comparison groups may affect outcome.

(8) *Selection-maturation interaction*: When subject groups are not randomly selected, it may be that a group's higher rate of maturation, rather than the treatment, accounts for the observed effect.

External validity. The term *external validity* refers to the extent to which the results of an experiment can be generalized to other subjects in other environments. Bracht and Glass (1968) have identified two types of external validity: (a) population validity, which is concerned with generalizability to other subjects; and (b) ecological validity, which is concerned with generalizability to other settings or environmental conditions.

In minimizing threats to population validity, the researcher needs to (a) be sure the sample is representative of the target population and (b) be aware of subject-treatment interaction—that is, different subjects have different learning styles.

Threats to ecological validity to which the researcher must attend include the following:

(1) *Independent variable*: An accurate description of the independent variable is necessary for replication and generalization of the results.

(2) *Dependent variables*: Accurate description of the dependent variables and measurement instruments used is necessary.

(3) *Multiple-treatment interference*: With subjects receiving more than one treatment it is difficult to determine treatment effects.

(4) *Hawthorne effect*: Subjects' behaviors are influenced by virtue of being part of a study and knowing it.

(5) *Experimenter or Rosenthal effect*: Something in the experimenter's behavior or personal affect inadvertently influences subjects' performance.

(6) *Novelty and disruption effects*: Any change within a setting that is normally routine may affect results more than in a setting where change is common.

(7) *Pretest and posttest sensitization*: The pretest may make subjects more receptive to treatment; in some cases, the posttest emphasizes treatment in ways that would not occur without it.

(8) *Interaction of history and treatment effect*: Outside events occurring during the treatment time may affect the outcome.

(9) *Interaction of time of measurement and treatment effects*: Because some treatments have immediate and/or short-term effects and some have delayed reactions, the dependent variable should be measured several times after treatment.

Research Designs

Keeping the need to control these threats in mind, the researcher has a number of research methods and designs from which to choose. In general there are four types of research methods: (a) experimental, (b) ex post facto, (c) descriptive and historical, and (d) survey (Ary et al., 1985).

Experimental research. Experimental designs include true experimental, factorial, and quasi-experimental. True experimental designs are highly recommended for research in education and counseling because of the high degree of validity controls they provide. The use of control groups and randomization contributes to the strength of these designs. These single-variable designs include (a) randomized subjects, posttest-only control group design; (b) randomized matched subjects, posttest-only control group design; (c) randomized subjects, pretest-posttest control group design; (d) Solomon three-group design; and (e) Solomon four-group design.

When more than one independent variable is manipulated, factorial designs are used in order to determine the effects of each variable on the dependent variable, as well as the interaction effects among the several variables. In one type of factorial design the researcher

acesses the effects of the independent variable as well as one or more attribute variables. In the other type the researcher manipulates more than one independent variable in order to analyze their main effects as well as interaction effects.

Ex post facto research. Quasi-experimental designs are used in classroom or counseling situations where randomization and control over experimental conditions are not possible. In these situations attention must be paid to the sources of internal and external validity threats in the design and interpretation of the study. Quasi-experimental designs include (a) non-randomized control group pretest-posttest design, (b) counterbalanced design, (c) one-group time-series design, and (d) control group time-series design.

Ex post facto research is research in which the experimenter does not have direct control over the independent variable because the variations have already occurred in the natural course of events or because they are inherently not manipulable. The researcher makes inferences about relations among variables, without direct intervention, from naturally occurring differences in independent and dependent variables (Kerlinger, 1986). These studies take into consideration such variables as intelligence, personality, home background, and other important factors that are out of the control of the researcher.

Descriptive and historical research. Descriptive and historical research are designed to determine what exists rather than to test hypotheses. The purpose is often to get information to assist in decision making or to explore a new area of research. Some types of descriptive designs are (a) surveys, (b) case studies, (c) developmental studies, (d) follow-up studies, (e) documentary analysis, (f) trend analyses, and (g) correlation studies.

Survey research. While one category of survey research is a specialized form of descriptive research, an explanatory survey is a specialized form of ex post facto research. It not only gathers information on variables, but attempts to explain relationships among these variables. The five steps in carrying out a survey are as follows: (a) Plan the topic, the population, the methods, and procedures; (b) get a representative, random sample; (c) construct the instrument to be used for personal or telephone interviews and/or questionnaires; (d) carry out the survey by pretesting the instrument, training interviewers, interviewing subjects, or distributing the questionnaires; and (e) process the data by coding, computer processing, interpreting the results, and reporting the findings (Ary et al., 1985).

Observation and Data Collection

Once the research method and experimental design have been decided upon, observation and data collection procedures must be specified. Problems and methods are interactive in the sense that problems dictate methods to a certain degree, but the availability, feasibility, and relevance of methods also influence problems. Methods of data collection help researchers make observations so that symbols or numerals can be assigned to the object or set of objects under study so they can bring empirical evidence to bear on research questions (Kerlinger, 1986). The researcher must check to be sure the procedures are sufficient to answer every question and test every hypothesis.

Methods. There are various methods of observation and data collection from which to choose. Kerlinger (1986) discusses five:

(1) *Interviews and questionnaires*: The carefully structured, pretested personal interview that includes open-ended questions is an excellent way to get information regarding people's feelings, intentions, attitudes, and so on. Drawbacks are that mailed questionnaires have low return rates and personal interviews require a great deal of time, energy, money, and skill.

(2) *Objective tests and scales*: These are the most widely used method of data collection and observation in education. (See the beginning of this chapter and also Chapter 6.) Whether using an existing measure or designing a new one, the researcher must pay attention to accepted psychometric procedures, reliability, and validity.

(3) *Available materials, projective methods, and content analysis*: Personal and soci-etal products, particularly verbal materials, are either produced in the course of living by individuals and groups or deliberately stimulated by researchers to provide measures of variables. These measures are obtained by content analysis and projective methods. This method is less objective than questionnaires, tests, or scales.

(4) *Observations of behavior and sociometry*: Researchers who use observation assign numerical values to human behavioral acts in order to accumulate data from which inferences can be drawn. Sociometry involves group members' observing each other and recording their reactions to each other for the researcher's assessment. Observation and sociometry are highly subjective and pose problems with respect to reliability and validity.

(5) *Q methodology (Stephenson, 1953)*: The Q technique involves sorting decks of cards called Q sorts and examining the correlations among the responses of different individuals. Subjects are presented with a deck of cards that contains a set of statements, words, pictures, or the like, which they rank order according to some criterion. Q methodology is not applicable to large samples and has some statistical weaknesses.

Data analysis. After specifying the data collection procedures, the researcher must select the data analysis methodology. Statistical procedures used to analyze data have been discussed earlier in this chapter. Keep in mind that statistical techniques should be selected on the basis of their appropriateness for answering the research question and their compatability with the research design. Procedures to be used for data presentation, such as tables, figures, and charts, should also be determined during the planning stage (Ary et al., 1985).

When all the preliminary decisions have been made and the previous steps have been clearly delineated in a written proposal, it is time to execute the research plan. The researcher proceeds to collect and organize the data as specified in the plan. Data analysis is often done by computer in order to achieve precision and to save on time and energy (Ary et al., 1985).

Communicating Results

After the results are known, the researcher is ready to evaluate the results and draw conclusions. The results of the study may be reported in a thesis or dissertation, a journal article, or a conference paper: in reporting the results of a study, the researcher should (a) draw only those conclusions supported by the data, (b) report the limitations of the study, (c) report internal and external validity problems, and (d) present the importance of the study accurately (Ary et al., 1985).

Research Theory and Issues

Research represents the scientific aspect of the counseling profession. Because the basic aim of science is to explain natural phenomena, and because such explanations are called theories, counseling research must be theory based. A theory can be defined as "a set of interrelated constructs (concepts), definitions, and propositions that present a systematic view of phenomena by certifying relations among variables, with the purpose of explaining and predicting the phenomena" (Kerlinger, 1986, p. 9). Although researchers may focus on the short-range goal of finding specific relations, theoretical research aims are superior because they are more general and more widely applicable.

Research Theory

According to Ary et al. (1985), theories serve several purposes. They summarize existing knowledge, they clarify and give meaning to isolated empirical findings, and they provide tentative explanations for observed events and relationships. Theories also stimulate the development of new knowledge by providing stimuli for further investigation. A sound theory should be parsimonious as well as consistent with observed facts and current knowledge. It should provide means for its verification as useful or not useful, and it

should stimulate new discoveries and indicate future research needs.

Although research and evaluation are treated together throughout most of this chapter, some distinction needs to be made between the two. Whereas research is concerned with the development of theories, evaluation emphasizes mission achievement or product delivery. Evaluation implies a judgment of the worth or value of a particular process, technique or program. According to Lewis and Lewis (1983), evaluation should be an integral part of the management cycle, which includes planning, budgeting, implementing, and evaluating. They suggest evaluation be part of ongoing self-assessment rather than a specialized operation that involves experts invading the organization from the outside.

The evaluation process consists of three basic steps: (a) State objectives in measurable terms, (b) design the means to meet these objectives, and (c) select or develop measures by which attainment of each objective will be determined. After the measures have been taken, outcome evaluation will determine whether or not the objectives have been met. Program strengths and weaknesses can then be analyzed with suggestions for future modification, if appropriate (Isaac & Michael, 1981).

Research Issues

Whether conducting research or evaluation studies, professional counselors need to be aware of many ethical and legal considerations.

Ethics. The AACD (1981) code of ethics provides ethical guidelines for research and publication. Counselors are cautioned to avoid activities that cause stress for subjects, to inform subjects of possible risks, and to remove harmful aftereffects as soon as the design allows. Researchers must protect human subjects from harm, inform them of the nature and purpose of the study, and allow them to withdraw their consent at any time during the study. The researcher must ensure confidentiality and protect subjects' rights to privacy.

In addition to the researcher's obligation to the subjects, there are professional obligations as well. The results of studies must (a) include information about all the variables and conditions, (b) be reported accurately, so as not to be misleading, and (c) protect the identity of subjects. Researchers should make original research available to others, give due credit for contributions and references, and submit manuscripts to only one journal at a time.

Legalities. Besides the ethical issues mentioned, counselor-researchers should pay attention to a number of legal considerations. Because counselors in some states do not have the right of privileged communication, they must exercise caution in the information they put into clients' charts and the information they release. Counselors must also beware of malpractice suits. According to Hopkins and Anderson (1986), counselors may be judged negligent if they (a) use procedures not in the realm of accepted practice, (b) use techniques for which they are not trained or competent, (c) fail to follow procedures known to be more helpful, (d) fail to explain potential hazards of treatment, (e) defame clients' character, or (f) invade clients' privacy.

Ongoing debate. Despite the information and training that counselors receive about research, there is an ongoing debate about whether and which kind of research counselors ought to be doing. Although counselors are mandated to conduct research, it is thought that the majority of counseling practitioners neither keep up with the published research nor conduct any kind of formal research on their own (Goldman, 1986).

Advocates of research and evaluation claim that traditional research allows theory and practice to evolve and solidify. Goldman (1986), however, believes that traditional research falls short of providing information that counselors can put into practice with clients. He advocates new approaches to research and suggests that counselors (a) study the individual rather than the group, (b) study the whole person rather than isolated parts, (c) focus on real life rather than laboratory situations, (d) use observation rather than questionnaires, (e) utilize case study methods and intensive experimental design for intensive analysis of individuals, and (f) study current and relevant concerns.

Vacc and Loesch (1987) see the debate over counselors' proficiency and conduct of research coming to an end. The new standards for counselor preparation (CACREP) and counselor certification (NBCC), as well as licensing standards, require counselors and counseling programs to have a certain level of competence in research in order to be accredited, certified, or licensed. Because research (i.e., making contributions to the theoretical and knowledge base of the counseling profession) is one of the four main components of professionalism, it is likely that counselors will become more, not less, involved in research of one sort or another as the profession grows and develops.

LEARNING OBJECTIVES

After studying the material in this chapter, you should be able to do the following:

(1) Understand basic statistical terminology.

(2) Differentiate between qualitative and quantitative data and among interval, ratio, nominal, and ordinal scales.

(3) Explain the use of descriptive and inferential statistics.

(4) Explain the use of t test, ANOVA, and chi-square.

(5) Discuss sampling techniques.

(6) Describe the procedure for hypothesis testing.

(7) Discuss the basic steps in planning and conducting a research study.

(8) Define independent, dependent, and control variables and be able to identify them in a study.

(9) Discuss the possible threats to internal and external validity and ways to control for them.

(10) Explain the four basic types of research.

(11) Be familiar with various methods of observation and data collection.

(12) Explain the theoretical bases for research.

(13) Differentiate between research and evaluation.

(14) Be aware of ethical issues in conducting research and evaluation.

(15) Discuss legal issues in research and evaluation.

TERMS AND NAMES
TO REMEMBER

Terms

You should have an understanding of the following terms and be able to define them in your own words.

ANOVA
chi-square
cluster sampling
content analysis
control variable
correlations
critical value
dependent variable
descriptive
descriptive statistics
experimental design
empirical
evaluation
ex post facto
external validity
F test
independent variable
inferential statistics
interaction effects
internal validity
interval
level of significance
mean
median
mode

nominal
nonprobability sampling
null hypothesis
ordinal
parameters
parsimonious
probability sampling
qualitative data
quantitative data
quartile deviation
quasi-experimental
range
ratio
research
research design
simple random sampling
statistics
standard deviation
stratified sampling
survey
systematic sampling
t test
theory
variability
variance

Names

You should be familiar with these people and be aware of their contributions to the counseling profession with regard to research and evaluation.

Gutman
Hawthorne
Likert
Pearson
Rosenthal

Solomon
Spearman
Stephenson
Thurstone
Tukey

FILL IN THE BLANKS

The following section reviews some of the major points in this content area. Check your knowledge of the area by filling in the appropriate name, term, or concept in each blank provided. Answer choices are found above, in the section containing terms and names to remember. You will find the correct answers at the end of the chapter.

(1) _____ scales are interval scales with an absolute zero point.

(2) Standard deviation is a measure of _____ _____.

(3) Measures of central tendency include _____ _____, _____ _____, and _____ _____.

(4) In research a variable that is a consequence of an antecedent variable is called a _____.

(5) A _____ scale places objects or individuals into categories.

(6) A researcher whose study involves manipulation of the independent variable in a controlled setting is conducting _____ _____.

(7) A theory that explains events in the simplest form possible and has few complexities and assumptions is said to be _____ _____.

(8) Population _____ are the characteristics of the larger group, while _____ refers to the characteristics of the sample.

(9) If the _____ is set at .01, the results of the study would be due to chance rather than treatment less than 1 time out of 100.

(10) Maturation, regression, and experimental mortality are examples of threats to _____.

(11) To compare the mean scores of two groups, the _____ _____ should be used.

(12) Interval and ratio data are _____, and nominal and ordinal are _____.

(13) In _____ research the independent
      variable is not within the control of the researcher.

(14) When two or more groups are being compared, the omnibus _____
      _____ can be used to determine if any
      significant differences exist.

(15) When _____ is used, each member of
      the population has an equal and independent chance of being chosen.

(16) The calculated and critical t values are compared to determine whether or
      not to reject the _____.

(17) _____ has to do with the
      generalizability of the results of a study.

(18) When all the elements of the population cannot be enumerated,
      _____ must be used to select subjects.

(19) In general, _____ is theory oriented and
      _____ is outcome oriented.

(20) When more than one independent variable is manipulated, factorial
      research designs are used to analyze main effects as well as _____
      _____.

(21) Experimental research is designed for hypothesis testing, whereas
      _____ research seeks to determine what
      exists.

(22) One measure of dispersion, _____, tells
      the difference between the highest and lowest values in the distribution.

(23) _____ refers to the strength of the
      relationship between two variables.

(24) _____ imply a relationship between
      treatment and outcome.

(25) _____ research may be either
      descriptive or ex post facto.

MATCHING TEST

Match the names in the left-hand column with the appropriate concepts in the right-hand column.

___ (1) Gutman

___ (2) Hawthorne

___ (3) Likert

___ (4) Pearson

___ (5) Rosenthal

___ (6) Solomon

___ (7) Spearman

___ (8) Stephenson

___ (9) Thurstone

___ (10) Tukey

(a) product-moment coefficient of correlation for linear, interval data

(b) cumulative scales

(c) post hoc multiple comparison test

(d) Q methodology

(e) an experimental effect that threatens internal validity

(f) coefficient of correlation for rank-ordered data

(g) equal-appearing interval scales

(h) summated rating scales

(i) research design with three or four groups

(j) an experimental effect in which some characteristic or behavior of the experimenter influences the subjects' behavior

CASE STUDY

An experimenter is interested in comparing the effects of two types of instruction in the basic counseling skills of paraphrasing and reflecting feelings. One group will be trained in traditional classroom methods, while the other group will use a self-guided computer learning system.

The 30 subjects in the study are enrolled in a master's level introductory counseling course. To be certain that the two groups are of equal ability, the researcher administers some measure of skill level and then establishes 15 pairs of subjects. Within each pair the researcher flips a coin to decide which member will be assigned to the classroom group and which will be assigned to the computer group.

The groups meet for two hours twice a week for three weeks. The classroom group meets with an instructor using traditional methods. The computer group meets in the computer lab, where subjects work independently on separate computer terminals. At the end of the three weeks, the subjects' counseling skills are again measured.

Analysis

(1) What is the name of the experimental design used?

_____

(2) What are some factors, other than skill level, that the researcher might want to consider in determining the pairs of subjects?

_____

_____

_____

_____

(3) What is the independent variable in this study?

_____

(4) What is the dependent variable?

_____

_____

(5) What are some control variables the researcher should consider in analyzing the results of this study?

_____

_____

(6) Consider each of the possible threats to internal validity and tell how this design controls for it or what limitations it presents.

history:

_____

_____

maturation:

_____

_____

testing:

_____

_____

instrumentation:

_____

_____

statistical regression:

_____

_____

selection:

_____

_____

mortality:

_____

_____

selection-maturation interaction:

_____

_____

(7) Discuss the threats to external validity and tell how they could be handled in this study.

population:

_____

treatment-subject interaction:

_____

independent variable:

_____

dependent variable:

_____

multiple treatment inference:

_____

history treatment interaction:

_____

time-treatment interaction:

_____

pretest-posttest sensitization:

_____

Hawthorne effect:

_____

novelty and disruption:

_____

experimenter effect:

_____

(8) State the null hypothesis for this study.

_____

_____

(9) Discuss the statistical procedures you would use in analyzing the data from this study.

_____

_____

_____

_____

(10) Discuss methods for disseminating the results of this study and to which journals it might be submitted.

_____

_____

_____

_____

MULTIPLE-CHOICE TEST

Check your understanding of this content area by responding to the following questions. You will find the answer key at the end of the chapter.

1. A researcher wants to measure client satisfaction with the counseling relationship. A 5-point rating scale is designed with response choices 5 = very satisfied, 4 = satisfied, 3 = neutral, 2 = dissatisfied, 1 = very dissatisfied. This is an example of a
   a. ratio scale
   b. Likert-type scale
   c. Thurstone-type scale
   d. nominal-type scale

2. An educator selected as her experimental subjects the 50 fifth-grade students who had the lowest achievement test scores. The internal validity of this study is most likely to be threatened by
   a. testing
   b. instrumentation
   c. Rosenthal effect
   d. statistical regression

3. Subjects in the control group of a weight-loss study are given gelatin capsules that they are led to believe are diet pills. The subjects react by losing weight. This effect is referred to as
   a. placebo effect
   b. interaction effect
   c. experimental effect
   d. main effect

4. A 95% confidence level means that
   a. there is a 95% chance the subjects will improve
   b. the alpha level has been set at .05
   c. 95 out of every 100 subjects will improve
   d. the null hypothesis will be rejected 5 out of every 100 times

5. Rose N. Thal designs an experimental study to compare the effects of a new counseling intervention with traditional counseling. The research design most appropriate for her study is
   a. Solomon four-group design
   b. one-group pretest-posttest design
   c. randomized subjects posttest-only control group design
   d. randomized subjects pretest-posttest control group design

6. A researcher reports a correlation of −1.67 between teacher praise and student off-task behavior. This correlation coefficient indicates that
   a. the researcher must have made some mistake
   b. teacher praise is inversely related to student off-task behavior
   c. there is a negative relationship between praise and off-task behavior
   d. teacher praise has little influence on student behavior

7. Standard deviation is associated with
   a. abnormal behavior
   b. normal behavior
   c. the mean
   d. achievement

8. In analyzing the results of his study, Dr. Know found some extreme scores. Which of the following measures of central tendency will be most affected by the extreme scores?
   a. mid-score
   b. mode
   c. mean
   d. median

9. A distinguishing feature of a ratio scale is

   a. ordered categories
   b. absolute zero point
   c. mutually exclusive groups
   d. continuum of responses

10. Which of the following research designs most effectively controls the threats to internal validity?

   a. randomized subjects pretest-posttest control group design
   b. static group comparison
   c. matched subjects posttest-only control group design
   d. Solomon four-group design

11. Once a researcher has chosen a general question to be answered in the study, the next step is to

   a. formulate the null hypothesis
   b. choose measurement instruments
   c. search the related literature
   d. select subjects for the study

12. Sometimes researchers are interested in the effects of more than one independent variable. Experiments of this nature, which allow more than one factor to vary, are known as

   a. variability studies
   b. dual-design scales
   c. multiple analyses
   d. factorial designs

13. Which of the following statements is not true regarding the interpretation of the Pearson product-moment coefficient of correlation?

   a. This correlation is most useful for ordinal data.
   b. This correlation does not necessarily indicate causation.
   c. The size of this correlation is in part a function of the variability of the two distributions to be correlated.
   d. Correlation coefficients should not be interpreted in terms of percentage of perfect correlations.

14. Dr. Dorm conducted a study to determine whether graduate and undergraduate students preferred to live in dormitories or off-campus apartments. His null hypothesis stated that there was no significant difference in the proportion of graduate and undergraduate students who prefer dorms or apartments. The best statistical procedure for testing this hypothesis is

   a. chi-square test of independence
   b. MANOVA
   c. omnibus F test
   d. t test for independent samples

15. A. T. Test conducted a study of teaching methods, comparing three groups. When he analyzed the data, a nonsignificant F test was observed. He should

   a. accept the null hypothesis
   b. fail to reject the null hypothesis
   c. conduct pairwise comparisons
   d. reject the null hypothesis

16. There is a .025 probability of error on either side of the normal curve when

   a. the alpha level is set at .025
   b. the confidence level is variable
   c. the confidence level is 75%
   d. the alpha level is set at .05

17. An intelligence test is administered to all the fourth graders in the school district. If the standard deviation is reported to be 10, then

   a. about two-thirds of the midrange scores fall between 90 and 100
   b. about two-thirds of the midrange scores fall between 95 and 105
   c. the mean must be 100
   d. the median is 50

18. The response choices on an attitude scale include good-bad, hard-easy, interesting-boring. This type of scale is called

   a. summated rating
   b. cumulative
   c. semantic differential
   d. equal-appearing interval

19. To infer a causal relationship three kinds of evidence are necessary. Which of these is not acceptable evidence?

    a. that a statistical relationship between X and Y has been established
    b. that the null hypothesis is rejected
    c. that X preceded Y in time
    d. that other factors did not determine Y

20. The single best way to achieve control in an experimental design is

    a. inference
    b. randomization
    c. statistical analysis
    d. observation

21. In controlling for external validity the experimentally accessible population should have characteristics similar to

    a. the target population
    b. the random sample
    c. general population
    d. the control group

22. Which of the following situations does not call for ex post facto research?

    a. Handicapped children have lower self-concepts than nonhandicapped children.
    b. Adolescents from single-parent homes drop out of high school more frequently than do adolescents from two-parent homes.
    c. Counselors in training who videotape counseling sessions attain a higher skill level than those who do not use videotape.
    d. Students with high IQs are more achievement oriented than those with low IQs.

23. One of the threats to external validity occurs when subjects act differently because they know they are participating in a study. This phenomenon is known as the

    a. Thurstone effect
    b. Solomon effect
    c. Hawthorne effect
    d. Rosenthal effect

24. In choosing measurement instruments, the most important considerations are

    a. reliability and validity
    b. reliability and objectivity
    c. methodology and validity
    d. generalizability and objectivity

25. Which of the following is not an acceptable method of gathering data for survey research?

    a. personal interviews
    b. group self-administered questionnaires
    c. telephone interviews
    d. all of the above are acceptable methods

ANSWER KEY

Fill in the Blanks

(1) ratio
(2) variability
(3) mean, median, mode
(4) dependent variable
(5) nominal
(6) experimental research
(7) parsimonious
(8) parameters, statistics
(9) level of significance
(10) internal validity
(11) *t* test
(12) quantitative, qualitative
(13) ex post facto
(14) *F* test
(15) simple random sampling
(16) null hypothesis
(17) external validity
(18) nonprobability sampling
(19) research, evaluation
(20) interaction effects
(21) descriptive
(22) range
(23) correlation
(24) inferential statistics
(25) survey

Matching

(1) b
(2) e
(3) h
(4) a
(5) j
(6) i
(7) f
(8) d
(9) g
(10) c

Multiple-Choice

1.	b	10.	d	18.	c
2.	d	11.	c	19.	b
3.	a	12.	d	20.	b
4.	b	13.	a	21.	a
5.	d	14.	a	22.	c
6.	a	15.	b	23.	c
7.	c	16.	d	24.	a
8.	c	17.	a	25.	d
9.	b				

CHAPTER 8

Professional Orientation

SUMMARY	167
Professional Organizations	**167**
History and Definition	167
Goals and Objectives	168
Organizational Structure	169
Credentialing	**170**
Accreditation	170
Certification	171
Licensure	171
Professional Development Issues	**172**
Ethical Considerations	172
Legal Aspects	173
Role Identity	174
LEARNING OBJECTIVES	175
TIME LINE	176
TERMS AND NAMES TO REMEMBER	177
Terms	**177**
Names	**177**
FILL IN THE BLANKS	178
MATCHING TEST	180
CASE STUDY	181
Analysis	**181**
MULTIPLE-CHOICE TEST	184
ANSWER KEY	187
Fill in the Blanks	**187**
Matching	**187**
Multiple-Choice	**187**

SUMMARY

Professional orientation includes goals and objectives of professional organizations, codes of ethics, legal considerations, standards of preparation, certification, and licensing and role identity of counselors and other personnel services of specialists. (Loesch & Vacc, 1986 p. 14)

Professional Organizations

Only recently has counseling come to be considered a profession rather than an occupation. Since its emergence early in the twentieth century, counseling has drawn from other social sciences, such as psychology, sociology, and anthropology. Professional counseling has gradually established its own identity and now meets the criteria of a profession set forth by Wittmer and Loesch (1986), who state that a profession is "a vocational activity having (1) an underlying body of theoretical and research knowledge, (2) an identifiable set of effective skills and activities, and (3) a publicly professed voluntary self-imposed set of behavioral guidelines" (p. 301).

History and Definition

Blocher (1987) traces the history of the counseling profession according to the settings, the clientele, and the goals of counseling professionals decade by decade. From the 1900s to the 1920s, counseling took place mainly in settlement houses and schools. Guidance workers, incensed at the abuses of the Industrial Revolution, helped youth leaving school and those already working in industry to prepare for and cope with the world of work.

Pioneers. Early leaders in the guidance movement were social reformers such as Jessie B. Davis, founder of the first school guidance program; Anna Reed and Eli Weaver, pioneers in school guidance; and David Hill, who took a scientific approach to social problems. Most notable was Frank Parsons, the "father of guidance," whose revolutionary work, *Choosing a Vocation* (1909), inspired the first vocational guidance conference in 1910. This eventually led to the founding of the first professional organization in the counseling field, the National Vocational Guidance Association (NVGA) in 1913. Counselors at this time employed Parsons's trait-and-factor approach.

The 1920s. During the 1920s and 1930s, counseling and guidance expanded into colleges and employment services. In addition to youth leaving school, college graduates and other job seekers could benefit from the educational and vocational guidance of counseling professionals. In the 1930s and 1940s, the field of testing and differential psychology had a great impact upon the guidance movement (Blocher, 1987). Influenced by the Army Alpha and Beta Group Test for screening military recruits in World War I, hundreds of group tests had been developed by the mid-1920s and became a focal point of counseling over the next couple of decades. Counselors also employed child case studies, directive counseling, and group guidance/information giving (Aubrey, 1986).

The 1930s and 1940s. In 1931 the process of counseling as a psychological process was first introduced in *Workbook in Vocations* (Proctor, Benefield, & Wrenn, 1931). At that time counselors could be found not only in some high schools and colleges, but also in junior high schools, the Veterans Administration, and rehabilitation agencies. Service recipients included children, adolescents, young adults, and veterans needing vocational, educational, or rehabilitative assistance. With the aftermath of World War II in the late 1940s came a revolution in the counseling profession. Psychiatry's inability to handle the large number of veterans and civilians in need of help opened the door for counseling to grow and develop.

The 1950s. In the 1950s, spurred by the work of Carl Rogers (1942, 1951), counseling began to emerge as a profession in its own right. The approach was humanistic and individual, testing was replaced by therapy techniques and

168

BECOMING A PROFESSIONAL COUNSELOR

methods, and the range of settings where counselors worked began to expand. Counseling theory was bolstered by advances in developmental psychology, learning theory, psychiatry, and sociology. Influenced by the pioneering work of Super (1953, 1955), guidance grew into career development (Aubrey, 1986). The passage of the National Defense Education Act (NDEA) in 1958 increased the number of counselor training programs, and within a few years the number of counselors working in schools and other settings had increased dramatically.

The 1960s. Just as the 1960s were a time of unrest and turmoil for the nation, the counseling profession struggled for a unified identity. Counselors were working with a full age range of clients, not only in schools, from elementary to university, but also in family services, corrections, and alcohol and drug treatment centers. A wide range of new methodologies were introduced, and counselors began to focus on the developmental needs of "normal" individuals. However, keeping their focus on individual intrapsychic issues, counselors missed the opportunity to respond adequately to societal factors such as the Vietnam War, the civil rights and women's movements, the proliferation of drug abuse, and the growth of the counterculture (Aubrey, 1986).

The 1970s. In the 1970s, the profession took a new turn as group work emerged as the new counseling technology. Individuals began to gather in groups in order to solve common problems and issues. In addition to groups led by professional counselors, there were many self-help groups, group homes and workshops, skill groups, and educational groups. Counselors moved into a wider range of settings, including community mental health agencies, private practice, and established health care systems. As counselors focused less on individual, intrapsychic issues and more on group, environment-oriented issues, they began "giving away" skills—such as parent effectiveness, assertiveness, and communication skills—to clients.

The 1980s. Although counseling is now recognized as a full-fledged profession, in the 1980s it experienced what Hayes (1984) has called an "identity crisis." The counseling profession made tremendous gains in terms of the nature and scope of services offered, the growth of professional organizations for counselors, the institution of credentialing, and the great numbers of counselor training programs housed in colleges and universities throughout the nation. Now this profession must continue to grow and respond maturely to the challenges of the 1990s.

The future. Aubrey (1986) believes that the shift of counselors to professional protectiveness rather than "giving skills away" and their return to traditional, medical model approaches, rather than educational, preventive, and environmental interventions, can be attributed to difficult economic times. Instead of falling back on safe and familiar methods, he asserts, the counseling profession needs to respond maturely to the calling to maintain gains and develop further professional expertise. To meet this challenge, according to Lewis and Lewis (1987), practitioners must learn to serve large groups as well as individuals, to educate as well as to counsel, and to attend to the environment as well as to the troubled individual. Professional counselors who develop these skills will be better equipped to compete successfully with social workers, psychologists, and even psychiatrists.

Goals and Objectives

Counselors who wish to promote their own unique professionalism belong to professional organizations. Vacc and Loesch (1987) cite three reasons for membership in these organizations: Professional organizations provide (a) the main source of information and activity whereby counselors can improve their skills, knowledge, and performance; (b) an avenue for counselors to associate and interact with one another; and (c) the most effective means for counselors to improve their profession.

Organizations. There are a number of professional organizations counselors can join. The American Association for Counseling and Development (AACD) is the main professional organization to which national certified counselors (NCCs) belong. AACD has 15 divisions to accommodate the various professional emphases to which counselors ascribe. Other organizations to which professional counselors may belong include (a) the American

Psychological Association (APA), especially Division 17, Counseling Psychology (Ph.D.s only); (b) the Association for Marriage and Family Therapy (AAMFT); (c) the American Educational Research Association (AERA), especially Division H, Counseling and Human Development; and (d) the National Rehabilitation Counselors Association (NRCA).

Mission. Although all the above-mentioned organizations are viable options for counselors, AACD will be used as an example of goals, objectives, and organizational structure of professional associations. At its annual meeting in March 1988, the AACD governing council made its goals and objectives clear by adopting this mission statement:

The mission of AACD is to be an Association of responsible professionals which functions in the present and prepares for the future in order to enhance human development . . . [and] advance the counseling and human development profession. . . .

[Counselors can achieve the goal to] *enhance human development* by

—informing the public about human development concerns;

—cooperating with other organizations to achieve mutual objectives;

—removing barriers to human development;

—promoting social policy that enhances human development; and

—supporting legislation that enhances human development.

[Professional counselors work toward the goal to] *advance the counseling and human development profession* by

—influencing graduate education standards;

—promoting ethical and responsible professional practice;

—demanding high standards of professional conduct;

—conducting professional education programs;

—promoting research;

—publishing professional literature;

—conducting professional meetings; and

—supporting legislation that is compatible with association goals and tax status.

Organizational Structure

AACD is organized into regions, which reflect geographical locations, as well as divisions, which reflect professional emphases. Membership in one of the four regions—southern, north Atlantic, midwestern, or western—is determined by an individual's residential address. Divisional membership is a matter of personal preference. Members may join as many of the 14 divisions and 2 organizational affiliates as they desire. These include the following:

- American College Personnel Association (ACPA)
- Association for Counselor Education and Supervision (ACES)
- National Career Development Association (NCDA)
- Association for Humanistic Education and Development (AHEAD)
- American School Counselors Association (ASCA)
- American Rehabilitation Counseling Association (ARCA)
- Association for Measurement and Evaluation in Counseling and Development (AMECD)
- National Employment Counselors Association (NECA)
- Association for Multicultural Counseling and Development (AMCD)
- Association for Religious and Value Issues in Counseling (ARVIC)
- Association for Specialists in Group Work (ASGW)
- American Mental Health Counselors Association (AMHCA)
- Public Offender Counselors Association (POCA)
- Association for Adult Development and Aging (AADA)
- Military Educators and Counselors Association (MECA)
- International Family Therapy Association (IFTA)

Counselors with good professional orientations are active participants in their state branches as well as their national divisions. They also demonstrate their concern for professionalism in counseling by seeking applicable professional credentials.

Credentialing

Professional orientation is an attitude adopted by counselors toward their counseling and related professional activities, which include voluntary adherence and contribution to, as well as support of, the attainment of the goals, objectives, and behaviors considered proper by members of the counseling profession. This attitude of professionalism implies not only self-improvement and development, but also improvement of the profession through such activities as research and publication, consultation, education, and public relations. Because professional activities enhance both the competence and the public image of professional counselors, AACD advocates three of them in particular: (a) accreditation, (b) licensure, (c) certification (Wittmer & Loesch, 1986).

Accreditation

Accreditation is a process by which "an association or agency grants public recognition to a school, institute, college, university, or specialized program of study having met certain established qualifications or standards" (Pennell, Proffitt, & Hatch, 1971, p. 3). Accreditation applies to programs rather than to academic departments or individuals. Within the counseling profession several accreditation options are available. Doctoral counseling psychology programs may be accredited by the American Psychological Association. Master's-level preparation programs for school counselors may be accredited by the National Council for Accreditation of Teacher Education. Master's-level counselor preparation programs for marriage and family counseling may be accredited by the American Association for Marriage and Family Therapists. The Council on Rehabilitation Education accredits master's-level rehabil-itation counseling programs. Programs housed in state colleges and universities may also be accredited by that state's Department of Education.

In addition to these, the Council for the Accreditation of Counseling and Related Educational Programs (CACREP), an affiliate of AACD, accredits three types of entry-level programs and one doctoral-level program. The master's-level programs include (a) school counseling, (b) student development in higher education (counseling, administrative, or developmental emphasis), and (c) counseling in community and other agency settings (optional mental health counseling emphasis). The advanced-level program is counselor education.

Although CACREP will be used as an example here, it should be noted that accrediting bodies have several commonalities. Accreditation (a) is voluntary, (b) is based on standards, (c) costs money, (d) necessitates self-evaluation, (e) has geographical limits, and (f) is not reciprocal. Even though education does not guarantee competence, accreditation is based on the premise that competent professionals must have had effective training (Wittmer & Loesch, 1986). It should also be noted that accreditation is a joint process between the accrediting body and the faculty and administration of the institution seeking accreditation.

Although affiliated with AACD, CACREP is a legally separate nonprofessional corporation created to implement standards of preparation for professional counselors. The founding of CACREP in 1981 was a culmination of efforts to set standards for counselor education that was begun by ACES in the 1950s and joined by ASCA in the 1960s. Rather than institute new accreditation standards, CACREP refined and broadened these earlier processes. Today, "with a constituency representing the full range of work settings for counselors and related practitioners, as well as an individual representing the public, the council renders rigorous and objective judgment on the quality of the professional preparation" (AACD, 1986, p. 1).

Once a program has applied for accreditation, an orderly procedure must be followed. First, the program faculty conduct a self-study to determine compliance with CACREP standards. Second, the application materials and self-study are evaluated by a review committee. Third, when the program is read, a site visit is implemented by the CACREP team. Fourth, the program faculty review and respond to the site visitation team report. Fifth, the CACREP council renders one of three possible decisions: (a) full approval for a several-year period, (b) provisional approval with two years to comply to recommendations, or (c) denial of approval (AACD, 1986).

Certification

Although individual counselors interested in developing their professionalism can control the credential of accreditation only by graduating from an accredited program of study, certification is one credential that is entirely within the individual's control. When individuals meet the criteria set forth by a counselor certification agency, they are allowed to use the title "certified counselor." Even though noncertified individuals may practice as counselors, this credential carries prestige in that the credentialing agency affirms that the certified individual can do counseling effectively (Wittmer & Loesch, 1986).

Certification for specific branches of counseling has been in existence since the late 1970s, when the Commission on Rehabilitation Counselor Certification (CRCC) began certifying rehabilitation counselors and the National Academy of Certified Clinical Mental Health Counselors (NACCMHC) began to certify mental health counselors. In an effort to establish a generic counselor certification requiring basic knowledge and skills necessary for all types of professional counseling, AACD established the National Board for Certified Counselors (NBCC) in 1982.

NBCC requires both knowledge and skill components. The knowledge component is evaluated in two ways. First, general minimum academic requirements must be met. In addition to a counseling theories course, applicants must have successfully completed academic experiences in six of the eight areas covered in the NBCC exam: (a) human growth and development; (b) social and cultural foundations; (c) the helping relationship; (d) group dynamics, processes, and counseling; (e) life-style and career development; (f) appraisal of individuals; (g) research and evaluation; and (h) professional orientation (Loesch & Vacc, 1986).

The second evaluation of the knowledge component is the NBCC counselor certification examination itself. The exam consists of 25 multiple-choice questions in each of the eight core curriculum areas mentioned above. A minimum criterion score is determined for each form of the exam. Those scoring above the minimum criterion score pass the exam and receive the designation national certified counselor (NCC). Initial certification lasts five years, and renewal is contingent upon completion of a minimum of 100 hours of professional development activities.

The skill component is evaluated by examining three aspects of the applicant's previous professional experience. One requirement is documentation of a supervised internship. Another requirement is two years of post-master's degree professional counseling experience of at least 20 hours per week (waived for graduates of CACREP-accredited programs). Finally, applicants must provide letters of reference attesting to their competence as counselors (Vacc & Loesch, 1987).

Since 1985, when NBCC merged with the National Certified Career Counselors (NCCC) to form a two-tier certification structure, NCCs who wish to specialize in career counseling can attain additional academic and professional experience and then take another exam in order to be designated NCCC. The American Association for Marriage and Family Therapy (AAMFT) provides another credential, similar to certification, for professional counselors who specialize in marriage and family counseling. Upon completion of an accredited program of study and the experience prescribed by AAMFT, a counselor can be granted "clinical member" status in that organization. Most of these organizations publish a registry, or list of certified individuals, so that the public can identify those who have met the standards for certification (Vacc & Loesch, 1987).

Licensure

Another credential of interest to counselors, licensure, refers to state laws that regulate the practice of counseling. This regulation is a practice act because it limits who may practice certain types of counseling. It is also a title control process that restricts the use of the title *licensed counselor* to those who have met the state requirements. States may license three classifications of counseling professionals: (a) psychologist, (b) marriage and family therapist, and (c) licensed professional counselor or mental health counselor. At the time of this writing, 31 states were offering licensure and/or certification for professional counselors; this number is constantly changing, however.

There are some important facts to remember with respect to professional credentials for counselors:

(1) They are voluntary.
(2) Counselor licensure is governed by the individual states, whereas national certification goes with the person.
(3) They imply adherence to minimum standards of academic preparation, supervised training experience, and professional experience.
(4) Licensure and registry require residency.
(5) Few credentialing agencies require work samples, but all consider personal characteristics, require examinations, charge fees, and require continuing professional development for renewal.
(6) Reciprocity of licensure is common from state to state; however, reciprocity between licensure and certification agencies are rare (Wittmer & Loesch, 1986).

Professional Development Issues

In addition to becoming actively involved in professional organizations and obtaining professional credentials, counselors need to pay attention to those aspects of professional development that govern their relationship with clients, that is, ethical and legal standards. Ethical standards are voluntary, self-imposed behavioral guidelines established by professional organizations to protect the best interests of the profession as well as the clients. Legal standards, or laws, are state statutes that apply to the practice of counseling within the state's jurisdiction.

Ethical Considerations

The ethical standards that apply to professional counselors are established by organizations such as AACD (and some of its divisions), APA, and AAMFT, and by certification agencies, such as NBCC and NACCMHC. Vacc and Loesch (1987) define ethics as those standards that "reflect value, moral, and social judgments . . . [and] communicate to both counselors and clients the value judgments, reflected in behavioral statements, made by professional counselors about how counselors should behave and how counseling should be practiced" (p. 215). Although adherence to ethical standards is voluntary (i.e., not mandated by law), the organizations themselves can impose sanctions upon counselors found guilty of unethical practice.

Code of ethics. NCCs must adhere to the *NBCC Code of Ethics* (1982, see Appendix A), which was adapted directly from the ethical standards of AACD (1981). This code of ethics contains eight major sections:

- *Section A: General*—includes professional development; data collection; responsibility to clients, co-workers, and agencies; professional qualifications; and fees
- *Section B: Counseling Relationship*—includes protection of clients' rights; confidentiality; duty to warn; record keeping; dual relationships; conflict of interest; and case consultation for both individual and group clients (See also Appendix B, Ethical Guidelines for Group Leaders of ASGW.)
- *Section C: Measurement and Evaluation*—includes counselor responsibilities in test selection, administration, scoring, interpretation, and dissemination of results (See also Appendix C, Respondents of Users of Standardized Tests.)
- *Section D: Research and Publication*—includes protection of human subjects;

planning and conduct of research; due credit; dissemination and interpretation of results; and simultaneous publication

- *Section E: Consulting*—includes characteristics and role definition of consultant; problem and goal delineation; fees; and referral
- *Section F: Private Practice*—includes advertisement; legal responsibility, professional affiliations; and termination
- *Section G: Personnel Administration*—includes mutual goals, responsibilities, and accountability of counselors and institutions in the management and administration of counseling program activities
- *Section H: Preparation Standards*—includes ethical responsibilities specific to trainers and educators and adherence to AACD/CACREP standards of preparation

Peer Monitoring. AACD and NBCC, like most professional organizations, hold their members responsible not only for following these ethical guidelines themselves, but also for monitoring their peers. Although ignoring the unethical behavior of a colleague is considered to be an ethical violation itself, Corey, Corey, and Callahan (1988) warn professional counselors to make a commitment first to monitoring the quality of their own behavior before passing judgment on others. However, when violations by other professionals do become obvious, they should be confronted first personally, then through the institution's channels, and finally through the procedures established by the state branch, division, or association (AACD, 1981).

Legal Aspects

Besides maintaining high ethical standards, counselors are required to abide by the legal statutes of the jurisdiction in which they practice. Unfortunately, the legal aspects of counseling are not as cut and dried as might be supposed. There is no general body of law governing helping relationships. Some court decisions may relate directly to the practice of counseling, while others apply only to medical helpers such as psychiatrists. Laws are established at the state level, and decisions rendered in one jurisdiction are not binding in another. Consequently, counselors must not only be knowledgeable about their legal responsibilities, they must also be aware that at times their ethical codes may conflict with legal principles (Van Hoose & Kottler, 1985).

Malpractice. As counselors have become more influential, more numerous, and more visible to the public, they have more often been held accountable for their actions; and along with other professionals, counselors are increasingly becoming the targets of malpractice suits. Malpractice litigation requires proof of three conditions: (a) that the counselor had a duty to the client, (b) that the counselor's conduct was negligent or improper, and (c) that there was a causal relationship between the counselor's negligence and the damage to the client (Van Hoose & Kottler, 1985). Some of the more common malpractice allegations include (a) infliction of mental distress, (b) defamation of character, (c) sexual harassment, (d) battery, (e) misrepresentation of professional service (Wittmer & Loesch, 1986), (f) failure to explain possible negative consequences of treatment, (g) invasion of privacy, and (h) failure to follow procedures known to be more helpful (Hopkins & Anderson, 1986). To prevent malpractice, counselors should be careful to act within the scope of their competence, to be open and honest with clients, to know their own limitations, to seek consultation on difficult cases, and to keep informed of landmark court decisions (Corey et al., 1988).

Legal concepts. Some legal concepts that counselors need to keep in mind include the following:

(1) *Duty to warn*: This refers to the counselor's obligation to inform potential victims when a client threatens to harm others.

(2) *Informed consent*: This applies to conduct of research and includes informing subjects about the nature of the research and obtaining subjects' signatures on informed consent forms.

(3) *Record keeping*: This includes exercising caution when placing materials in clients' records and obtaining written

permission before releasing information from clients' files (Vacc & Loesch, 1987).

(4)   *Privileged communication*: This exists for counselors in only a few states. It legally protects professionals from disclosing information about clients, but, according to Corey et al. (1988), a counselor must provide information about a client when (a) the counselor is acting in a court-appointed capacity, (b) the client intends to commit suicide or some other crime, (c) the counselor is being sued by a client, (d) insanity is the client's legal defense, (e) criminal action is involved, (f) child abuse or neglect is involved, or (g) the client needs psychiatric hospitalization.

Role Identity

Role identity, like ethical and legal concerns, is another professional development issue for counselors. Blocher (1987) suggests that the basis for counselors' identity problems is that they do much more than counsel. He discusses five distinct delivery modes, or ways of providing counseling services, that define the professional role:

(1)   *One-to-one counseling*: This is the traditional help-giving model from which the counseling profession got its name. The professional offers psychological assistance to the client in a face-to-face situation, stressing problem solving, decision making and stress management in practical situations, rather than curing psychopathology.

(2)   *Group counseling*: The professional counselor offers psychological assistance in a face-to-face situation with more than one client at a time. The group simulates real-life situations, and the members provide a support system for one another.

(3)   *Consultation*: In this mode the counselor, as consultant, works with another professional, the consultee, to help a third party, the client. In this way counselors can affect a greater number of people and increase the total pool of human services resources within an organization or community.

(4)   *Training*: Counselors who engage in training, or psychological education, may be providing immediate help to individuals in need and preventing future problems at the same time. Teaching psychological principles and communication skills promotes positive personality development and growth.

(5)   *Organizational development*: In this mode the counselor facilitates improvement of an organization's environment, which, in turn, improves the organizational performance and the well-being of the members.

In summary, counselors play a variety of roles in a wide range of settings. Nevertheless, these roles do not clearly distinguish counselors from other service providers such as psychotherapists, psychologists, and social workers. Therefore, counselors must continue to develop their professional orientation and their professional identity as they act in the best interests of their clients and continually seek to improve themselves. As Wittmer and Loesch (1986) so aptly point out, "When counselors do behave as professionals, the benefits are both personal and societal" (p. 328).

LEARNING OBJECTIVES

After studying the material in this chapter, you should be able to do the following:

(1) Define counseling as a profession.

(2) Discuss the history of the counseling profession.

(3) Understand the goals and objectives of professional organizations for counselors, especially AACD.

(4) Explain the organizational structure of AACD, including its divisions and their purposes.

(5) Define and discuss credentials for counselors, including accreditation, certification, and licensure.

(6) Be aware of professional development issues.

(7) Discuss the concept of professional orientation.

(8) Understand the AACD and NBCC codes of ethics and be able to apply them to real-life situations.

(9) Be able to explain and apply legal concepts that apply to the counseling profession.

(10) Discuss the five delivery modes that make up the role identity of a professional counselor.

TIME LINE

You should be aware of important developments in the evolution of professional orientation for counselors.

1909	beginning of vocational guidance	1973	ARVIC and ASGW join APGA
1910	first vocational guidance conference	1974	Family Educational Rights and Privacy Act (Buckley Amendment)
1913	NVGA formed		
1915	*Vocational Guidance Journal*	1975	Title IX of Education Amendment Act
1931	*Workbook in Vocations* defines counseling process	1977	U.S. Department of Health, Education and Welfare defines licensure
1942	client-centered counseling	1977	ACES Guidelines for Doctoral Preparation
1950	ACES, standards for graduate programs in counseling		
		1978	AMHCA joins APGA
1952	APGA formed (merger of NVGA, ACES, ACPA, AHEAD)	1979	ACES standards for entry- and advanced-level preparation
1953	ASCA joins APGA	1981	CACREP established by APGA
1958	NDEA	1982	NBCC established by APGA
1965	AMECD joins APGA	1983	APGA becomes AACD
1966	NECA joins APGA	1985	NCCC merges with NBCC
1967	ASCA, standards for secondary school counselors	1986	AADA and MECA join AACD
		1988	International Family Therapy joins AACD
1970s	CRCC and NACCMHC certification		
1971	ACES, Commission on Standards and Accreditation	1989	AACD approves Standards for Supervision
1972	AMCD joins APGA	1990	_____

TERMS AND NAMES
TO REMEMBER

Terms

You should have an understanding of the following terms and be able to define them in your own words.

accreditation
assertiveness
certification
clinical member
confidentiality
conflict of interest
credentialing
defamation of character
dual relationships
duty to warn
entry-level program
ethics
guidance
legal standards
licensure

malpractice
negligence
privileged communication
professional association
professional orientation
provisional approval
reciprocity
regions
registry
self-help groups
self-study
site visit
skill groups
standards of preparation
workshops

Names

You should be familiar with the names of these organizations and be aware of the purposes they serve.

American Association for Marriage and
  Family Therapy
American College Personnel Association
American Mental Health Counselors
  Association
American Rehabilitation Counseling
  Association
American School Counselors Association
Association for Adult Development and Aging
Association for Counselor Education and
  Supervision
Association for Humanistic Education and
  Development
Association for Measurement and Evaluation
  in Counseling and Development
Association for Multicultural Counseling and
  Development

Association for Religious and Value Issues in
  Counseling
Association for Specialists in Group Work
Commission on Rehabilitation Counselor
  Certification
Council for Accreditation of Counseling and
  Related Educational Programs
Military Educators and Counselors
  Association
National Academy of Certified Clinical
  Mental Health Counselors
National Career Development Association
National Employment Counselors
  Association
Public Offender Counselors Association

FILL IN THE BLANKS

The following section reviews some of the major points in this content area. Check your knowledge of the area by filling in the appropriate name, term, or concept in each blank provided. Answer choices are found above, in the section containing terms and names to remember. You will find the correct answers at the end of the chapter.

(1) To be convicted of _____ a counselor's conduct must have been negligent or improper.

(2) If a particular counseling program has not quite met all of the CACREP's standards, it may be given _____ for two years.

(3) Early Counselors were _____ workers.

(4) Counselors who meet the educational and experiential requirements may become _____ of AAMFT.

(5) Many professional credentialing agencies publish a _____ _____ that lists all their certified members.

(6) Counselors who are devoted to self-improvement as well as improvement of the counseling profession are said to have good _____ _____ .

(7) Although professional _____ are not legally binding, they are enforced by professional organizations.

(8) Before conducting research with human subjects, professional counselors should obtain _____ .

(9) In most jurisdictions _____ is a legal standard that does not apply to counselors.

(10) Counseling programs that wish to be accredited by CACREP must first conduct a _____ to determine compliance with CACREP standards.

(11) Counselors working in agency settings may be required to seek _____ _____ certification.

(12) The professional credential _____ goes with the program of study, while _____ and _____ go with the person.

(13) When a counselor hears in a counseling session that a client threatens to harm another person, the counselor's _____ _____ must be exercised.

(14) _____ are for counseling students seeking a master's or specialist degree.

(15) A counselor does not violate _____ by consulting with another professional about a difficult case as long as the identity of the client is not revealed.

(16) Counselors' geographical locations determine to which _____ _____ of AACD they belong.

(17) During the 1970s _____ became a popular way for people to solve common problems without professional help.

(18) After evaluating a counseling program's application materials, a _____ is conducted by the CACREP team.

(19) Licensure is a professional _____ regulated by individual states.

(20) Counselors are guilty of _____ when they date or have other nonprofessional involvements with clients.

(21) In addition to _____'s general counselor certification, counselors who specialize in working with disabled persons may seek certification from _____.

(22) Counselors can "give their skills away" in _____ _____ training groups and other types of _____.

(23) In the 1970s _____ were established to provide a means to teach disabled clients employment skills and enable them to earn money.

(24) A counselor who slanders a client may be accused of _____ _____.

(25) In addition to face-to-face counseling, the _____ _____ of a professional counselor may include consultation, training, and organizational development.

MATCHING TEST

Match the acronyms of the professional association in the left-hand column with the populations they serve in the right-hand column.

___	(1) ACPA	(a) test takers
___	(2) ACES	(b) minorities
___	(3) ASCA	(c) members of the armed services
___	(4) ARCA	(d) college students
___	(5) AMECD	(e) counselees with spiritual issues
___	(6) NECA and NCDA	(f) counseling students
___	(7) AMCD	(g) school children
___	(8) ARVIC	(h) people on probation or parole
___	(9) ASGW	(i) people with disabilities
___	(10) AMHCA	(j) workers, businesses, and industry
___	(11) POCA	(k) agency clients
___	(12) AADA	(l) adults through the life span
___	(13) MECA	(m) counseling group members

CASE STUDY

You are a second-semester male intern in a university counseling center. You have been seeing Lucy, a graduate student in health education, for one and a half semesters. Lucy's presenting problems were loneliness and depression. Before beginning graduate school, she had attended a four-year commuter college in her hometown, where she lived a very stable, though protective, home life with her parents and two younger brothers. She was an excellent student, always on the dean's list, and had a group of friends with whom she had attended junior high, high school, and college.

Lucy's move to graduate school at the large state university where you are interning is her first attempt at independence from her parents. She was having difficulty adjusting, feeling lost and alone, and unsure about how to make social contacts. By her second semester she has gotten involved in some departmental activities and has made a few friends. She has been hired as a graduate assistant to teach a health issues class for student athletes. Because of her connection with the athletic department, Lucy is often able to obtain choice tickets for university sporting events. Lucy is not a sports fan, so she has given tickets to you on several occasions.

This time Lucy has tickets for the gymnastics finals. She tells you that she does enjoy gymnastics and would like to attend the meet with you. She tells you that you have been so helpful to her in coming "out of her shell" that she hardly ever feels lonely and depressed any more. She likes the social nature of her sessions with you and would like to get to know you better on a more personal basis.

Analysis

(1) Is it ethical for you to accept tickets from your client? Why or why not?

_____

_____

_____

_____

_____

(2) Does it make a difference whether you asked for the tickets or not? Discuss.

_____

_____

_____

_____

_____

(3)   Given the recent social nature of the sessions, should you suggest termination of counseling for Lucy?

_____

_____

_____

_____

_____

(4)   What are the ethical ramifications if you decide to attend the gymnastics meet with Lucy?

_____

_____

_____

_____

_____

(5)   If you do attend, what effect do you think this social relationship would have on the therapeutic process with this client?

_____

_____

_____

_____

_____

(6)   Do you see any potential for malpractice in this case? If so, discuss.

_____

_____

_____

_____

_____

Notes

_____

_____

_____

_____

_____

_____

_____

_____

_____

_____

_____

_____

_____

_____

_____

_____

_____

_____

_____

_____

MULTIPLE-CHOICE TEST

Check your understanding of this content area by responding to the following questions. You will find the answer key at the end of the chapter.

1. In the course of her intake session with an NCC, a client reveals that she has been seeing a psychiatrist in the area for the past year. The *NBCC Code of Ethics* requires the counselor to

   a. contact and receive the approval of the psychiatrist before entering into a counseling relationship with this client
   b. do cotherapy with the psychiatrist
   c. work with the client on different issues from those the psychiatrist does
   d. reassure the client that confidentiality will not allow you to reveal this information to anyone

2. The main function of early counselors was

   a. important change
   b. marriage and family therapy
   c. vocational guidance
   d. skill training groups

3. A counselor is not bound by confidentiality when

   a. the client signs an informed consent form
   b. the client is taking medication
   c. the client's mental condition is unstable
   d. the client's condition indicates danger to self or others

4. Who retains responsibility for ethical research practice conducted in a mental health agency?

   a. the supervisor of the unit
   b. the client's individual counselors
   c. the human subjects committee
   d. the principal investigator

5. You are conducting a community education class for the mental health center for which you work. One of the participants approaches you during the break to inquire about individual counseling with you. Since you do have a small private practice, you

   a. make an appointment to see the client the next day
   b. tell the client to call your agency's intake department to schedule an appointment
   c. make an appointment to see the client after the community education class has ended
   d. tell your client to call your private office the next evening to schedule an appointment

6. According to the *AACD Code of Ethics*, counseling programs

   a. must present a variety of theoretical orientations so students can choose
   b. must include active listening skills
   c. should maintain an equal number of male and female students
   d. should call in experts to teach the theories presented to students

7. When it becomes obvious that a client's wishes are in direct conflict with your own value system, as an ethical counselor, you should

   a. convince the client that your way of thinking is in his or her best interest
   b. explain your difficulty to the client and promise to try not to let it interfere with the counseling process
   c. explain your difficulty to the client and refer him or her to another counselor
   d. not reveal your views to the client

8. Group leaders are responsible for providing information about group work and group services to clients. Which of the following is not one of those responsibilities?

    a. protect members by defining confidentiality, its importance, and the difficulty of enforcement

    b. keep experimental activities secret so the group will not be inhibited

    c. inform members that participation is voluntary and they may leave the group at any time

    d. explain the goals and purpose of the group to each member ahead of time

9. Which of the following is not covered by the code of ethics regarding personnel administration?

    a. members must select staff members with the same theoretical orientation

    b. members must provide in-service professional development for staff

    c. members must submit to professional review and evaluation

    d. members must establish a working relationship with supervisors and subordinates

10. In your internship at a community mental health center you are counseling a severely disturbed woman with suicidal ideation. You are not only overwhelmed, but also concerned about professional liability. The best course of action for you to take would be to

    a. see the client on a daily basis until she becomes more stable

    b. terminate the relationship immediately

    c. refer the client to a more experienced, crisis-oriented counselor

    d. be sure to document all sessions, paying special attention to confidentiality

11. The preparation standards of AACD

    a. give the requirements for passing the counselor certification exam

    b. delineate the responsibilities of counselor training programs

    c. offer guidelines for initial sessions with clients

    d. list the minimum qualifications for acceptance into a counselor education program

12. Which of the following is not of concern to a counselor submitting a research article for publication in a professional journal?

    a. make original research data available to qualified others for replication

    b. report unfavorable as well as favorable results

    c. consult the *Publication Manual of the American Psychological Association* for style

    d. all of the above are legitimate concerns

13. Licensure is a "practice control" act because it

    a. requires counselors to have a certain amount of practice, or experience, before obtaining it

    b. applies only to counselors in private practice

    c. permits counselors to do a certain type of counseling in a given state

    d. limits the number of hours counseling agencies may operate

14. Fees paid to counselors by insurance companies are known as

    a. third-party payments

    b. premiums

    c. sliding-scale fees

    d. reimbursements

15. Counseling has recently come to be considered a profession. Which of the following is not a necessary component of a profession?

    a. an underlying body of theoretical knowledge

    b. standards for licensure and certification

    c. an identifiable set of skills and activities

    d. a publicly professed code of ethics

16. One of Super's contributions to the counseling field was

    a. his psychodynamic model
    b. the work *Choosing a Vocation*
    c. changing guidance into career development
    d. his *Handbook on Vocations*

17. In the 1960s, counselors focused their attention on

    a. working with individuals
    b. social issues
    c. test administration
    d. mental health centers

18. Which of the following is not part of the role identity of a modern-day counselor?

    a. training and development specialist
    b. expert advice-giver
    c. organizational consultant
    d. individual and group therapist

19. The term *psychological education* refers to

    a. Psychology 101 and 102
    b. graduate school training in psychological principles
    c. insights gained through individual sessions with a psychologist
    d. teaching personal and interpersonal skills to promote the growth of individuals

20. Which of these is not a necessary condition for malpractice litigation?

    a. the counselor had a duty to the client
    b. the counselor behaved improperly or negligently
    c. the counselor's negligence caused damage to the client
    d. all of these are necessary conditions

21. In a large public agency the responsibility for maintaining ethical standards among the professional staff lies with

    a. front-office administration
    b. the individual supervisors throughout the agency
    c. the professional staff itself
    d. the state administrators

22. Which of the following is true of both legal and ethical standards for professional counselors?

    a. they are behavioral guidelines
    b. they are state regulated
    c. they govern the counselor-client relationship
    d. a and c are correct

23. Which of the following are eligible for state licensure as counselors?

    a. only mental health counselors
    b. psychologists, marriage and family therapists, and mental health counselors
    c. psychologists, mental health counselors, and psychiatric social workers
    d. marriage and family therapists, mental health counselors, and social workers

24. Membership in the divisions of AACD

    a. is by member choice
    b. is determined by the member's geographical location
    c. depends upon the member's academic degree specialization area
    d. is limited by the state

25. Which event had the greatest impact on the growth of the counseling profession?

    a. the passage of NDEA
    b. the change from APGA to AACD
    c. the founding of NVGA
    d. the passage of P.L. 94-142

ANSWER KEY

Fill in the Blanks

(1) malpractice
(2) provisional approval
(3) guidance
(4) clinical members
(5) registry
(6) professional orientation
(7) ethics
(8) informed consent
(9) privileged communication
(10) self-study
(11) NACCMHC
(12) accreditation, certification, licensure
(13) duty to warn
(14) entry-level programs
(15) confidentiality
(16) region
(17) self-help groups
(18) site visit
(19) credential
(20) dual relationships
(21) NBCC Commission on Rehabilitation Counselor Certification
(22) assertiveness, skill groups
(23) workshops
(24) defamation of character
(25) role identity

Matching

(1) d
(2) f
(3) g
(4) i
(5) a
(6) j
(7) b
(8) e
(9) m
(10) k
(11) h
(12) l
(13) c

Multiple-Choice

1. a	10. c	18. b
2. c	11. b	19. d
3. d	12. d	20. d
4. d	13. c	21. c
5. b	14. a	22. d
6. a	15. b	23. b
7. c	16. c	24. a
8. b	17. a	25. a
9. a		

Study Tips

Whether you are using this manual to prepare for a counselor certification examination or to get ready to take your doctoral comprehensive exams, some general guidelines for study may help you to use your preparation time more effectively.

GENERAL GUIDELINES

If you are to be successful in reaching your goal—that is, passing a major exam—you must first make it the number one priority in your life. Once this commitment has been made, set up a study schedule for yourself. It is unrealistic to assume you can cram all your studying into the week or the weekend preceding the exam. Plan to spend a couple of hours a day for six to eight weeks prior to the examination date. This will allow you to make a comprehensive review of the material rather than a panic-stricken attempt to cram it all in at the last minute.

Time Management

Time is life. It is irreversible and irreplaceable. To waste your time is to waste your life, but to master your time is to master your life and make the most of it. (Lakein, 1973, p. 11)

Once you have decided to make preparation for the exam your top priority, block out a time every day to spend studying. If you choose an eight-week schedule, you can devote one week to each content area, approximately 10 hours if you take weekends off. When possible, choose your most productive time of day. For example, if you are a "morning person," plan your study time early in the day. This may involve re-arranging your daily schedule to revolve around your study time, but remember that it is only temporary, and the rewards will be substantial.

As you begin to study each content area, gather the materials you will need. In addition to the chapter of this book related to each area, you may have course notes, textbooks, and so on that you will want to have available. Although some of the content areas represent material taught in several courses, we have attempted to review each area comprehensively through the summaries and various study exercises. However, there may be an answer you do not understand or that you disagree

with, or a particular topic in which you think you are deficient. Having additional resources at your fingertips will save time and frustration.

Lakein, in his best-seller *How to Get Control of Your Time and Your Life* (1973), suggests a number of techniques that you may find helpful.

Work smarter, not harder. Make effective use of your time by taking a few minutes each day to plan and organize. Break the task down into small steps. These chapters lend themselves to this: (a) Read the summary; (b) study the time line; (c) look up terms in the glossary; (d) complete the matching test, and so on. If you are having trouble getting started, choose one task that can be accomplished in about five minutes and start with that. Promise yourself a short break or a small reward after accomplishing the five-minute task. This may well be enough to get you going in the study session.

Be prepared to use time that is usually wasted. Carry study materials with you at all times. The perforated pages of this book are easily torn out and folded to fit into a purse or pocket. When there is an unexpected delay such as a traffic jam or you must wait for an appointment or meeting, use the time to review your study materials instead of pacing or complaining.

Stress the benefits. When motivation to study becomes a problem, it might help to consider two types of benefits to be expected: (a) pluses that will start when you have completed your studying and passed the exam, and (b) minuses that will stop once you have passed. In the plus category you might include self-satisfaction, better job opportunities, advancing in your program of study, and pay increase, among others. Minuses that will stop might include worrying about whether or not you will pass, being stymied in your program of study or your job, and self-doubt. Make a list of the benefits and keep it in view in your study area.

Avoid procrastination. Before you actually begin an organized program of study, or once you have been involved in it for a week or two, you may find myriad reasons for not following your plan. When this happens, you need to figure out what escape routes you are using and close them off temporarily. You can also give yourself a pep talk, stressing the benefits. If you find you are never "in the mood" during your designated study time, you may need to revise your schedule to take advantage of times when you are more open to studying. Sometimes it helps to make a commitment to another person. Joining a study group or finding a partner with whom to study once a week may force you to stick to your resolve to master one area per week.

The Wellness Approach

Wellness is a way of life—a lifestyle you design to achieve your highest potential for well-being. (Travis & Ryan, 1988, p. xiv)

The wellness model stresses self-responsibility and self-appreciation. It is a holistic approach that involves taking care of not only your physical self, but also your mental, emotional, social, and spiritual aspects. Focusing on one to the exclusion of others leads to imbalance and, eventually, illness.

Holistic approach. When trying to achieve your highest potential academically/mentally, don't forget to take care of the rest of your needs. Students preparing for major exams often overexert themselves mentally while neglecting other important areas of their lives. The result may be ineffective studying, information overload, and poor performance.

Physical illness at the time of, or shortly after, an exam is not uncommon.

Instead, take a holistic approach to your exam preparation. You may decrease your sleep in order to create more time for studying, so be sure your sleep time is restful and undisturbed. Use sleep time to process information and motivate yourself, either by suggesting thoughts to yourself before falling asleep or listening to a tape. One of the authors used a self-hypnosis tape with suggestions related to study motivation and successful passage of comprehensive exams with great results.

Stress management. Studying for exams is very stressful, so consider some stress management techniques. Be sure to engage in aerobic exercise regularly. This not only keeps you in shape, it increases energy and promotes feelings of well-being. Control your diet by eliminating or reducing caffeine, alcohol, sodium, and sugar. These substances, especially when taken in excess, may contribute to illness, lack of energy, and mood swings.

Use some form of relaxation every day. This may be self-hypnosis, meditation, yoga, listening to music, reading, or any other activity that gives you a feeling of relaxation and well-being. Although you may have to curtail some social activities temporarily, a well-planned study schedule should allow some time for fun and social interaction. To ease your frazzled nerves, pay special attention to your emotional needs during times of intense study. Spiritual outlets can help you keep things in perspective as you appeal to a higher power either within or outside yourself.

NATIONAL COUNSELOR EXAM

The National Board for Certified Counselors, an affiliate of the American Association for Counseling and Development (AACD), was incorporated in 1982. The purposes of NBCC are to establish and monitor a national certification process for professional counselors. NBCC maintains a registry of those counselors who have met its standards in training, experience, and performance on the National Counselor Examination (NCE), and it makes this list available to the public. Although certification is a voluntary process, no fewer than 16 states use NCE scores as a criterion for licensure of professional counselors.

Purpose of Certification

According to the 1990 NCE application packet, there are four purposes for counselor certification: (a) to promote professional accountability and visibility, (b) to identify to their peers and also to the public those counselors who have met NBCC standards, (c) to advance cooperation among those organizations involved in professional credentialing activities, and (d) to encourage national certified counselors (NCCs) to continue their professional growth and development.

Testing Procedure

The NCE is offered twice per year (spring and fall) at a number of sites throughout the country, with at least one site in each state. The test consists of 200 multiple-choice items that must be completed within four hours. Each of the eight sections consists of 25 items, 20 that are scored and 5 that are being tested for addition to the item pool. Scores are reported as the number of correct responses (out of 20) for each section of the exam, and as totals. If your total score meets or exceeds the minimum criterion for that form of the exam, you become an NCC.

Test Format

The NCE is a multiple-choice test similar to the practice tests in this book. NBCC does not release information regarding test items, nor does it make old forms of the NCE available. Therefore, the items in this volume have not been prepared by NBCC, but are similar to those practice items that are included in the NCE application packet.

Because of the multiple-choice format, it is imperative that you read each question carefully. Often one particular word or emphasis may change the meaning of the question. Mark the best answer for each question. If you are unsure, try to eliminate choices that are obviously wrong and then pick the one that seems most correct. You will not be penalized for guessing, so be sure to choose an answer for every question. If time allows, go back over your answers. Use caution in changing answers, because often your first inclination is correct.

COMPREHENSIVE EXAMS

If your doctoral program is accredited by the Council for the Accreditation of Counseling and Related Educational Programs (CACREP), your course of study should correspond closely to the content areas of the NBCC exam. Although individual departments are free to determine the nature of their comprehensive exams, most likely the format will be essay rather than multiple-choice. Nevertheless, the study materials in this volume should prove helpful as a review of the core areas.

Depending upon the information given by your department, you may need to modify the study plan suggested here, but the basic elements should remain the same. Given the intensity of preparation for qualifying exams, the formation of study/support groups is highly recommended. This book can serve as an organizational guide for the study group. Individuals in the group can work through one chapter of this study guide each week and then meet to process and discuss the information. The case studies may be especially useful in helping students to conceptualize and apply general ideas. Group members can also make up sample essay questions for each other to answer and quiz each other on pertinent references.

Whether you aim to become a national certified counselor or to be accepted as a candidate for the Ph.D. in a counseling or related educational program, you will find this book a useful organizational tool and guide for your studies. Good luck!

Glossary

abnormal behavior: maladaptive behavior that interferes with optimal functioning and growth of the individual and, ultimately, the society.

abuse: mistreatment of one human being by another, as in child abuse or spouse abuse, or misuse of a substance, as in alcohol or drug abuse.

accreditation: a professional credential applicable to programs deemed to have met certain established qualifications or standards.

achievement test: an appraisal instrument designed to measure formal (i.e., school) learning.

ageism: discrimination or negative attitude toward persons based upon the fact that they are elderly.

androgyny: characteristic of a human being incorporating both masculine and feminine attributes in one personality.

aptitude battery: a set of appraisals designed to predict achievement prior to instruction or selection.

attending: a particular type of behavior displayed by a counselor toward a client that includes appropriate eye contact, body and verbal language, following free from value judgments and distractions.

attitude test: an appraisal instrument that measures the tendency to respond favorably or unfavorably toward specific groups, institutions, or objects.

behavioral view: a theory of helping that focuses on observable and measurable behaviors and precise goals set by the clients, sees clients as products of their environments, and seeks to change environmental contingencies in order to change client behavior.

career guidance: a type of vocational education that normally occurs in school settings and consists of an organized program to promote self-understanding, understanding of work and society changes, leisure awareness, and avenues for self-fulfillment.

career counseling: a type of individual, adult counseling that focuses on career development needs by promoting the self-discovery and decision-making skills needed to make effective career and lifestyle choices.

career development: a life-span process that involves searching for the psychological meaning of vocationally relevant acts, and of work itself.

certification: a title control process by which an agency grants recognition to an individual who has fulfilled the standards of the agency, thereby earning the right to use the title "certified."

classical conditioning: a model of learning that involves the conditioning of new stimuli to existing responses.

client-centered: a theory of helping that emphasizes the process of being, rather than the outcome, with the counselor facilitating in the process of helping clients find their own direction.

194   BECOMING A PROFESSIONAL COUNSELOR

cognitive therapy: a theory of helping that assists clients in identifying automatic, illogical, and irrational thoughts and generating more adaptive alternative thoughts that lead to more satisfying behaviors.

cohesiveness: an aspect of group dynamics that refers to the attractiveness of the counseling group for its members.

confidentiality: the ethical responsibility of the counselor to safeguard clients from unauthorized disclosure of information about themselves.

consultation: a helping relationship involving collaboration between two professionals, the consultant and the consultee, focusing on issues that cause human problems in the consultee's workplace.

counselor: a helper who is trained to work with normal populations to prevent problems or to remedy them at their early stages, taking a developmental, educational approach in order to assist clients in achieving more effective personal, social, educational, and career development and adjustment.

culture: a way of life of a people; the sum total of their beliefs about and procedures for coping with their environment. Cross-cultural counseling takes into account cultural, social class, racial, and ethnic differences between counselor and client.

data, people, and things: part of the classification system in the DOT based on interest requirements. Jobs are classified on a continuum from low to high interest in ideas and information (data), interpersonal relations (people), and physical objects (things).

disabled: physically, mentally, or emotionally handicapped.

discrimination: the act of treating people differently because of their age, sex, race, or culture.

DOT: *Dictionary of Occupational Titles,* a publication of the U.S. Department of Labor that contains an alphabetically arranged list of occupational titles and their descriptions.

empathy: a counselor skill that involves reflecting the client's feelings in such a way as to demonstrate understanding of the client by the counselor.

ethics: a set of standards of right or wrong that have been established by a profession.

evaluation: a judgment of the worth or value of a particular process, technique, or program.

experimental design: the conceptual framework within which a research project is conducted; a research plan that serves to establish the conditions for the comparisons required by the hypotheses of the experiment and to enable the experimenter, through statistical analysis of the data, to make a meaningful interpretation of the results of the study.

external validity: the generalizability or representativeness of the findings of a research project; that is, the extent to which the results of an experiment can be generalized to different subjects, settings, and measuring instruments.

feedback: the verbalization of an individual's perceptions and reactions to another's verbal or nonverbal behavior.

genuineness: a counselor response that demonstrates the ability to be real or honest with clients; counselor verbalizations are congruent with inner feelings.

group dynamics: the area of social psychology that focuses on advancing knowledge about the nature of group life; social forces and interplay operative within the group at any time.

group process: the study of how groups work; the continuous, ongoing movement of the group toward the achievement of its goals.

group roles: members' functions within the group; task and maintenance roles help the group move toward goals, while personal/individual roles detract from the group when self-orientation is at odds with the group.

informed consent: an ethical standard that requires group leaders to identify clearly for the members the nature and goals of the group and the responsibilities and rights of the members.

intelligence test: an appraisal instrument designed to measure IQ.

interest inventory: a series of items having no correct answers, designed to indicate preference for one activity over another.

internal validity: criteria for evaluating the soundness of causal relationships in a research study, that is, for determining whether or not the independent variable made a difference.

intervention: a facilitative response by the counselor to the client.

learning theory: explanation of human development that focuses on perception, learning, and cognition; includes classical, operant, and vicarious conditioning.

licensure: the process by which an agency of government grants permission to an individual to engage in a given occupation upon finding that the applicant has attained the minimal degree of competence necessary to ensure that the public health, safety, and welfare will be reasonably well protected.

life-career rainbow: a career development tool that depicts the life span in terms of six life roles and five life stages.

life-style: an individual's total way of being in the world, including aspects of work, home/family, and leisure life.

malpractice: the failure to render proper service, through ignorance or negligence, resulting in injury or loss to the client; departing from usual practice or not exercising due care.

maturation: the process of growth and development.

mean: a measure of central tendency sometimes referred to as the arithmetic average; found by summing all values and dividing by the number of cases.

median: the midpoint in a series of measurements after all values have been placed in sequence.

norms: in group counseling, standard rules of conduct in the group, formal or informal, visible or invisible, spoken or unspoken; in appraisal, the distribution of scores obtained from a standardized group (i.e., representatives of specified populations).

OOH: *Occupational Outlook Handbook,* a resource guide published by the U.S. Department of Labor that contains career information for use in guidance.

operant conditioning: a type of learning in which the individual actively operates or acts on the environment in order to achieve some goal.

prejudice: an irrational attitude or behavior directed against an individual or a group, or their supposed characteristics.

prevention: counselor activities aimed at reducing the incidence and severity of problems. Primary prevention, aimed at total populations, promotes the development of healthy behaviors through information and education. Secondary prevention, or early intervention, is aimed at high-risk groups or persons in the early stages of a problem, and focuses on reducing the duration and/or intensity of the disorder. Tertiary prevention (rehabilitation or treatment) is designed to facilitate a full, effective return to the highest possible level of functioning.

privileged communication: a legal concept that means clients are protected by state law from having their confidences revealed in a court of law without their permission. Note: Laws differ by state and do not apply equally to all helping professionals.

professional orientation: attitude adopted by professional counselors toward their counseling and related professional activities that includes voluntarily adhering to, supporting, and contributing to the achievement and improvement of the goals, objectives, and behaviors deemed

196   BECOMING A PROFESSIONAL COUNSELOR

appropriate by the members of the profession.

qualitative data: measurement based upon ordinal scales (unequal differences between successive categories of the trait being measured) or nominal scales (derived from mutually exclusive categories without regard to order).

quantitative data: measurement based upon ratio scales that have equal intervals and an absolute zero.

reflection: a counselor response that restates the client's statement, communicating its content and affect with accuracy and equal intensity.

registry: a publicly distributed list of names of persons who have met some identified set of minimum qualifications.

reinforcement: the consequence of a behavior that increases the likelihood of the behavior reoccurring; in positive reinforcement, stimuli are presented; in negative reinforcement, stimuli are removed.

reliability: the extent to which individual differences are measured consistently as determined by coefficients of stability, equivalence, and internal consistency or homogeneity.

research: organized scientific efforts that seek the advancement of knowledge.

respect: a counselor response that demonstrates to clients that the counselor has faith in their ability to solve their own problems.

roles: functions assumed by individuals based on their place in a family (family roles), their longevity (age roles), or their gender (sex roles). Too many different functions cause role conflict and role strain; successful balance of roles leads to role integration.

sampling: selecting a representative portion of a population to participate in a research study.

self-actualization: the inherent tendency of the organism to develop all its capacities in ways that serve to maintain or enhance the organism.

sexism: discrimination against persons because of their gender.

stages: periods of growth, exploration, establishment, maintenance, and decline in development and their relationship to chronological age.

Standards of Counselor Preparation: a set of guidelines established by ACES to which counselor training programs must adhere in order to be accredited by CACREP.

statistics: a science concerned with the presentation, analysis, and interpretation of data obtained from samples of observations.

stereotyping: making a judgment about a person or group based upon a preconceived notion rather than fact.

trait theory: a way of classifying individuals according to a series of personality constructs, or traits, that can be used to predict behavior under given circumstances.

trait-and-factor theory: a matching approach to career development that assumes that success in a chosen field may be achieved by matching an individual's personal characteristics with the characteristics required for a particular occupation.

unconditional positive regard: a counselor's nonpossessive caring or acceptance of the individuality of each client.

validity: the extent to which measurements or items correspond with criteria.

variable: an attribute that is regarded as reflecting or expressing some concept or construct and that takes on different values. Dependent variables are those that are consequences of antecedent variables and that are the object of research studies; independent variables are antecedent variables that are manipulated in research studies to determine their effect on the dependent variables.

vicarious conditioning: learning that takes place through observation of the behavior of others (i.e., models).

APPENDIX A

NBCC Code of Ethics

NATIONAL BOARD FOR CERTIFIED COUN-
SELORS CODE OF ETHICS
Approved on July 1, 1982
Amended on February 21, 1987

PREAMBLE

The National Board for Certified Counselors (NBCC) is an educational, scientific, and professional organization dedicated to the enhancement of the worth, dignity, potential, and uniqueness of each individual and, thus, to the service of society. This code of ethics enables the NBCC to clarify the nature of ethical responsibilities for present and future certified counselors.

Section A: General

1. Certified counselors influence the development of the profession by continuous efforts to improve professional practices, services, and research. Professional growth is continuous throughout the certified counselor's career and is exemplified by the development of a philosophy that explains why and how a certified counselor functions in the helping relationship. Certified counselors must gather data on their effectiveness and be guided by their findings.

2. Certified counselors have a responsibility to the clients they are serving and to the institutions within which the services are being performed. Certified counselors also strive to assist the respective agency, organization, or institution in providing the highest caliber of professional services. The acceptance of employment in an institution implies that the certified counselor is in agreement with the general policies and principles of the institution. Therefore, the professional activities of the certified counselor are in accord with the objectives of the institution. If, despite concerted efforts, the certified counselor cannot reach agreement with the employer as to acceptable standards of conduct that allow for changes in institutional policy that are conducive to the positive growth and development of clients, then terminating the affiliation should be seriously considered.

3. Ethical behavior among professional associates (i.e., both certified and non-certified

counselors) must be expected at all times. When accessible information raises doubt as to the ethical behavior of professional colleagues, whether certified counselors or not, the certified counselor must take action to attempt to rectify this condition. Such action uses the respective institution's channels first and then uses procedures established by the NBCC.

4. Certified counselors neither claim nor imply professional qualifications which exceed those possessed, and are responsible for correcting any misrepresentations of these qualifications by others.

5. Certified counselors must refuse a private fee or other remuneration for consultation or counseling with persons who are entitled to these services through the certified counselor's employing institution or agency. The policies of some agencies may make explicit provisions for staff members to engage in private practice with agency clients. However, should agency clients desire private counseling or consulting service, they must be apprised of other options available to them. Certified counselors must not divert to their private practices, legitimate clients in their primary agencies or of the institutes with which they are affiliated.

6. In establishing fees for professional counseling services, certified counselors must consider the financial status of clients and the respective locality. In the event that the established fee status is inappropriate for a client, assistance must be provided in finding comparable services of acceptable cost.

7. Certified counselors seek only those positions in the delivery of professional services for which they are professionally qualified.

8. Certified counselors recognize their limitations and provide services or only use techniques for which they are qualified by training and/or experience. Certified counselors recognize the need, and seek continuing education, to assure competent services.

9. Certified counselors are aware of the intimacy in the counseling relationship, maintain respect for the client, and avoid engaging in activities that seek to meet their personal needs at the expense of the client.

10. Certified counselors do not condone or engage in sexual harassment which is defined as deliberate or repeated comments, gestures, or physical contacts of a sexual nature.

11. Certified counselors avoid bringing their personal or professional issues into the counseling relationship. Through as awareness of the impact of stereotyping and discrimination (i.e., biases based on age, disability, ethnicity, gender, race, religion, or sexual preference), certified counselors guard the individual rights and personal dignity of the client in the counseling relationship.

12. Certified counselors are accountable at all times for their behavior. They must be aware that all actions and behaviors of the counselor reflect on professional integrity and, when inappropriate, can damage the public trust in the counseling profession. To protect public confidence in the counseling profession, certified counselors avoid public behavior that is clearly in violation of accepted moral and legal standards.

13. Certified counselors have a social responsibility because their recommendations and professional actions may alter the lives of others. Certified counselors remain fully cognizant of their impact and are alert to personal, social, organizational, financial, or political situations or pressures which might lead to misuse of their influence.

14. Products or services provided by certified counselors by means of classroom instruction, public lectures, demonstrations, written articles, radio or television programs or other types of media must meet the criteria cited in Sections A through F of these Standards.

Section B: Counseling Relationship

1. The primary obligation of certified counselors is to respect the integrity and promote the welfare of a client, regardless of whether the client is assisted individually or in a group relationship. In a group setting, the certified counselor is also responsible for taking reasonable precautions to protect individuals from physical and/or psychological trauma resulting from interaction within the group.

2. The counseling relationship and information resulting from it remains confidential, consistent with the legal obligations of the certified counselor. In a group counseling setting, the certified counselor sets a norm of confidentiality regarding all group participants' disclosures.

3. Certified counselors know and take into account the traditions and practices of other professional groups with whom they work and co-operate fully with such groups. If a person is receiving similar services from another professional, certified counselors do not offer their own services directly to such a person. If a certified counselor is contacted by a person who is already receiving similar services from another professional, the certified counselor carefully considers that professional relationship and proceeds with caution and sensitivity to the therapeutic issues as well as the client's welfare. Certified counselors discuss these issues with clients so as to minimize the risk of confusion and conflict.

4. When a client's condition indicates that there is a clear and imminent danger to the client or others, the certified counselor must take reasonable personal action or inform responsible authorities. Consultation with other professionals must be used where possible. The assumption of responsibility for the client's behavior must be taken only after careful deliberation, and the client must be involved in the resumption of responsibility as quickly as possible.

5. Records of the counseling relationship, including interview notes, test data, correspondence, audio or visual tape recordings, electronic data storage, and other documents are to be considered professional information for use in counseling. They should not be considered a part of the records of the institution or agency in which the counselor is employed unless specified by state statute or regulation. Revelation to others of counseling material must occur only upon the expressed consent of the client; certified counselors must make provisions for maintaining confidentiality in the storage and disposal of records. Certified counselors providing information to the public or to subordinates, peers, or supervisors have a responsibility to ensure than the content is general;

unidentified client information should be accurate and unbiased, and should consist of objective, factual data.

6. Certified counselors must ensure that data maintained in electronic storage are secure. The data must be limited to information that is appropriate and necessary for the services being provided and accessible only to appropriate staff members involved in the provision of services by using the best computer security methods available. Certified counselors must also ensure that the electronically stored data are destroyed when the information is no longer of value in providing services.

7. Data derived from a counseling relationship for use in counselor training or research shall be confined to content that can be disguised to ensure full protection of the identity of the subject/client and shall be obtained with informed consent.

8. Certified counselors must inform clients before or at the time the counseling relationship commences, of the purposes, goals, techniques, rules and procedures, and limitations that may affect the relationship.

9. All methods of treatment by certified counselors must be clearly indicated to prospective recipients and safety precautions must be taken in their use.

10. Certified counselors who have an administrative, supervisory and/or evaluative relationship with individuals seeking counseling services must not serve as the counselor and should refer the individuals to other professionals. Exceptions are made only in instances where an individual's situation warrants counseling intervention and another alternative is unavailable. Dual relationships with clients that might impair the certified counselor's objectivity and professional judgement must be avoided and/or the counseling relationship terminated through referral to another competent professional.

11. When certified counselors determine an inability to be of professional assistance to a potential or existing client, they must, respectively, not initiate the counseling relationship or immediately terminate the relationship. In either event, the certified counselor must suggest appropriate alternatives. Certified

counselors must be knowledgeable about referral resources so that a satisfactory referral can be initiated. In the event that the client declines a suggested referral, the certified counselor is not obligated to continue the relationship.

12. Certified counselors may choose to consult with any other professionally competent person about a client and must notify clients of this right. Certified counselors must avoid placing a consultant in a conflict-of-interest situation that would preclude the consultant's being a proper party to the certified counselor's efforts to help the client.

13. Certified counselors who counsel clients from cultures different from their own must gain knowledge, personal awareness, and sensitivity pertinent to the client populations served and must incorporate culturally relevant techniques into their practice.

14. When certified counselors are engaged in intensive, short-term therapy, they must ensure that professional counseling assistance is available to the client(s) during and following the counseling.

15. Certified counselors must screen prospective group counseling participants, especially when the emphasis is on self-understanding and growth through self-disclosure. Certified counselors must maintain an awareness of each group participant's welfare throughout the group process.

16. When electronic data and systems are used as a component of counseling services, certified counselors must ensure that the computer application, and any information it contains, is appropriate for the respective needs of clients and is non-discriminatory. Certified counselors must ensure that they themselves have acquired a facilitation level of knowledge with any system they use including hands-on application, search experience, and understanding of the uses of all aspects of the computer-based system. In selecting and/or maintaining computer-based systems that contain career information, counselors must ensure that the system provides current, accurate, and locally relevant information. Certified counselors must also ensure that clients are intellectually, emotionally, and physically compatible to using the computer application and understand its purpose and operation. Client

use of a computer application must be evaluated to correct possible problems and assess subsequent needs.

17. Certified counselors who develop self-help/stand-alone computer software for use by the general public, must first ensure that it is initially designed to function in a stand-alone manner, as opposed to modifying software that was originally designed to require support from a counselor. Secondly, the software must include program statements that provide the user with intended outcomes, suggestions for using the software, descriptions of inappropriately used applications, and descriptions of when and how counseling services might be beneficial. Finally, the manual must include the qualifications of the developer, the development process, validation data, and operating procedures.

Section C: Measurement and Evaluation

1. Certified counselors must provide specific orientation or information to an examinee prior to and following the administration of assessment instruments or techniques so that the results may be placed in proper perspective with other relevant factors. The purpose of testing and the explicit use of the results must be made known to an examinee prior to testing.

2. In selecting assessment instruments or techniques for use in a given situation or with a particular client, certified counselors must evaluate carefully the instrument's specific theoretical bases and characteristics, validity, reliability and appropriateness. Certified counselors are professionally responsible for using invalidated information carefully.

3. When making statements to the public about assessment instruments or techniques, certified counselors must provide accurate information and avoid false claims or misconceptions concerning the meaning of psychometric terms. Special efforts are often required to avoid unwarranted connotations or terms such as IQ and grade-equivalent scores.

4. Because many types of assessment techniques exist, certified counselors must recog-

nize the limits of their competence and perform only those functions for which they have received appropriate training.

5. Certified counselors must note when tests are not administered under standard conditions or when unusual behavior or irregularities occur during a testing session, and the results must be designated as invalid or of questionable validity. Unsupervised or inadequately supervised assessments, such as mail-in tests, are considered unethical. However, the use of standardized instruments that are designed to be self-administered and self-scored, such as interest inventories, is appropriate.

6. Because prior coaching or dissemination of test materials can invalidate test results, certified counselors are professionally obligated to maintain test security. In addition, conditions that produce most favorable test results must be made known to an examinee (e.g., penalty for guessing).

7. Certified counselors must consider psychometric limitations when selecting and using an instrument, and must be cognizant of the limitations when interpreting the results. When tests are used to classify clients, certified counselors must ensure that periodic review and/or retesting are made to prevent client stereotyping.

8. An examinee's welfare, explicit prior understanding, and agreement are the factors used when determining who receives the test results. Certified counselors must see that appropriate interpretation accompanies any release of individual or group test data (e.g., limitations of instrument and norms).

9. Certified counselors must ensure that computer-generated test administration and scoring programs function properly thereby providing clients with accurate test results.

10. Certified counselors, who are responsible for making decisions based on assessment results, must have appropriate training and skills based on educational and psychological measurement, validation criteria, test research, and guidelines for test development and use.

11. Certified counselors must be cautious when interpreting the results of instruments that possess insufficient technical data, and must explicitly state to examinees the specific purposes for the use of such instruments.

12. Certified counselors must proceed with caution when attempting to evaluate and interpret performances of minority group members or other persons who are not represented in the norm group on which the instrument was standardized.

13. Certified counselors who develop computer-based test interpretations to support the assessment process, must ensure that the validity of the interpretations is established prior to the commercial distribution of the computer application.

14. Certified counselors recognize that test results may become obsolete, and avoid the misuse of obsolete data.

15. Certified counselors must avoid the appropriation, reproduction, or modification of published tests or parts thereof without acknowledgement and permission from the publisher.

Section D: Research and Publication

1. Certified counselors will adhere to relevant guidelines on research with human subjects. These include the:

 a. Ethical Principles in the Conduct of Research with Human Participants, Washington, D.D.: American Psychological Association Inc., 1982
 b. Code of Federal Regulation, Title 45, Subtitle A, Part 46, as currently issued.
 c. Ethical Principles of Psychologists, American Psychological Association, Principle #9: Research with Human Participants.
 d. Buckley Amendment.
 e. current federal regulations and various state rights privacy acts.

2. In planning research activities involving human subjects, certified counselors must be aware of and responsive to all pertinent ethical principles and ensure that the research problem, design, and execution are in full compliance with the principles.

3. The ultimate responsibility for ethical research lies with the principal researcher,

though others involved in the research activities are ethically obligated and responsible for their own actions.

4. Certified counselors who conduct research with human subjects' are responsible for the subjects' welfare throughout the experiment and must take all reasonable precautions to avoid causing injurious psychological, physical, or social effects on their subjects.

5. Certified counselors, who conduct research, must abide by the following basic elements of informed consent:

   a. a fair explanation of the procedures to be followed, including an identification of those which are experimental
   b. a description of the attendant discomforts and risks
   c. a description of the benefits to be expected
   d. a disclosure of appropriate alternative procedures that would be advantageous for subjects
   e. an offer to answer any inquiries concerning the procedures
   f. an instruction that subjects are free to withdraw their consent and to discontinue participation in the project or activity at any time

6. When reporting research results, explicit mention must be made of all the variables and conditions known to the investigator that may have affected the outcome of the study or the interpretation of the data.

7. Certified counselors who conduct and report research investigations must do so in a manner that minimizes the possibility that the results will be misleading.

8. Certified counselors are obligated to make available sufficient original research data to qualified others who may wish to replicate the study.

9. Certified counselors who supply data, aid in the research of another person, report research results, or make original data available, must take due care to disguise the identity of respective subjects in the absence of specific authorization from the subjects to do otherwise.

10. When conducting and reporting research, certified counselors must be familiar with, and give recognition to, previous work on the topic, must observe all copyright laws, and must follow the principles of giving full credit to those to whom credit is due.

11. Certified counselors must give due credit through joint authorship, acknowledgement, footnote statements, or other appropriate means to those who have contributed significantly to the research and/or publication, in accordance with such contributions.

12. Certified counselors should communicate to other counselors the results of any research judged to be of professional value. Results that reflect unfavorably on institutions, programs, services, or vested interests must not be withheld.

13. Certified counselors who agree to cooperate with another individual in research and/or publication must incur an obligation to cooperate as promised in terms of punctuality of performance and with full regard to the completeness and accuracy of the information required.

14. Certified counselors must not submit the same manuscript, or one essentially similar in content, for simultaneous publication consideration by two or more journals. In addition, manuscripts that are published in whole or substantial part in another journal or published work should not be submitted for publication without acknowledgement and permission from the previous publication.

Section E: Consulting

Consultation refers to a voluntary relationship between a professional helper and help-needing individual, group, or social unit in which the consultant is providing help to the client(s) in defining and solving a work-related problem or potential work-related problem with a client or client system.

1. Certified counselors, acting as consultants, must have a high degree of self awareness of their own values, knowledge, skills, limitations, and needs in entering a helping relationship that involves human and/or organizational change. The focus of the consulting relationship must be on the issues to be

resolved and not on the person(s) presenting the problem.

2. In the consulting relationship, the certified counselor and client must understand and agree upon the problem definition, subsequent goals, and predicted consequences of interventions selected.

3. Certified counselors must be reasonably certain that they, or the organization represented, have the necessary competencies and resources for giving the kind of help that is needed or that may develop later, and that appropriate referral resources are available to the consultant.

4. Certified counselors in a consulting relationship must encourage and cultivate client adaptability and growth toward self-direction. Certified counselors must maintain this role consistently and not become a decision maker for clients or create a future dependency on the consultant.

5. Certified counselors conscientiously adhere to the NBCC Code of Ethics when announcing consultant availability for services.

Section F: Private Practice

1. Certified counselors should assist the profession by facilitating the availability of counseling services in private as well as public settings.

2. In advertising services as a private practitioner, certified counselors must advertise in a manner that accurately informs the public of the professional services, expertise, and techniques of counseling available.

3. Certified counselors who assume an executive leadership role in a private practice organization do not permit their names to be used in professional notices during periods of time when they are not actively engaged in the private practice of counseling.

4. Certified counselors may list their highest relevant degree, type and level of certification and/or license, address, telephone number, office hours, type and/or description of services, and other relevant information. Listed information must not contain false, inaccurate,

misleading, partial, out-of-context, or otherwise deceptive material or statements.

5. Certified counselors who are involved in a partnership/corporation with other certified counselors and/or other professionals, must clearly specify the separate specialities of each member of the partnership or corporation, in compliance with the regulations of the locality.

6. Certified counselors have an obligation to withdraw from a private practice counseling relationship if it violates the Code of Ethics, the mental or physical condition of the certified counselor renders it difficult to carry out an effective professional relationship, or the counseling relationship is no longer productive for the client.

Appendix: Certification Examination

1. Applicants for the NBCC Counselor Certification Examination must have fulfilled all current eligibility requirements, and are responsible for the accuracy and validity of all information and/or materials provided by themselves or by others for fulfillment of eligibility criteria.

2. Participation in the NBCC Counselor Certification Examination by any person under the auspices of eligibility ascribed to another person (i.e., applicant) is prohibited. Applicants are responsible for ensuring that no other person participates in the NBCC Counselor Certification Examination through use of the eligibility specifically assigned to the applicant.

3. Participants in the NBCC Counselor Certification Examination must refrain from the use of behaviors and/or materials which would afford them unfair advantage for performance on the Examination. These behaviors and/or materials include, but are not limited to, any form of copying of responses from another participant's answer sheet, use of unauthorized notes or other informational materials, or communication with other participants during the Examination.

4. Participants in the NBCC Counselor Certification Examination must, at the end of the regularly scheduled Examination period,

return all Examination materials to the test administrator.

5. After completing the NBCC Counselor Certification Examination, participants must not disclose, in either verbal or written form, items which appeared on the Examination form.

Acknowledgment

Reference documents, statements, and sources for the development of the NBCC Code of Ethics were as follows:

The Ethical Standards of the American Association for Counseling and Development, Responsible Uses for Standardized Testing (AMECD), codes of ethics of the American Psychological Association, National Academy of Certified Clinical Mental Health Counselors, and the National Career Development Association, handbook of Standards for Computer-Based Career Information Systems (ASCI) and Guidelines for the Use of Computer-Based Career Information and Guidance Systems (ASCI).

Ethical Guidelines for Group Counselors

ETHICAL GUIDELINES FOR GROUP COUN-
SELORS
*Approved by the Association for Specialists in
Group Work (ASGW) Executive Board, June 1,
1989*

PREAMBLE

One characteristic of any professional group
is the possession of a body of knowledge, skills,
and voluntarily, self-professed standards for
ethical practice. A Code of Ethics consists of
those standards that have been formally and
publicly acknowledged by the members of a
profession to serve as the guidelines for professional conduct, discharge of duties, and the
resolution of moral dilemmas. By this document, the Association for Specialists in Group
Work (ASGW) has identified the standards of
conduct appropriate for ethical behavior
among its members.

The Association for Specialists in Group
Work recognizes the basic commitment of its
members to the Ethical Standards of its parent
organization, the American Association for
Counseling and Development (AACD) and
nothing in this document shall be construed to
supplant that code. These standards are
intended to complement the AACD standards
in the area of group work by setting and by
stimulating a greater concern for competent
group leadership.

The group counselor is expected to be a professional agent and to take the processes of
ethical responsibility seriously. ASGW views
"ethical process" as being integral to group
work and view group counselors as "ethical
agents." Group counselors, by their very nature
in being responsible and responsive to their
group members, necessarily embrace a certain
potential for ethical vulnerability. It is incumbent upon group counselors to give consider-
able attention to the intent and context of their
actions because the attempts of counselors to
influence human behavior through group
work always have ethical implications.

The following ethical guidelines have been
developed to encourage ethical behavior of
group counselors. These guidelines are written
for students and practitioners, and are meant to
stimulate reflection, self-examination, and discussion of issues and practices. They address

the group counselor's responsibility for providing information about group work to clients and the group counselor's responsibility for providing group counseling services to clients. A final section discusses the group counselor's responsibility for safeguarding ethical practice and procedures for reporting unethical behavior. Group counselors are expected to make known these standards to group members.

Ethical Guidelines

1. *Orientation and providing Information:* Group counselors adequately prepare prospective or new group members by providing as much information about the existing or proposed group as necessary.

- Minimally, information related to each of the following areas should be provided.

   (a) Entrance procedures, time parameters of the group experience, group participation expectations, methods of payment (where appropriate), and termination procedures are explained by the group counselor as appropriate to the level of maturity of group members and the nature and purpose(s) of the group.

   (b) Group counselors have available for distribution, a professional disclosure statement that includes information on the group counselor's qualifications and group services that can be provided, particularly as related to the nature and purpose(s) of the specific group.

   (c) Group counselors communicate the role expectations, rights, and responsibilities of group members and group counselor(s).

   (d) The group goals are stated as concisely as possible by the group counselor including "whose" goal it is (the group counselor's, the institution's, the parent's, the law's, society's, etc.) and the role of group members in influencing or determining the group's goal(s).

   (e) Group counselors explore with group members the risks of potential life changes that may occur because of the group experience and help members explore their readiness to face these possibilities.

   (f) Group members are informed by the group counselor of unusual or experimental procedures that might be expected in their group experience.

   (g) Group counselors explain, as realistically as possible, what services can and cannot be provided within the particular group structure offered.

   (h) Group counselors emphasize the need to promote full psychological functioning and presence among group members. They inquire from prospective group members whether they are using any kind of drug or medication that may affect functioning in the group. They do not permit any use of alcohol and/or illegal drugs during group sessions and they discourage the use of alcohol and/or drugs (legal or illegal) prior to group meetings which may affect the physical or emotional presence of the member or other group members.

   (i) Group counselors inquire from prospective group members whether they have ever been a client in counseling or psychotherapy. If a prospective group member is already in a counseling relationship with another professional person, the group counselor advises the prospective group member to notify the other professional of their participation in the group.

   (j) Group counselors clearly inform group members about the policies pertaining to the group counselor's willingness to consult with them between group sessions.

(k) In establishing fees for group counseling services, group counselors consider the financial status and the locality of prospective group members. Group members are not charged fees for group sessions where the group counselor is not present and the policy of charging for sessions missed by a group member is clearly communicated. Fees for participating as a group member are contracted between group counselor and group member for a specified period of time. Group counselors do not increase fees for group counseling services until the existing contracted fee structure has expired. In the event that the established fee structure is inappropriate for a prospective member, group counselors assist in finding comparable services of acceptable cost.

2. *Screening of Members:* The group counselor screens prospective group members (when appropriate to their theoretical orientation). Insofar as possible, the counselor selects group members whose needs and goals are compatible with the goals of the group, who will not impede the group process, and whose well-being will not be jeopardized by the group experience. An orientation to the group (i.e., ASGW Ethical Guideline #1) is included during the screening process.

• Screening may be accomplished in one or more ways, such as the following:

(a) Individual interview

(b) Group interview of prospective group members

(c) Interview as part of a team staffing

(d) Completion of a written questionnaire by prospective group members.

3. *Confidentiality:* Group counselors protect members by defining clearly what confidentiality means, why it is important, and the difficulties involved in enforcement.

(a) Group counselors take steps to protect members by defining confidentiality and the limits of confidentiality (i.e., when a group member's condition indicates that there is clear and imminent danger to the member, other, or physical property, the group counselor takes a reasonable personal action and/or informs responsible authorities).

(b) Group counselors stress the importance of confidentiality and set a norm of confidentiality regarding all group participants' disclosures. The importance of maintaining confidentiality is emphasized before the group begins and at various times in the group. The fact that confidentiality cannot be guaranteed is clearly stated.

(c) Members are made aware of the difficulties involved in enforcing and ensuring confidentiality in a group setting. The counselor provides examples of how confidentiality can non-maliciously be broken to increase members' awareness, and helps to lessen the likelihood that this breach of confidence will occur. Group counselors inform group members about the potential consequences of intentionally breaching confidentiality.

(d) Group counselors can only ensure confidentiality on their part and not on the part of the members.

(e) Group counselors video or audio tape a group session only with the prior consent and the members' knowledge of how the tape will be used.

(f) When working with minors, the group counselor specifies the limits of confidentiality.

(g) Participants in a mandatory group are made aware of any reporting procedures required of the group counselor.

(h) Group counselors store or dispose of group member recourse (written, audio, video, etc.) in ways that maintain confidentiality.

(i) Instructors of group counseling courses maintain the anonymity of group members whenever discussing group counseling cases.

4. *Voluntary/Involuntary Participation:* Group counselors inform members whether participation is voluntary or involuntary.

(a) Group counselors take steps to ensure informed consent procedures in both voluntary and involuntary groups.

(b) When working with minors in a group, counselors are expected to follow the procedures specified by the institution in which they are practicing.

(c) With involuntary groups, every attempt is made to enlist the cooperation of the members and their continuance in the group on a voluntary basis.

(d) Group counselors do not certify that group treatment has been received by members who merely attend sessions but did not meet the defined group expectations. Group members are informed about the consequences for failing to participate in a group.

5. *Leaving a Group:* Provisions are made to assist a group member to terminate in an effective way.

(a) Procedures to be followed for a group member who chooses to exit a group prematurely are discussed by the counselor with all group members either before the group begins, during a pre-screening interview, or during the initial group session.

(b) In case of legally mandated group counseling, group counselors inform members of the possible consequences for premature self termination.

(c) Ideally, both the group counselor and the member can work cooperatively to determine the degree to which a group experience is productive or counterproductive for that individual.

(d) Members ultimately have a right to discontinue membership in the group, at a designated time, if the predetermined trial period proves to be unsatisfactory.

(e) Members have the right to exit a group, but it is important that they be made aware of the importance of informing the counselor and the group members prior to deciding to leave. The counselor discusses the possible risks of leaving the group prematurely with a member who is considering this option.

(f) Before leaving a group, the group counselor encourages members (if appropriate) to discuss their reasons for wanting to discontinue membership in the group. Counselors intervene if other members use undue pressure to force a member to remain in the group.

6. *Coercion and Pressure:* Group counselors protect member rights against physical threats, intimidation, coercion, and undue peer pressure insofar as is reasonably possible.

(a) It is essential to differentiate between "therapeutic pressure" that is part of any group and "undue pressure," which is not therapeutic.

(b) The purpose of a group is to help participants find their own answers, not to pressure them into doing what the group thinks is appropriate.

(c) Counselors exert care not to coerce participants to change in directions which they clearly state they do not choose.

(d) Counselors have responsibility to intervene when others use undue pressure or attempt to persuade members against their will.

(e) Counselors intervene when any member attempts to act out aggression in a physical way that might harm another member or themselves.

(f) Counselors intervene when a member is verbally abusive or inappropriately confrontive to another member.

7. *Imposing Counselor Values:* Group counselors develop an awareness of their own values and needs and the potential impact they have on the interventions likely to be made.

(a) Although group counselors take care to avoid imposing their values on members, it is appropriate that they expose their own beliefs, decisions, needs, and values, when concealing them would create problems for the members.

(b) There are values implicit in any group, and these are made clear to potential members before they join the group. (Examples of certain values include: expressing feelings, being direct and honest, sharing personal material with others, learning how to trust, improving interpersonal communication, and deciding for oneself.)

(c) Personal and professional needs of group counselors are not met at the members' expense.

(d) Group counselors avoid using the group for their own therapy.

(e) Group counselors are aware of their own values and assumptions and how these apply in a multicultural context.

(f) Group counselors take steps to increase their awareness of ways that their personal reactions to members might inhibit the group process and they monitor their countertransference. Through an awareness of the impact of stereotyping and discrimination (i.e.,

biases based on age, disability, ethnicity, gender, race, religion, or sexual preference), group counselors guard the individual rights and personal dignity of all group members.

8. *Equitable Treatment:* Group counselors make every reasonable effort to treat each member individually and equally.

(a) Group counselors recognize and respect differences (e.g., cultural, racial, religious, lifestyle, age, disability, gender) among group members.

(b) Group counselors maintain an awareness of their behavior toward individual group members and are alert to the potential detrimental effects of favoritism or partiality toward any particular group member to the exclusion or detriment of any other member(s). It is likely that group counselors will favor some members over others, yet all group members deserve to be treated equally.

(c) Group counselors ensure equitable use of group time for each member by inviting silent members to become involved, acknowledging nonverbal attempts to communicate, and discouraging rambling and monopolizing of time by members.

(d) If a large group is planned, counselors consider enlisting another qualified professional to serve as a co-leader for the group sessions.

9. *Dual Relationships:* Group counselors avoid dual relationships with group members that might impair their objectivity and professional judgment, as well as those which are likely to compromise a group member's ability to participate fully in the group.

(a) Group counselors do not misuse their professional role and power as group leader to advance personal or social contacts with members throughout the duration of the group.

(b) Group counselors do not use their professional relationship with group members to further their own interest either during the group or after the termination of the group.

(c) Sexual intimacies between group counselors and members are unethical.

(d) Group counselors do not barter (exchange) professional services with group members for services.

(e) Group counselors do not admit their own family members, relatives, employees, or personal friends as members to their groups.

(f) Group counselors discuss with group members the potential detrimental effects of group members engaging in intimate inter-member relationships outside of the group.

(g) Students who participate in a group as a partial course requirement for a group course are not evaluated for an academic grade based upon their degree of participation as a member in a group. Instructors of group counseling courses take steps to minimize the possible negative impact on students when they participate in a group course by separating course grades from participation in the group and by allowing students to decide what issues to explore and when to stop.

(h) It is inappropriate to solicit members from a class (or institutional affiliation) for one's private counseling or therapeutic groups.

10. *Use of Techniques:* Group counselors do not attempt any technique unless trained in its use or under supervision by a counselor familiar with the intervention.

(a) Group counselors are able to articulate a theoretical orientation that guides their practice, and they are able to provide a rationale for their interventions.

(b) Depending upon the type of an intervention, group counselors have training commensurate with the potential impact of a technique.

(c) Group counselors are aware of the necessity to modify their techniques to fit the unique needs of various cultural and ethnic groups.

(d) Group counselors assist members in translating in-group learnings to daily life.

11. *Goal Development:* Group counselors make every effort to assist members in developing their personal goals.

(a) Group counselors use their skills to assist members in making their goals specific so that others present in the group will understand the nature of the goals.

(b) Throughout the course of a group, group counselors assist members in assessing the degree to which personal goals are being met, and assist in revising any goals when it is appropriate.

(c) Group counselors help members clarify the degree to which the goals can be met within the context of a particular group.

12. *Consultation:* Group counselors develop and explain policies about between-session consultation to group members.

(a) Group counselors take care to make certain that members do not use between-session consultations to avoid dealing with issues pertaining to the group that would be dealt with best in the group.

(b) Group counselors urge members to bring the issues discussed during between-session consultations into the group if they pertain to the group.

(c) Group counselors seek out consultation and/or supervision regarding ethical concerns or when encountering difficulties which interfere with their effective functioning as group leaders.

(d) Group counselors seek appropriate professional assistance for their own personal problems or conflicts that are likely to impair their professional judgment and work performance.

(e) Group counselors discuss their group cases only for professional consultation and educational purposes.

(f) Group counselors inform members about policies regarding whether consultations will be held confidential.

13. *Termination from the Group:* Depending upon the purpose of participation in the group, counselors promote termination of members from the group in the most efficient period of time.

(a) Group counselors maintain a constant awareness of the progress made by each group member and periodically invite the group members to explore and reevaluate their experiences in the group. It is the responsibility of group counselors to help promote the independence of members from the group in a timely manner.

14. *Evaluation and Follow-up:* Group counselors make every attempt to engage in ongoing assessment and to design follow-up procedures for their groups.

(a) Group counselors recognize the importance of ongoing assessment of a group, and they assist members in evaluating their own progress.

(b) Group counselors conduct evaluation of the total group experience at the final meeting (or before termination), as well as ongoing evaluation.

(c) Group counselors monitor their own behavior and become aware of what they are modeling in the group.

(d) Follow-up meetings might be with individuals, groups, or both to determine the degree to which: (i) members have reached their goals, (ii) the group had a positive or negative effect on the participants, and (iii) members could profit from some type of referral. Information is requested for possible modification of future groups. If there is no follow-up meeting, provisions are made available for individual follow-up meetings to any member who needs or requests such a contact.

15. *Referrals:* If the needs of a particular member cannot be met within the type of group being offered, the group counselor suggests other appropriate professional referrals.

(a) Group counselors are knowledgeable of local community resources for assisting group members regarding professional referrals.

(b) Group counselors help members seek further professional assistance, if needed.

16. *Professional Development:* Group counselors recognize that professional growth is a continuous, ongoing, developmental process throughout their career.

(a) Group counselors maintain and upgrade their knowledge and skill competencies through educational activities, clinical experiences, and participation in professional development activities.

(b) Group counselors keep abreast of research findings and new developments as applied to groups.

Safeguarding Ethical Practice and Procedures for Reporting Unethical Behavior

The preceding remarks have been advanced as guidelines which are generally representative of ethical and professional group practice. They have not been proposed as rigidly defined prescriptions. However, practitioners who are thought to be grossly unresponsive to the ethical concerns addressed in the document may be subject to a review of their practices by the AACD Ethics Committee and ASGW peers.

- For consultation and/or questions regarding these ASGW Ethical Guidelines or group ethical dilemmas, you may contact the Chairperson of the ASGW Ethics Committee. The name, address, and telephone number of the current ASGW Ethics Committee Chairperson may be acquired by telephoning the AACD office in Alexandria, Virginia at 703/823-9800.
- If a group counselor's behavior is suspected as being unethical, the following procedures are to be followed:

    (a) Collect more information and investigate further to confirm the unethical practice as determined by the ASGW Ethical Guidelines.

    (b) Confront the individual with the apparent violation of ethical guidelines for the purposes of protecting the safety of any clients and to help the group counselor correct any inappropriate behaviors. If unsatisfactory resolution is not reached through this contact then:

    (c) A complaint should be made in writing, including the specific facts and dates of the alleged violation and all relevant supporting data. The complaint should be included in an envelope marked "CONFIDENTIAL" to ensure confidentiality for both the accuser(s) and the alleged violator(s) and forward to all of the following sources:

    1. The name and address of the Chairperson of the state Counselor Licensure Board for the respective state, if in existence.
    2. The Ethics Committee c/o The President American Association for Counseling and Development 5999 Stevenson Avenue Alexandria, Virginia 22304
    3. The name and address of all private credentialing agencies in which the alleged violator maintains credentials or holds professional membership.

APPENDIX C

Responsibilities of Users
of Standardized Tests

American Association for Counseling and Development

INTRODUCTION

During the past several years, individual APGA members have been under increasing pressure from their various constituencies to define, provide and employ safeguards against the misuse of standardized tests. APGA as an organization has also been challenged by individuals and agencies to provide leadership in the face of growing concern about the effects of testing on clients of all ages and all subpopulations, and in all settings.

At the 1976 APGA convention, the board of directors requested action on the development of a statement on the responsible use of standardized tests. A committee representing all APGA divisions and regions spent two years studying the issues and developing the following statement.

To furnish perspective for the work of this committee, a review of relevant literature was conducted and each member of the committee received copies of numerous position papers, reports, articles and monographs that added to understanding the issues and the consequences of alternative principles.

Among these papers were the interim report of the 1975-76 APGA Committee on Standardized Testing: the 1972 APGA / AMEG Statement on the Responsible Use of Tests; position papers of individual divisions and of other professional organizations such as the American Educational Research Association and the National Council on Measurement in Education; journal articles; and conference presentations.

The committee's statement is intended to be sensitive to current and emerging problems and concerns that are generic to all APGA divisions/regions and to address these problems

NOTE: AACD is in the process of a major revision of the *Responsibilities of Users of Standardized Tests.*

SOURCE: American Personnel & Guidance Association, *APGA Policy Statement: Responsibilities of Users of Standardized Tests.* Copyright 1980 by American Personnel & Guideance Association. Reprinted by permission.

Originally published in Guidepost. October 5, 1978. Reprinted by the Association for Measurement and Evaluation in Guidance, a division of the American Personnel and Guidance Association.

and concerns with principles that are specific enough to serve as a template to develop division/region statements addressed to the specific disciplines/settings of individual divisions/regions.

Target Audience

The statement is intended to present the position and address the needs of the professional members of APGA divisions and regions. Although this position may provide guidance for test developers, teachers, administrators, parents, press or the general public, it is not designed to represent these audiences. The statement is built on the assumption that test data of themselves are neutral and that guidelines are needed to promote constructive use of tests.

Organization and Focus

The statement is organized into eight sections: Introduction, Decision Rules, Test Selection, Qualifications of Test Users, Test Administration, Scoring of Tests, Test Interpretation and Communication. Each section is directed toward the various uses and decisions that must be made by the test user (e.g., whether to test, which test(s) to use, what data to obtain, how to interpret, etc.). The committee developed a classification system for the uses of standardized tests and treated only those issues that fit into the use classification scheme.

The next step was to define issues related to the classification system. Issues were sought from individuals, professional statements, literature and the popular press. Issues were examined in terms of their relevance to APGA members and to their importance in terms of the possible consequences to the person(s) tested.

Only the principles underlying each issue are specified. These principles are appropriate as standards for all APGA divisions and regions. Divisions and regions are encouraged to develop their own statements, expanding on each principle with specific procedures and examples and appropriate to their members. The principles are grouped around similar issues and are indexed for easy reference.

Decision Rules

In human service agencies, decisions about client needs may be made on the basis of direct observation or historical information alone. Further refinement of direct observation and historical data can often be obtained by employing standardized tests.

Deciding whether to test creates the possibility of three classes of errors relative to the agency functions of description, diagnosis, prescription, selection, placement, prediction, growth evaluation, etc.

First, a decision not to test can result in misjudgments that stem solely from inadequate data.

Second, tests may be used well, producing data that could improve accuracy in decisions affecting the client but that are not utilized.

Third, tests may be misused through inappropriate selection, improper administration, inaccurate scoring, incompetent interpretation or indiscriminate, inadequate, or inaccurate communication.

To reduce the chance for errors, the responsible practitioner will always determine in advance why a given test should be used. This provides protection and benefits for both the client and the agency. Having a clearly developed rationale increases the probable benefits of testing by indicating how a particular set of information, when used by an individual or set of individuals, will contribute to a sounder decision without prejudice to either the client or the agency.

The guidelines that follow are intended to provide decision rules to help agencies and practitioners avoid charges of irresponsible practice.

Defining Purposes for Testing

1. Decide whether you will be testing to evaluate individuals, groups or both.

2. Identify your interests in the particular target population in terms of the agency's purposes and capabilities.

3. Determine limits to diagnosis, prediction or selection created by age, racial, sexual, ethnic or cultural characteristics of those to be tested.

4. Develop specific objectives and limits for the use of test data in relation to each of the component service areas of placement/selection, prediction (expectancies), description/diagnosis and growth studies (assessing change over time).

A. Placement. If the purpose is selection or placement (selection is a simple in-out sort of placement), the test selector and interpreter must know about the programs or institutions in which the client may be placed and be able to judge the consequences of such placement or exclusion for the client.

B. Prediction/expectancies. If the purpose is prediction, the persons deciding to test and/or interpret the results must understand the pitfalls of labeling, stereotyping and prejudging people. Ways to avoid these potentially invidious outcomes should be known.

C. Description/diagnosis. If the purpose is diagnosis or description, the selector or interpreter should understand enough about the general domain being measured to be able to identify those aspects adequately measured and those not.

D. Growth/change assessment. If the purpose is to examine growth, the person designing the study and interpreting the results needs to know the many problems associated with such measurement:

1. the unreliability of change measures;
2. the pitfalls in using norms as reference points;
3. the associated problems of articulation and comparability;
4. the limitations of scoring scales, such as grade equivalents, that may not have the comparable meaning which they appear to have at different scale levels.

Determining Information Needs

1. Assess the consequences for the clients of both testing or not testing.
2. Determine what decisions can be made with existing information to avoid unnecessary data-gathering efforts.

3. Limit data gathering to those functions or aptitude, achievement, interests/attitudes/values and perceptual-motor skills that are directly relevant in making decisions about delivery of services to a particular individual or group.
4. Identify whether the test being considered can provide acceptable levels of precision (reliability) for the decision being made.
5. Identify whether the data obtained can be cross-validated against other available data as a part of the decision-making process.
6. Determine the amount and form of data to be shared on the basis of maximum relevance to the agency's purposes and capabilities.

Identifying Users of Test Information

1. Data should be prepared so that they can be comprehended by the persons using the data for decision-making.
2. Limit access to users specifically authorized by the law or by the client.
3. Identify obsolescence schedules so that stored personal test data may be systematically reclassified and relocated to historical files or destroyed.
4. Process personal data used for research or program evaluation so as to assure individual anonymity.

Qualifications of Test Users

All professional personnel and guidance workers should have formal training in psychological and educational measurement and testing. Nevertheless, it is unreasonable to expect that this training necessarily makes one an expert or even that an expert always has all the knowledge and skill appropriate to any particular situation. Thus, questions of user qualifications should always arise when testing is being considered.

Those who participate in any aspect of testing should be qualified to do so. Lack of proper qualifications leads to misuse, errors and sometimes damage to clients. Each professional is responsible for making judgment on this matter in each situation and cannot leave that responsibility either to clients or to those in authority.

In many instances information or skills that may be lacking can be acquired quite readily by those with a background of professional training and experience. In all instances it is incumbent upon the individual to obtain that training or arrange for proper supervision and assistance when engaged in, or planning to engage in, testing.

The requisite qualifications for test users depend on four factors: (1) the particular role of the user; (2) the setting in which the use takes place; (3) the nature of the test; and (4) the purpose of the testing.

These factors interact with each other but may nevertheless be considered separately for the purposes of these standards.

Roles of Test Users, Selectors, Administrators, Scorers and Interpreters

A test user may play all of these roles or any subset of them when working with other professional personnel. In some situations each role may be the responsibility of a different person. The knowledge and skills that pertain to these roles are listed under the sections so headed. The general principle is that the test users should engage in only those testing activities for which their training and experience qualify them.

Settings and Conditions of Test Use

Counselors and personnel workers should assess the quality and relevance of their knowledge and skills to the situation before deciding to test or to participate in a testing program.

Characteristics of Tests

Tests differ in many ways, and users need to understand the peculiarities of the instruments they are using.

Purposes of Testing

The purpose of the testing dictates how the test is used and thus may influence requisite qualifications of users beyond those entailed by their testing roles. Technically proper use for ill-understood purposes may constitute misuse.

Test Selection

Tests should be selected for a specific measurement purpose, use and interpretation. The selection of tests should be guided by information obtained from a careful analysis of the following major considerations:

What are the characteristics of the population to be tested?
What knowledge, skills, abilities, or attitudes are to be assessed?
What are the purposes for testing?
How will the test scores be used and interpreted?

When complete answers to these questions have been obtained, selection or development of tests should be directed toward obtaining measures that are congruent with the stated needs for assessment in terms of the purposes, content, use interpretation and particular characteristics of the individuals who are to be tested.

Selection of tests must also be guided by the criteria of technical quality recommended by the measurement profession and published by APA/AERA/NCME in "Standards for Educational and Psychological Tests" (1974). Full recognition and analysis of these considerations should become the focus of a process to select appropriate tests. The responsible test selector will:

Select Appropriate Tests

1.   Select tests that have been demonstrated, to the satisfaction of professional specialists, as appropriate for the characteristics of the population to be tested.

2. Select tests that are within the level of skills of administration and interpretation possessed by the practitioner.

3. Determine whether a common test or different tests are required for the accurate measurement of groups with different characteristics.

4. Recognize that different tests for cultural, ethnic and racial groups constitute inefficient means for making corrections for differences in prior life experiences, except where different languages are involved.

5. Determine whether persons or groups that use different languages should be tested in either or both languages and in some instance by prior testing for bilingualism.

Relate Evidence or Validity to Particular Usage

1. Apply tests or selection only when they should predictive validity for the specific tasks or competencies needed in an educational or employment assignment to maintain legal prescriptions for non-discriminatory practices in selection, employment or placement.

2. Determine validity of a test (whether the test measures what it claims to measure) through evidence of the constructs used in developing the measures, the correlation of the test performance with another appraisal of the characteristics being measured, or the predictions of specified behavior from the test performance.

3. Determine that the content of the test has high congruence with the users' definition of the knowledge and skills that are the desired criteria of human performance to be appraised.

4. Confirm that the criteria of human performance to be appraised are contained in the tasks and results of the testing procedure.

Employ User Participation in Test Selection

Actively involve the persons who will be using the tests (administering, scoring, summarizing, interpreting, making decisions) in the selection of tests that are congruent with the locally determined purposes, conditions and uses of the measurement.

Select Tests to Satisfy Local Use

1. Give specific attention to how the test is designed to handle the variation of motivation among persons taking the test, the variation or bias in response to the test content and the effects of the presence or absence of guessing in the responses to the test questions.

2. Determine whether tests standardized for nationwide use show evidence that such tests yield comparable results for individuals or groups with cultural differences.

3. Identify and analyze the effects of working speed and language facility in relation to the criteria of human performance that are expected to result from the test.

Consider Technical Characteristics of Tests

1. Select only published or locally developed tests that have documented evidence of the reliability of consistency of the measure.

2. Select tests that have documented evidence of the effectiveness of the measure for the purpose to be served: placement/selection, prediction (expectancy), description/diagnosis, or growth studies (change over time). A test is rarely equally effective for the four common test uses.

3. Consider the procedures used in standardization and norming for relevance to the local population and the desired use and interpretation.

4. Use separate norms for men and women only when empirical evidence indicates this is necessary to minimize bias.

5. Determine the degree of reliability (or validity) demanded of a test on the basis of the nature of the decisions to be based on test scores.

6. A test for final diagnosis or selection requires a higher degree of reliability than an initial screening test.

7. Explicitly list and use the ease and accuracy of the procedures for scoring, summarizing and communicating test performance as criteria for selecting a test.

8. Recognize that the technical characteristics and norms of standardized tests may vary when used with different populations. The selection process should include trial administrations to verify that the test is functioning with the technical characteristics and desired results for the local population and local uses.

Practical constraints of cost, conditions and time for testing must be considered but not used as the primary criteria for test selection.

Test Administration

Test administration includes all procedures that are used to ensure that the test is presented consistently in the manner specified by the test developers and used in the standardization and that the individuals being tested have orientation and conditions that maximize opportunity for optimum performance.

Standardized tests should provide manuals giving specific directions for administering, scoring and interpreting tests. Tests developed for a specific local purpose, use or population should be administered in a prescribed and consistent manner to obtain optimum performance from the individuals being tested. Effective administration of tests requires that the administrator have knowledge and training with the instruments and the processes of presentation.

Orientation

1. Inform testing candidates, relevant institutions or agencies and the community about the testing procedure. The orientation should describe the purposes and contents sampled by the test, how it is administered and how the scores will be reported and used.

2. Provide annual training for test administrators by qualified professional specialists if your agency or institution uses tests or sponsors testing programs.

3. Routinely review the test materials and administration conditions well in advance of the time for testing so that full preparation will ensure standardized administration and recognition of any irregularities that may occur.

4. Ensure that the orientation is sufficient to make the test relevant for the individual or group being tested before beginning test administration.

5. Ensure that all persons being tested have the specified practice with sample problems or test taking skills prior to their performance on the test.

6. Demonstrate the techniques and requirements for marking machine-scorable answer sheets. Check all individuals taking a test for competency in the techniques of recording their answers prior to the specific period of testing.

Qualifications of Test Administrators

1. Administer standardized tests only if you are qualified by training and experience as competent to administer particular tests.

2. Know the exact population and procedures used in standardizing the test and determine that the test is appropriate for the local population that is to be tested.

3. Acquire extensive training required to administer, score or interpret tests requiring test-specific training.

Giving Directions

1. Administer standardized tests with the verbatim instructions, exact sequence and timing and the identical materials that were used in the test standardization.

2. Present all tests (whether standardized, published or locally constructed) in an identical manner to ensure that the test is a fair and comparable demonstration of the performance of each individual taking the test.

Recognize that taking a test may be a new and frightening experience or stimulate anxiety or frustration for some individuals. Communicate to the examinees that they should attempt each task with positive application of their skills and knowledge and the anticipation that they will do their best.

Testing Conditions

1. Devote concentrated attention to observing the condition and reactions of the individuals being tested. Observe those being tested and identify environmental, health or emotional conditions that should be recorded and considered as invalidating elements for the test performance.

2. Possess and demonstrate clear verbal articulation, calmness and positive anticipation, empathy for social identification with the examinees, and, impartial treatment for all being tested.

3. Determine whether the testing environment (seating, work surfaces, lighting, heating, freedom from distractions, etc.) is conducive to the best possible performance of the test-takers.

4. Administer tests in physical facilities and psychological climates that allow each individual being tested to achieve optimum performance.

5. Record any deviation from standardized test administration procedure (such as used to accommodate handicapping conditions) and make it a permanent attachment to the test score or record.

6. Develop and complete for each test a systematic and objective procedure for observing and recording the behavior of those being tested (and recording conventional or deviant conditions of testing). Attach this record to the test scores of the persons tested.

7. Provide a written record of any circumstances that may have increased or reduced the opportunity of an individual being tested to demonstrate his or her best performance.

8. Accept responsibility for seeing that invalid or questionable test scores are not recorded, or not recorded without written qualification of the conditions that may have affected optimum test performance.

9. Arrange assistance from trained personnel in provided uniform conditions and in observing the conduct of the examinees when large groups of individuals must be tested.

Professional Collaboration

Recognize that in institutional settings, and wherever skill and knowledge can be pooled and responsibility shared, it is the qualifications of the team as a whole that count rather than those of individuals. However, coordination and consistency must be maintained.

Test Scoring

The measurement of human performance depends on accurate and consistent application of defined procedures for crediting the responses made by persons being tested. The procedures for scoring and recording test performance must be continuously audited for consistency and accuracy.

1. Routinely rescore a sample of the test answer sheets to verify the accuracy of the initial scoring.

2. Employ systematic procedures to verify the accuracy and consistency of matching scoring of answer sheets.

3. Obtain a separate and independent verification that appropriate scoring rules and normative conversions are used for each person tested.

4. Verify as accurate the computation of raw scores and the conversion of raw scores to normative or descriptive scales prior to release of such information to the tested person or to users of the test results.

5. Routinely check machine or manual reports of test results for accuracy. The person performing this task must be qualified to recognize inappropriate or impossible scores.

6. Develop and use systematic and objective procedures for observing and recording the conditions and behaviors of persons being tested and make this a part of the scores or test results that are reported.

7. Clearly label the scores that are reported and the date that a particular test was administered.

Test Interpretation

Test interpretation encompasses all the ways we assign value to the scores.

A test can be described as a systematic set or series of standard observations of performances that all fall in some particular domain. Typically each observation yields a rating of the performance (such as right or wrong and pass or fail), then these ratings are counted and this count becomes the basis of the scores. Such scores are usually much more stable than the result of any single performance. This score reliability creates the possibility of validity greater than can be obtained from unsystematic or nonaggregated observations.

The proper interpretation of test scores starts with understanding these fundamental characteristics of tests. Given this, the interpretation of scores from a test entails knowledge about (1) administration and score procedures; (2) scores, norms, and related technical features; (3) reliability; and (4) validity.

Adequate test interpretation requires knowledge and skill in each of these areas. Some of this information can be mastered only by studying the manual and other materials of the test; no one should undertake the interpretation of scores on any test without such study.

Administration and Scoring

Standard procedures for administering and scoring the test limit the possible meanings of scores. Departures from standard conditions and procedures modify and often invalidate the criteria for score interpretation.

1. The principles in the section on administration and scoring need to be understood by those engaged in interpretation.

2. Ascertain the circumstances peculiar to the particular administration and scoring of the test.

    A. Examine all reports from administrators, proctors, and scorers concerning irregularities or conditions, such as excessive anxiety, which may have affected performance.

    B. Weigh the possible effects on test scores of examiner-examinee differences in ethnic and cultural background, attitudes and values in light of research on these matters. Recognize that such effects are probably larger in individual testing situations.

    C. Look for administrators' reports of examinee behavior that indicate the responses were made on some basis other than that intended—as when a student being tested for knowledge of addition-number-facts adds by making tallies and then counting them.

3. Consider differences among clients in their reaction to instructions about guessing and scoring.

4. Recognize or judge the effect of scorer biases and judgment when subjective elements enter into scoring.

Scores, Norms, and Related Technical Features

The result of scoring a test is usually a number (or a set of numbers) called a raw score. Raw scores taken by themselves are not usually interpretable. Some additional steps must be taken.

The procedures either translate the numbers directly into descriptions of their meaning (e.g., pass or fail) or into other numbers called derived scores (e.g., standard scores) whose meaning stems from the test norms.

To interpret test scores, these procedures and the resulting descriptions or derived scores need to be thoroughly understood. Anything less than full understanding is likely to produce at least some, and probably many, serious errors in interpretation. The following are imperatives for interpreting tests:

1. Examine the test manuals, handbooks, users' guides and technical reports to determine what descriptions or derived scores are produced and what unique characteristics each may have.

2. Recognize that direct score interpretations such as mastery and nonmastery in criterion-referenced tests depend on arbitrary rules or standards.

   A. Report number or percent of items right in addition to the indicated interpretation whenever it will help others understand the quality of the examinee's test performance.

   B. Recognize that the difficulty of a fixed standard, such as 80 percent right, will vary widely from objective to objective. Such scores are not comparable in the normative sense.

   C. Recognize that when each score is classified as pass-fail, master-nonmastery or the like, that each element is being given equal weight.

3. Use the derived scores that fit the needs of the current use of the test.

   A. Use percentile ranks for direct comparison of individuals to the norm or reference group.

   B. Use standard scores or equal unit scaled scores whenever means and variances are calculated or other arithmetic operations are being used.

4. Recognize that only those derived scores that are based on the same norm group can be compared.

5. Consider the effect of any differences between the tests in what they measure when one test or form is equated with another, as well as the errors stemming from the equating itself.

   Give greater credence to growth or change shown by the same test (including level and form) than to equated measures except where practice effects or feedback have destroyed the validity of a second use.

6. Evaluate the appropriateness of the norm groups available as bases for interpreting the scores of clients.

   A. Use the norms for the group to which the client belongs.

   B. Consider using local norms and derived scores based on these local norms whenever possible.

7. Acquire knowledge of specific psychological or educational concepts and theories before interpreting the scores of tests based on such knowledge.

Reliability

Reliability is a prerequisite to validity. Generally, the greater the number of items the greater the reliability of the test. The degree to which a score or a set of scores may vary because of measurement error is a central factor in interpretation.

1. Use the standard error of measurement to obtain a rough estimate of the probable variation in scores due to unreliability.

2. Use the reliability coefficient to estimate the proportion of score variance that is not due to error.

3. Consider the sources of variance attributable to error in the particular reliability indexes reported in relationship to the uses being made of the scores.

4. Assess reported reliabilities in light of the many extraneous factors that may have artificially raised or lowered these estimates, such as test speededness, sample homogeneity or heterogeneity, restrictions in range and the like.

5. Distinguish indexes of rater reliability (i.e., of objectivity) from test reliability.

Validity

Proper test interpretation requires knowledge of the validity evidence available for the test as used. Its validity for other uses is not relevant. The purpose of testing dictates how a test is used. Technically proper use for ill-understood purposes may constitute misuse. The nature of the validity evidence required for a test is a function of its use.

Prediction—developing expectancies: The relationship of the test scores to an independently developed criterion measure is the basis for predictive validity.

1. Consider both the reliability and the relevance of the criterion measures used.

2. Use cross-validation data to judge the validity of predictions.

3. Question the meaning of an apparently valid predictor that lacks both construct and content validity. Assess the role of underlying and concomitant variables.

4. Consider the validity of a given measure in the context of all the predictors used or available. Does the measure make an independent contribution to the prediction over and above that provided by other measures?

5. Consider the pitfalls of labeling, stereotyping and prejudging people. The self-fulfilling prophecies that may result are often undesirable.

Placement/selection: Predictive validity is the usual basis for valid placement. Consider the evidence of validity for each alternative (i.e., each placement) when inferring the meaning of scores.

1. Obtain accurate information about the programs or institutions in which the client may be placed in order to judge the consequences of such placement.

2. Estimate the probability of favorable outcomes for each possible placement (e.g., both selection and rejection) before judging the import of the scores.

3. Consider the possibility that outcomes favorable from an institutional point of view may differ from those that are favorable from the examinees' point of view.

4. Examine the possibility that the clients' group membership (race, sex, etc.) may alter the reported validity relationships.

5. Use all the available evidence about the individual to infer the validity of the score for that individual. Each single piece of information about an individual, (e.g., test score, teacher report, or counselor opinion) improves the probability that proper judgments and decisions can be made.

    A. Test scores should be considered in context; they do not have absolute meaning.

    B. Single test scores should not be the sole basis for placement or selection.

Description/diagnosis: Distinguish between those descriptions and diagnoses using psychological constructs that can be validated only indirectly and those for which content specifications suffice.

1. Identify clearly the domain specified by those asserting content validity.

Assess the adequacy of the content sampling procedures used in writing and selecting items.

2. Identify the dimensions of the construct being measured when multiple scores from a battery or inventory are used for description.

   A. Examine the content validity and/or the construct validity of each score separately.

   B. Consider the relative importance of the various subtests, parts, objectives or elements yielding separate scores and judge the weight they each should be given in interpretation.

   C. Recognize that when scores are summed or averaged, their weight is a function of their variances.

   D. Recognize that when each score is classified as pass-fail, mastery-nonmastery or the like, each element is being given equal weight.

3. Examine the completeness of the description provided, recognizing that no set of test scores completely describes a human being.

Growth—Studies of change: Valid assessment of growth or change requires both a test having descriptive validity and a procedure for establishing that the scores obtained differ from those that might arise when no change has occurred.

1. Report as possibilities all the interpretations the study or evaluation design permits. Point out those interpretations that are precluded by the design used.

   A. When standard procedures such as the RMC models (see Tallmadge, G.K., and Horst, D.P., A procedural guide for validating achievement gains in educational projects; Mountain View, Calif: RMC Research Corp., Dec. 1975) for measuring growth in achievement are employed, use the descriptions

of strengths and weaknesses provided.

   B. Look for naturally occurring control groups not part of design whenever possible.

2. Consider the strengths and weaknesses of the particular tests used with respect to this use.

   Consider the possibility of floor or ceiling effects, the content changes level to level, the adequacy of articulation in multilevel tests, the comparability of alternate forms, the adequacy of the score-equating across forms, and the comparability of timing of the testing to that of the norming.

3. Recognize the unreliability of individual score differences as measures of change.

4. Recognize the unreliability of individual score differences as measures of change.

5. Recognize the need for equal interval scales when trying to assess the amount of change.

Communicating Test Results

Communication consists of reporting data in such a way that it is comprehensible and informative. The responsible practitioner reports test data with a concern for the user's need for information and the purposes of evaluating the significance of the information.

There must also be a concern for the right of the individual tested to be informed regarding how the results will be used for his or her benefit (informed consent), who will have access to the results (right to privacy), and what safeguards exist to prevent misuse.

Where standardized test data are being used to enhance decisions about an individual, the practitioner's responsibilities are as follows:

Know the Manual

1. Become thoroughly familiar with the publisher's manual before attempting to "explain" any results.

224

BECOMING A PROFESSIONAL COUNSELOR

2. Develop skills needed to communicate results of tests, using concepts that are frequently misunderstood before communicating results to clients, the public, or other recipients of the information.

Know the Limits

1. Inform the person receiving the test information that "scores" are approximations, not absolutes, and indicate the SEM or the margin of error in some other way, such as by reporting score intervals rather than points.

2. Candidly discuss with the person receiving the test information any qualifications necessary to understand potential sources of bias for a given set of test results relative to their use with a specific individual.

3. Emphasize that test data represent just one source of information and should rarely, if ever, be used alone for decision making.

Informed Consent

1. Inform the person receiving the test information of any circumstances that could have affected the validity or reliability of the results.

2. Inform the examinee of what action will be taken by the agency and who will be using the results.

3. Obtain the consent of the examinee before using test results for any purpose other than that advanced prior to testing.

Right to Privacy

Inform the examinee of steps to be taken to correct any erroneous information that may be on file as a result of testing.

Where standardized test data are being used to describe groups for the purpose of evaluation, the practitioner's responsibilities are as follows:

Background information

1. Include background information to improve the accuracy of understanding about any numerical data.

2. Identify the purposes for which the reported data would be appropriate.

Politics

Be aware that public release of test information provides data for all kinds of purposes and that some of these may be adverse to the interests of those tested.

Averages and Norms

1. Clarify in particular that "average" on a standardized test is a range, not a point, and typically includes the middle 50 percent of the group being considered.

2. Qualify all group data in terms of the appropriateness of the norms for that group.

Agency Policies

1. Work for agency test-reporting policies designed to strengthen and protect the benefits of the groups being measured.

2. Work within the agency to establish procedures for periodic review of internal test use.

Counseling Services:
Consumer Rights and Responsibilities

Consumer Rights

- Be informed of the qualifications of your counselor: education, experience, and professional counseling certification(s) and state license(s).
- Receive an explanation of services offered, your time commitments, and fee scales and billing policies prior to receipt of services.
- Be informed of limitations of the counselor's practice to special areas of expertise (e.g., career development, ethnic groups, etc.) or age group (e.g., adolescents, older adults, etc.).
- Have all that you say treated confidentially and be informed of any state laws placing limitations on confidentiality in the counseling relationship.
- Ask questions about the counseling techniques and strategies and be informed of your progress.
- Participate in setting goals and evaluating progress toward meeting them.

- Be informed of how to contact the counselor in an emergency situation.
- Request referral for a second opinion at any time.
- Request copies of records and reports to be used by other counseling professionals.
- Receive a copy of the code of ethics to which your counselor adheres.
- Contact the appropriate professional organization if you have doubts or complaints relative to the counselor's conduct.
- Terminate the counseling relationship at any time.

Consumer Responsibilities

- Set and keep appointments with your counselor. Let him/her know as soon as possible if you cannot keep an appointment.

SOURCE: Reprinted with the permission of the National Board for Certified Counselors. NBCC endorsement of the publication in which this document appears is neither intended nor implied.

- Pay your fees in accordance with the schedule you pre-established with the counselor.
- Help plan your goals.
- Follow through with agreed upon goals.
- Keep your counselor informed of your progress toward meeting your goals.
- Terminate your counseling relationship before entering into arrangements with another counselor.

This statement was prepared by the National Board for Certified Counselors and Chi Sigma Iota to help you understand and exercise your rights as a consumer of counseling services. NBCC and BSI believe that clients who are informed consumers are able to best use counseling services to meet their individual needs.

References

Adler, A. (1963). *The practice and theory of individual psychology.* Patterson, NJ: Littlefield, Adams. (Original work published 1930)

Aiken, L. R. (1976). *Psychological testing and assessment* (2nd ed.). Boston: Allyn & Bacon.

Allport, G. W. (1961). *Patterns and growth in personality.* New York: Holt, Rinehart & Winston.

Allport, G. W., & Odbert, H. S. (1936). Trait names: A psycholexical study. *Psychological Monographs, 47,* 2-11.

Allport, G. W., Vernon, P. E., & Lindzey, G. (1960). *Study of values: Manual* (3rd ed.). Chicago: Riverside.

American Association for Counseling and Development (AACD). (1981). *Ethical standards of the American Association for Counseling and Development.* Alexandria, VA: Author.

American Association for Counseling and Development (AACD). (1986). *Accreditation procedures manual for counseling and related educational programs.* Alexandria, VA: Author.

American Personnel and Guidance Association. (1978, October 5). Responsibilities of users of standardized tests. *Guidepost, 21*(5), 5-8.

American Psychiatric Association. (1987). *Diagnostic and statistical manual of mental disorders* (3rd ed., rev.). Washington, DC: Author.

Anastasi, A. (1988). *Psychological testing* (6th ed.). New York: Macmillan.

Anderson, J. (1979). Social work practice with groups in the generic base of social work

practice. *Social Work with Groups, 2,* 281-293.

Ary, D., Jacobs, L. C., & Razavieh, A. (1985). *Introduction to research in education* (3rd ed.). New York: Holt, Rinehart & Winston.

Association for Specialists in Group Work. (1980). *Ethical guidelines for group leaders of the Association for Specialists in Group Work.* Alexandria, VA: American Association for Counseling and Development.

Atkinson, D. R., Morten, G., & Sue, D. W. (1983). *Counseling American minorities: A cross-cultural perspective* (2nd ed.). Dubuque, IA: William C. Brown.

Aubrey, R. F. (1986). The professionalization of counseling. In M. D. Lewis, R. L. Hayes, & J. A. Lewis (Eds.), *An introduction to the counseling profession.* Itasca, IL: F. E. Peacock.

Axelson, J. A. (1985). *Counseling and development in a multicultural society.* Monterey, CA: Brooks/Cole.

Bandura, A. (1969). *Principles of behavior modification.* New York: Holt, Rinehart & Winston.

Bandura, A. (1977). *Social learning theory.* Englewood Cliffs, NJ: Prentice-Hall.

Beck, A. T. (1985). Cognitive therapy, behavior therapy, psychoanalysis and pharmacotherapy: A cognitive continuum. In M. Mahoney & A. Freeman (Eds.), *Cognition and psychotherapy.* New York: Plenum.

Bee, H. L., & Mitchell, S. K. (1984). *The developing person: A lifespan approach* (2nd ed.). New York: Harper & Row.

Belkin, G. S. (1988). *Introduction to counseling* (3rd ed.). Dubuque, IA: William C. Brown.

Bell, A. P., & Weinberg, M. S. (1978). *Homosexualities: A study of diversity among men and women.* New York: Simon & Schuster.

Bem, S. L. (1975). Androgyne vs. the tight little lives of fluffy women and chesty men. *Psychology Today.*

Benoit-Smullyan, E. (1944). Status, status types, and status interrelations. *American Sociological Review, 9,* 151-161.

Berne, E. (1964). *Games people play.* New York: Grove.

Blau, P. (1964). *Exchange and power in social life.* New York: John Wiley.

Blocher, D. H. (1987). *The professional counselor.* New York: Macmillan.

Borders, L. D., & Leddick, G. R. (1987). *Handbook of counseling supervision.* Alexandria, VA: American Association for Counseling and Development.

Borow, H. (1961). Vocational development research: Some problems of logical and experimental form. *Personnel and Guidance Journal, 40,* 21-25.

Bracht, G. H., & Glass, G. V. (1968). The external validity of experiments. *American Educational Research Journal, 5,* 437-474.

Brimm, O. E. L. (1965). American attitudes toward intelligence tests. *American Psychologist, 20,* 125-130.

Brooks, L. (1984). Counseling special groups: Women and ethnic minorities. In D. Brown, L. Brooks, & Associates, *Career choice and development.* San Francisco: Jossey-Bass.

Brown, D. (1981). Emerging models of career development groups for persons at mid-life. *Vocational Guidance Quarterly, 29,* 332-340.

Brown, D. (1984). Mid-life career change. In D. Brown, L. Brooks, & Associates, *Career choice and development.* San Francisco: Jossey-Bass.

Buss, A. H., & Plomin, R. A. (1975). *Temperament theory of personality development.* New York: John Wiley.

Butler, R. (1974). Successful aging and role of the life review. *Journal of American Geriatric Society.*

Byrne, D., & Kelley, K. (1981). *An introduction to personality.* Englewood Cliffs, NJ: Prentice-Hall.

Campbell, D. T., & Stanley, J. C. (1966). *Experimental and quasi-experimental designs for research.* Chicago: Rand McNally.

Caplan, G. (1963). Types of mental health consultation. *American Journal of Orthopsychiatry, 3,* 470-481.

Carkhuff, R. R. (1969). *Helping and human relation* (Vol. 2). New York: Holt, Rinehart & Winston.

Cartwright, D., & Zander, A. (1968). *Group dynamics research and theory.* New York: Harper & Row.

Cattell, R. (1946). *Description and measurement of personality.* Yonkers, NY: World Book.

Cattell, R. B. (1948). Concepts and methods in the measurement of group syntality. *Psychological Review, 55,* 48-63.

Cattell, R. B., Eber, H. W., & Tatsuoka, M. M. (1970). *Handbook for the Sixteen Personality Factor Questionnaire.* Champaign, IL: Institute for Personality and Ability Testing.

Chambless, D. L., & Goldstein, A. J. (1979). Behavioral psychotherapy. In R. J. Corsini & Contributors, *Current psychotherapies* (2nd ed.). Itasca, IL: F. E. Peacock.

Chance, P. (1979). *Learning and behavior.* Belmont, CA: Wadsworth.

Coleman, J. C., Butcher, J. N., & Carson, R. C. (1980). *Abnormal psychology and modern life.* Glenview, IL: Scott, Foresman.

Conyne, R. K. (Ed.). (1985). *The group worker's handbook: Varieties of group experience.* Springfield, IL: Charles C Thomas.

Corey, G., & Corey, M. S. (1982). *Groups: Process and practice.* Monterey, CA: Brooks/Cole.

Corey, G., Corey, M. S., & Callahan, P. (1988). *Issues and ethics in the helping professions.* Pacific Grove, CA: Brooks/Cole.

Crites, J. O. (1973). *Career maturity inventory.* Monterey: California Test Bureau/McGraw-Hill.

Cronbach, L. (1984). *Essentials of psychological testing* (4th ed.). New York: Harper & Row.

Dagley, J. C., Gazda, G. M., & Pistole, M. C. (1986). Groups. In M. D. Lewis, R. L. Hayes, & J. A. Lewis (Eds.), *An introduction to the counseling profession.* Itasca, IL: F. E. Peacock.

Davis, J. B. (1914). *Vocational and moral guidance.* Boston: Ginn.

Dillard, J. M. (1983). *Multicultural counseling: Toward an ethnic and cultural relevance in human encounters.* Chicago: Nelson-Hall.

Draguns, J. G. (1981). Counseling across cultures: Common themes and distinct approaches. In J. B. Pedersen, J. G. Draguns, W. J. Lonner, & J. E. Trimble (Eds.), *Counseling across cultures* (rev., expanded ed., pp. 3-21). Honolulu: University Press of Hawaii.

Drummond, R. J. (1988). *Appraisal procedures for counselors and helping professionals.* Columbus, OH: Merrill.

Edwards, A. L. (1957). *Techniques of attitude scale construction.* New York: Appleton.

Egan, G. (1988). *The skilled helper.* Belmont, CA: Wadsworth.

Ellis, A. (1979). Rational-emotive therapy. In R. J. Corsini & Contributors, *Current psychotherapies* (2nd ed.). Itasca, IL: F E. Peacock.

Erikson, E. H. (1963). *Childhood and society* (2nd ed.). New York: Norton.

Festinger, L. (1957). *A theory of cognitive dissonance.* Stanford, CA: Stanford University Press.

Frankl, V. (1967). *Psychotherapy and existentialism: Selected papers on logotherapy.* New York: Simon & Schuster.

French, J. R. P., Jr., & Snyder, R. (1959). Leadership and interpersonal power. In D. Cartwright (Ed.), *Studies in social power.* Ann Arbor, MI: Institute for Social Research.

Freud, S. (1922). *Group psychology and the analysis of the ego.* London: International Psychoanalytic Press.

Freud, S. (1961). Some psychical consequences of the anatomical distinction between the sexes. In J. Strackey (Ed. and Trans.), *The standard edition of the complete psychological works of Sigmund Freud* (Vol. 19). London: Hogarth. (Original work published 1925)

Gallesich, J. (1985). Toward a meta-theory of consultation. *Counseling Psychologist, 13,* 336-354.

Gazda, G. M. (1973). *Human relations development.*

Gazda, G. M. (1984). *Group counseling: A developmental approach* (3rd ed.). Boston: Allyn & Bacon.

Gelatt, H. B. (1962). Decision-making: A conceptual frame of reference for counseling. *Journal of Counseling Psychology, 9,* 240-245.

Gendlin, E. (1981). *Focusing.* New York: Bantam.

Gessell, A. (1925). *The mental growth of the pre-school child.* New York: Macmillan.

Gibson, R. L., & Mitchell, M. H. (1986). *Introduction to counseling and guidance* (2nd ed.). New York: Macmillan.

Ginsberg, L. H. (Ed.). *Lifespan development psychology: Normative life crises.* New York: Academic Press.

Ginzberg, E. (1984). Career development. In D. Brown, L. Brooks, & Associates, *Career choice and development.* San Francisco: Jossey-Bass.

Ginzberg, E., Ginsburg, S. W., Axelrod, S., & Herma, J. R. (1951). *Occupational choice: An approach to a general theory.* New York: Columbia University Press.

Glasser, W. (1981). *Stations of the mind.* New York: Harper & Row.

Glasser, W. (1984). Reality therapy. In R. J. Corsini & Contributors, *Current psychotherapies* (3rd ed.). Itasca, IL: F. E. Peacock.

Goldhaber, D. (1986). *Life-span human development.* New York: Harcourt Brace Jovanovich.

Goldman, L. (1986). Research and evaluation. In M. D. Lewis, R. L. Hayes, & J. A. Lewis (Eds.), *An introduction to the counseling profession.* Itasca, IL: F. E. Peacock.

Harary, F., Norman, R. A., & Cartwright, D. (1965). *Structural models: An introduction to the theory of directed graphs.* New York: John Wiley.

Harris, T. A. (1969). *I'm OK—you're OK.* New York: Harper & Row.

Havighurst, R. J. (1964). Youth in exploration and man emergent. In H. Borow (Ed.), *Man in a world at work.* Boston: Houghton Mifflin.

Hayes, R. (1984). An alternative to rearranging our prejudice. In G. Walz & L. Benjamin (Eds.), *Shaping counselor education programs in the next five years: An experimental prototype for the counselor of tomorrow* (pp. 107-120). Ann Arbor, MI: ERIC/ CAPS.

Hayes, R. L. (1986). Human growth and development. In M. D. Lewis, R. L. Hayes, & J. A. Lewis (Eds.), *An introduction to the* counseling profession. Itasca, IL: F. E. Peacock.

Herr, E. L. (1986). Life-style and career development. In M. D. Lewis, R. L. Hayes, & J. A. Lewis (Eds.), An introduction to the counseling profession. Itasca, IL: F. E. Peacock.

Herr, E. L., & Cramer, S. H. (1988). Career guidance and counseling through the life span: Systematic approaches (3rd ed.). Glenview, IL: Scott, Foresman.

Hershenson, D. B., & Power, P. W. (1987). Mental health counseling theory and practice. New York: Pergamon.

Hill, R. C. (1972). The strength of black families. New York: Emerson Hall.

Holland, J. L. (1953). Holland's Vocational Preference Inventory. Palo Alto, CA: Consulting Psychologists Press.

Holland, J. L. (1973). Making vocational choices: A theory of careers. Englewood Cliffs, NJ: Prentice-Hall.

Holland, J. L. (1977). The Self-Directed Search. Palo Alto, CA: Consulting Psychologists Press.

Holland, J. L., et al. (1980). The Vocational Exploration and Insight Kit (VEIK). Palo Alto, CA: Consulting Psychologists Press.

Homans, G. (1961). Social behavior: Its elementary forms. New York: Harcourt Brace Jovanovich.

Hopkins, B. R., & Anderson, B. S. (1986). The counselor and the law (2nd ed.). Washington, DC: American Association for Counseling and Development Press.

Huck, S. W., Cormier, W. H., & Bounds, W. G., Jr. (1974). Reading statistics and research. New York: Harper & Row.

Hultsch, D. F., & Deutsch, F. (1981). Adult development and aging: A lifespan perspective. New York: McGraw-Hill.

Isaac, S., & Michael, W. B. (1981). Handbook in research and evaluation (2nd ed.). San Diego: EdITS.

Isaacson, L. E. (1985). Basics of career counseling. Boston: Allyn & Bacon.

Ivey, A. E. (1988). Intentional interviewing and counseling. Pacific Grove, CA: Brooks/ Cole.

Jennings, H. H. (1943). Leadership and isolation. New York: Longmans, Green.

Johnson, D. W., & Johnson, F. P. (1987). Joining together group theory and group skills. Englewood Cliffs, NJ: Prentice-Hall.

Jung, C. G. (1928). Contributions to analytic psychology. New York: Harcourt.

Jung, C. G. (1933). Psychological types. New York: Harcourt.

Jung, C. G. (1964). Man and his symbols. Garden City, NY: Doubleday.

Katz, M. (1963). Decisions and values: A rationale for secondary school guidance. New York: College Entrance Examination Board.

Katz, M. (1973). The name and nature of vocational guidance. In H. Borow (Ed.), Career guidance for a new age (pp. 83-134). Boston: Houghton Mifflin.

Katz, M. (1980). SIGI: An interactive aid to career decision-making. Journal of College Student Personnel, 21(1), 34-40.

Kaufmann, Y. (1979). Analytical psychotherapy. In R. J. Corsini & Contributors, Current psychotherapies (2nd ed.). Itasca, IL: F. E. Peacock.

Kegan, R. (1982). The evolving self: Problem and process in human development. Cambridge, MA: Harvard University Press.

Kelly, G. A. (1955). The psychology of personal constructs. New York: Norton.

Kempler, W. (1974). Principles of Gestalt family therapy. Costa Mesa, CA: Kempler Institute.

Kerlinger, F. N. (1986). Foundations of behavioral research (3rd ed.). New York: Holt, Rinehart & Winston.

Kissen, M. (1981). Exploring general systems processes in group settings. Psychotherapy: Theory, Research and Practice, 18, 424-430.

Klein, A. (1972). Effective group work. New York: Association Press.

Kohlberg, L. (1984). Essays on moral development: Vol. 2. The psychology of moral development. San Francisco: Harper & Row.

Krajewski, J. P. (1986). Psychotherapy with gay men and lesbians. In T. S. Stein & C. J. Cohen (Eds.), Contemporary perspectives on psychotherapy with lesbians and gay men. New York: Plenum Medical.

Krumboltz, J. D., Mitchell, A. M., & Jones, G. B. (1976). A social learning theory of career selection. Counseling Psychologist, 6, 71-81.

Kübler-Ross, E. (1969). *On death and dying.* New York: Macmillan.

Kurpius, D. J. (1978). Consultation theory and process: An integrated model. *Personnel and Guidance Journal, 56,* 335-338.

Kurpius, D. J. (1986). The helping relationship. In M. D. Lewis, R. L. Hayes, & J. A. Lewis (Eds.), *An introduction to the counseling profession.* Itasca, IL: F. E. Peacock.

Lakein, A. (1973). *How to get control of your time and your life.* New York: Signet.

Levinson, D. J. (1978). *The seasons of a man's life.* New York: Knopf.

Lewin, K. (1951). *Field theory in social science.* New York: Harper & Row.

Lewis, J. A., Dana, R. Q., & Blevins, G. A. (1988). *Substance abuse counseling: An individualized approach.* Pacific Grove, CA: Brooks/Cole.

Lewis, J. A., & Lewis, M. D. (1983). *Community counseling: A human services approach.* New York: John Wiley.

Lewis, J. A. & Lewis, M. D. (1989). *Community Counseling.* Pacific Grove, CA: Brooks/Cole.

Lewis, M. D., Hayes, R. L., & Lewis, J. A. (1986). *An introduction to the counseling profession.* Itasca, IL: F. E. Peacock.

Lewis, M. D., & Lewis, J. A. (1987). *Management of human service programs.* Monterey, CA: Brooks/Cole.

Lewis, R. G., & Ho, M. K. (1975). Social work with Native Americans. *Social Work, 20,* 379-382.

Likert, R. (1932). A technique for the measurement of attitudes. *Archives of Psychology, 140.*

Litwack, L. (1986). Appraisal of the individual. In M. D. Lewis, R. L. Hayes, & J. A. Lewis (Eds.), *An introduction to the counseling profession.* Itasca, IL: F. E. Peacock.

Loesch, L. C., & Vacc, N. A. (1986). *National counselor certification examination technical manual.* Alexandria, VA: National Board for Certified Counselors and American Association for Counseling and Development.

Loevinger, J. (1976). *Ego development: Conceptions and theories.* San Francisco: Jossey-Bass.

Maccoby, E. E., & Jacklin, C. N. (1974). *Psychology of sex differences.* Stanford, CA: Stanford University.

Maslow, A. (1954). *Motivation and personality.* New York: Harper.

Maslow, A. (1962). *Toward a psychology of being.* New York: Van Nostrand.

Meador, B. D., & Rogers, C. R. (1984). Person-centered therapy. In R. J. Corsini & Contributors, *Current psychotherapies* (3rd ed.). Itasca, IL: F. E. Peacock.

Mehrens, W. A. (1976). *Readings in measurement and evaluation in education and psychology.* New York: Holt, Rinehart & Winston.

Meichenbaum, D. (1977). *Cognitive behavior therapy.* New York: Plenum.

Miller, A. L., & Tiedeman, D. V. (1972). Decision making for the 70s: The cubing of the Tiedeman paradigm and its application in career education. *Focus on Guidance, 5,* 1-15.

Mitchell, J. V. (Ed.). (1983). *Tests in print III.* Lincoln: University of Nebraska Press.

Mitchell, L. K., & Krumboltz, J. D. (1984). Social learning approach to career decision making. In D. Brown, L. Brooks, & Associates, *Career choice and development* (pp. 235-280). San Francisco: Jossey-Bass.

Moreno, J. L. (1934). *Who shall survive?* Washington, DC: Nervous and Mental Diseases.

Mosak, H. H. (1979). Adlerian psychotherapy. In R. J. Corsini & Contributors, *Current psychotherapies* (2nd ed.). Itasca, IL: F. E. Peacock.

Murray, H. A. (1938). *Explorations in personality.* New York: Oxford University Press.

Myers, I. B. (1962). *The Myers-Briggs Type Indicator manual.* Princeton, NJ: Educational Testing Service.

Myers, I. B., & Briggs, K. S. (1985). *Myers-Briggs Type Indicator.* Palo Alto, CA: Consulting Psychologists Press. (Original work published 1925)

National Vocational Guidance Association, Board of Directors. (1982). Vocational/career counseling competencies. *NVGA Newsletter, 22,* 6.

Noll, V. H., & Scannell, D. P. (1972). *Introduction to educational measurement* (3rd ed.). Boston: Houghton Mifflin.

Olsen, M. (1968). *The process of social organization.* New York: Holt, Rinehart & Winston.

Osgood, C. E., Suci, G. J., & Tannenbaum, P. H. (1957). *The measurement of meaning.* Urbana: University of Illinois Press.

Padilla, A. M., Ruiz, R. A., & Alvarez, R. (1983). In D. R. Atkinson, G. Morten, & D. W. Sue, *Counseling American minorities: A cross-cultural perspective* (2nd ed.). Dubuque, IA: William C. Brown.

Parsons, F. (1909). *Choosing a vocation.* Boston: Houghton Mifflin.

Pavlov, I. (1927). *Conditioned reflexes.* New York: Dover.

Pennell, N. Y., Proffitt, J. R., & Hatch, T. D. (1971). *Accreditation and certification in relation to allied health manpower.* Washington, DC: U. S. Department of Health, Education and Welfare, Public Health Service.

Perry, W. G., Jr. (1970). *Forms of intellectual and ethical development in the college years.* New York: Holt, Rinehart & Winston.

Piaget, J. (1952). *The origins of intelligence in children.* New York: International Universities Press. (Original work published 1936)

Proctor, W. M., Benefield, W., & Wrenn, C. G. (1931). *Workbook in vocations.* Boston: Houghton Mifflin.

Riker, H. C. (1981). Preface. In J. E. Myers (Ed.), *Counseling older persons: Vol. 3. Trainers manual for basic helping skills* (pp. xvii-xx). Washington, DC: American Personnel and Guidance Association.

Rhyne, J. (1973). *The gestalt art experience.* Monterey, CA: Brooks/Cole.

Riegel, K. F. (1975). Adult life crises: A dialectical interpretation of development. In N. Datan & L. H. Ginsberg (Eds.), *Lifespan development psychology: Normative life crises.* New York: Academic Press.

Roe, A. (1957). Early determinants of vocational choice. *Journal of Counseling Psychology, 4,* 212-217.

Roe, A. (1976). *Classification of occupations by group and level.* Bensenville, IL: Scholastic Testing Service.

Rogers, C. R. (1942). *Counseling and psychotherapy.* Boston: Houghton Mifflin.

Rogers, C. R. (1951). *Client-centered therapy.* Boston: Houghton Mifflin.

Rogers, C. R. (1957). The necessary and sufficient conditions of therapeutic personality change. *Journal of Consulting Psychology, 21,* 95-103.

Rogers, C. R. (1961). *On becoming a person.* Boston: Houghton Mifflin.

Russell, M. L. (1978). Behavior consultation: Theory and process. *Personnel and Guidance Journal, 56,* 346-350.

Santrock, J. W. (1986). *Life-span development* (2nd ed.). Dubuque, IA: William C. Brown.

Saslow, C. A. (1982). *Basic research methods.* Reading, MA: Addison-Wesley.

Satir, V. (1967). *Conjoint family therapy: A guide to theory and technique.* Palo Alto, CA: Science and Behavior.

Satir, V. (1983). *Conjoint family therapy.* Palo Alto, CA: Science and Behavior.

Sax, G. (1980). *Principles of educational and psychological measurement* (2nd ed.). Belmont CA: Wadsworth.

Schein, E. H. (1969). *Process consultation: Its role in organization development.* Reading, MA: Addison-Wesley.

Schlossberg, N. K. (1984). *Counseling with adults in transition: Linking practice with theory.* New York: Springer.

Schutz, W. C. (1958). *FIRO: A three dimensional theory of interpersonal behavior.* New York: Rinehart.

Shaw, M. E. (1981). *Group dynamics: The psychology of small group behavior.* New York: McGraw-Hill.

Shertzer, B., & Stone, S. C. (1980). *Fundamentals of counseling* (3rd ed.). Boston: Houghton Mifflin.

Simkin, J. S. (1979). Gestalt therapy. In R. J. Corsini & Contributors, *Current psychotherapies* (2nd ed.). Itasca, IL: F. E. Peacock.

Simon, H. A. (1957). *Models of man: Social and rational.* New York: John Wiley.

Skinner, B. F. (1953). *Science and human behavior.* New York: Macmillan.

Stephenson, W. (1953). *The study of behavior.* Chicago: University of Chicago Press.

Sue, D. W. (1983a). Counseling Chinese Americans. In D. R. Atkinson, G. Morten, & D. W. Sue, *Counseling American minorities: A cross-cultural perspective* (2nd ed.). Dubuque, IA: William C. Brown. (Original work published 1972)

Sue, D. W. (1983b). Ethnic identity: The impact of two cultures on the psychological development of Asians in America. In

D. R. Atkinson, G. Morten, & D. W. Sue, *Counseling American minorities: A cross-cultural perspective* (2nd ed.). Dubuque, IA: William C. Brown. (Original work published 1973)

Sue, D. W., & Sue, D. (1977, September). Barriers to effective cross-cultural counseling. *Journal of Counseling Psychology.*

Sullivan, H. S. (1953). *The interpersonal theory of psychiatry.* New York: Norton.

Super, D. E. (1953). A theory of vocational development. *American Psychologist, 8,* 185-190.

Super, D. E. (1955). Transition: From vocational guidance to counseling psychology. *Journal of Counseling Psychology, 3,* 2-9.

Super, D. E. (1969). Vocational development theory: Persons, positions, processes. *Counseling Psychologist, 1,* 2-9.

Super, D. E. (1980). A life-span, life space approach to career development. *Journal of Vocational Behavior, 16,* 282-298.

Tharp, R. G., & Wetzel, R. (1969). *Behavior modification in the natural environment.* New York: Academic Press.

Thibaut, J., & Kelley, H. (1959). *The social psychology of groups.* New York: John Wiley.

Thomas, A., & Chess, S. (1977). *Temperament and development.* New York: Brunner/Mazel.

Thorndike, E. L. (1913). *The psychology of learning.* New York: Teachers College.

Thorndike, R. H., & Hagen, E. P. (1977). *Measurement and evaluation in psychology and education* (4th ed.). New York: John Wiley.

Thurstone, L., & Chave, E. (1929). *The measurement of attitude.* Chicago: University of Chicago Press.

Tiedeman, D. V., & Miller-Tiedeman, A. (1984). Career decision making: An individualistic perspective. In D. Brown, L. Brooks, & Associates, *Career choice and development* (pp. 281-310). San Francisco: Jossey-Bass.

Tiedeman, D. V., & O'Hara, R. P. (1963). *Career development: Choice and adjustment.* New York: College Entrance Examination Board.

Toseland, R. W., & Rivas, R. F. (1984). *An introduction to group work practice.* New York: Macmillan.

Travis, J. W., & Ryan, R. S. (1988). *Wellness workbook.* Berkeley, CA: Ten Speed.

Tuckman, B. (1963). Developmental sequence in small groups. *Psychological Bulletin, 63,* 384-399.

U.S. Department of Labor. (1978). *Dictionary of occupational titles* (4th ed.). Washington, DC: Government Printing Office.

U.S. Department of Labor. (1980). *Occupational outlook handbook.* Washington, DC: Government Printing Office.

Vacc, N. A., & Loesch, L. C. (1987). *Counseling as a profession.* Muncie, IN: Accelerated Development.

Van Hoose, W. H., & Kottler, J. A. (1985). *Ethical and legal issues in counseling and psychotherapy.* San Francisco: Jossey-Bass.

Van Hoose, W. H., & Worth, M. R. (1982). *Adulthood in the life cycle.* Dubuque, IA: William C. Brown.

Vontress, C. E. (1973). Counseling: Racial and ethnic factors. *Focus on Guidance, 5,* 1-10.

Vontress, C. E. (1985). Theories of counseling: A comparative analysis. In R. J. Samuda & A. Wolfgang (Eds.), *Intercultural counseling and assessment: Global perspectives* (pp. 19-31). Toronto: C. J. Hogrefe.

Vontress, C. E. (1986). Social and cultural foundations. In M. D. Lewis, R. L. Hayes, & J. A. Lewis (Eds.), *An introduction to the counseling profession.* Itasca, IL: F. E. Peacock.

Watson, J. B. (1919). *Psychology from the standpoint of a behaviorist.* Philadelphia: J. B. Lippincott.

Weinberg, G. (1972). *Society and the healthy homosexual.* Garden City, NY: Anchor.

Williamson, E. G. (1939). *How to counsel students.* New York: McGraw-Hill.

Williamson, E. G. (1950). *Counseling adolescents.* New York: Harper & Bros.

Wittmer, J. P., & Loesch, L. C. (1986). Professional orientation. In M. D. Lewis, R. L. Hayes, & J. A. Lewis (Eds.), *An introduction to the counseling profession* (pp. 301-330). Itasca, IL: F. E. Peacock.

Wolpe, J. (1966). The comparative clinical status of conditioning therapies and psychoanalysis. In J. Wolpe, A. Salter, & L. Reyna (Eds.), *The conditioning therapies.* New York: Holt, Rinehart & Winston.

Woodman, N. J., & Lenna, H. R. (1980). *Counseling with gay men and women: A guide for facilitating positive life-styles.* San Francisco: Jossey-Bass.

Yalom, I. D. (1975). *The theory and practice of group psychotherapy* (2nd ed.). New York: Basic Books.

About the Authors

Sheri A. Wallace is a doctoral candidate in counselor education at the University of Florida, Gainesville. She received her M.A. in counseling from Governors State University, University Park, Illinois, and her B.S. in education from Chicago State University. She has worked as an elementary school teacher in Calumet Park, Illinois, and as a consultant and educator for Tri-City Community Mental Health Center in East Chicago, Indiana. She has been a college instructor at Santa Fe Community College and a substance abuse counselor at Vista Pavilion in Gainesville. Her primary interest area is health promotion for business and industry.

Michael D. Lewis (Ph.D., University of Michigan) is Professor of Psychology and Counseling at Governors State University. He also is Chairperson for the Employee Assistance Program of the Association for Counselor Education and Supervision and is President of the Illinois Specialist in Group Work. He has worked with several human service organizations and has held academic positions at Florida Atlantic University, DePaul University, and Eastern Michigan University. Lewis has authored or coauthored 11 books and has published numerous articles in professional journals.

TO THE OWNER OF THIS BOOK

We hope that you have enjoyed *Becoming a Professional Counselor*. We would like to know as much about your experiences with this workbook as possible. Only through your comments and the comments of others can we learn how to make future editions more useful to readers. Please take the time to fill out the following form and send it to the authors, Sheri A. Wallace and Michael D. Lewis, c/o Editorial Production—Books, Sage Publications, P.O. Box 5084, Newbury Park, CA 91359.

School: _____ Your Instructor's Name: _____

(1) My purpose in using this book was:

_____

_____

(2) What I like *most* about this book is:

_____

_____

(3) What I like *least* about this book is:

_____

_____

(4) My specific suggestions for improving this book are:

_____

_____

(5) Some ways in which I used this book in class were:

_____

_____

(6) Some ways in which I used this book outside of class were:

_____

(7) Some of the book's exercises that were used most meaningfully were:

_____

_____

(8) My general reaction to this book is:

_____

_____

(9) In the space below, or in a separate letter, please write any other comments about the book that you would like to make. We welcome your suggestions.

_____

_____

_____

(10) If this book was used for a course, please tell us the name of the course:

_____

(11) My exam results were:

_____

Thank you!